The Pointless Joy

of

Freedom

John David

The Pointless Joy
of
Freedom

*Talks Inspired by Ancient and
Contemporary Spiritual Wisdom*

OPEN SKY PRESS
www.openskypress.com

The Pointless Joy of Freedom

Published by Open Sky Press Ltd.
483 Green Lanes, London N13 4BS
office@openskypress.com

Distribution Open Sky Press
Rheinstr. 54, D-51371 Hitdorf
Germany

First Edition
© Open Sky Press Ltd. 2018

ISBN 978-0-9574627-9-3

Cover design by Divya
Cover portrait by Arsen
All paintings by John David
Artwork by Divya
Photographs: Open Sky House Archive

Printed in Poland

OPEN SKY PRESS
www.openskypress.com

Acknowledgements

Open Sky Press has received so much support from friends and residents of Open Sky House in putting out this book, *The Pointless Joy of Freedom.*

Over the last two years, audio files of my meetings have been sent to friends living in India who ably transcribed them. Recently Kabir organised Daemian, Chetan and Gautham.

Devi and Kabir sifted through the mounds of transcriptions, sorting and choosing the material to be edited. Great thanks for the love and care they lavished on this enormous task. In addition, Kabir helped to select the quotations and wrote the accompanying letters. Devi edited and proofed the texts together with myself.

The beautiful design of the book was done within Open Sky Press by Divya and Tara. The formatting was done by Kabir, and he was assisted by Chanda, whose experience and knowledge helped on various other aspects of the book.

Divya designed the cover over days of intense colour printing to get it all just right. She also designed the biography pages. The biographies were compiled by Kabir.

Devi, a long time member of Open Sky House and now living in Australia, offered constant support in all aspects of producing this book. In particular as the editor of the English edition and final proof reader.

Kabir has made a huge contribution to this book. He has become an assistant editor and an assistant to myself in putting the whole project together and finally arranging the printing and distribution.

Thank you all for your support.

John David Nov 2017

Books and Films

Other Books by John David

Arunachala Talks in English and German
Arunachala Shiva in English, German, Russian
Papaji Amazing Grace in English and German
The Great Misunderstanding in English, German, Russian, Spanish
Blueprints for Awakening – European Masters in English and German
Blueprints for Awakening – Indian Masters in English, German, Russian

Films by John David
With subtitles in many languages

Art from Inner Stillness
The Great Misunderstanding
The Pointless Joy of Freedom
Satori – Metamorphosis of an Awakening
Blueprints for Awakening – Indian Masters
Arunachala Shiva – Commentaries on 'Who Am I?'
Blueprints for Awakening – European Spiritual Masters

Other books by Open Sky Press

Fire of Freedom by Papaji, in German
Thus Spake Papaji by Papaji, in German and Spanish
Nan Yar by Sri Ramana Maharshi, in English, German, Russian, Spanish

Contents

Chapter 6   Self-Enquiry [195]

Chapter 7   The Self [243]

Postscript

Introduction

The Pointless Joy of Freedom has been created over two years, containing some fifty talks I gave in public *Satsang* meetings and retreats in the Open Sky House Communities in Hitdorf Germany, Tripillya Ukraine and Denia Spain.

Since the 1960s when I was in my twenties, my interest in understanding myself and in attaining true freedom and peace led me to devote considerable years to spiritual practice, working with my first master Osho and later with Papaji.

I spent fifteen years of focused meditation and inner work under Osho's guidance. He had a wide knowledge of ancient and contemporary masters and gave wonderful talks introducing his disciples to a huge range of spiritual knowledge from many traditions. During my five-year stay with Papaji I dived deeply into Self-enquiry which was an important teaching from his master Sri Ramana Maharshi.

Osho's talks encouraged my already keen interest, and over the years I have continued to read works by and about great spiritual teachers. Allowing these words from wise teachers, past and present, to seep into my consciousness opened up my heart and mind. They also prompted me to seek out many living masters and record their teachings in the *Blueprints for Awakening* books and films.

The Pointless Joy of Freedom has grown out of talks I have given over the last couple of years where I have been inspired to share and explore some of these important teachings of my 'spiritual heroes' with my students. Of course the wisdom is not contained in the words themselves. They are not something for the mind to chew on and grow fat and 'wise'. Their value lies in the internal experience of the one who hears them, in recognizing the Truth in what they reveal.

These talks all happened spontaneously in my retreats and weekly Sat TV meetings from 2015 to 2017. They were broadcasted live through the Internet, mainly from our studio in the Open Sky House in Hitdorf. The meeting participants were mostly familiar residents who have lived with me for some time. Occasionally from around the world someone would enter the meeting via Skype and dialogue with me. These talks are all available on www.sattv.tv in the English archive. You can use topic search as a means to find a particular subject.

The talks for *The Pointless Joy of Freedom* have been selected to fit into seven broad categories, taking us from our initial interest in self-knowledge through to a deeper understanding and a movement away from suffering. This leads to a fair amount of repetition throughout the book. Over the last twenty years of sharing I have noticed our tendency not to hear, and so repetition is quite a good strategy. It reinforces those fundamental, essential understandings that can easily be brushed over in the mind's 'search' for something more 'profound'. In truth, until we are ready to suspend our belief that 'I know', there is no space for any other perspective or understanding.

The thirty masters whose quotes have been selected here have all touched and inspired me during more than forty years' involvement in the spiritual world. Most of them have some degree of wider exposure in the spiritual world. There are figures from history like Gautama Buddha, Jesus and Lao Tzu, who had religions founded on their behalf. There are more recent masters like Georges Gurdjieff, J. Krishnamurti and Irina Tweedie. Both Nisargadatta Maharaj and Neem Karoli Baba are a constant presence, even though I missed their physical presence. Contemporary masters, Ram Dass, Paul Lowe, Adyashanti and Eckhart Tolle I feel as kindred spirits.

Osho and Papaji are my direct masters and my gratitude to Sri Ramana Maharshi has inspired me to conduct a retreat at his beloved Arunachala for the last eighteen years. This retreat has allowed me to have an annual visit to India from which I draw much inspiration, and until their recent passing I had many friends from those interviewed for *Blueprints for Awakening* who could be relied on to keep me honest. In particular Swami Dayananda, Thuli Baba and Ma Souris. I have received countless inspiration from so many great beings that I feel constantly blessed.

When I began to seriously consider a book about my spiritual heroes I realised how many had influenced my spiritual understanding over a lifetime. Although I have used the words of these men and women as pointers to a deeper understanding of both human suffering and pointless joy, there is just as much inspiration, opportunity for reflection and insight in the words and actions of the two-year-old next door.

Rather than focusing on the words themselves, our insight will come when we turn our attention to our own experience of what they are pointing to. Enjoy the inspiration you can get from the thirty full-page biographies and find your own spiritual heroes. Don't take life too seriously; it seems to me God is everywhere, even if you are having fun. The title of this book, *The Pointless Joy of Freedom*, suggests that life is not so serious and that spiritual life, which is not really different from life, doesn't need to be arduous and serious but rather full of pointless joy. Enjoy your freedom.

John David Nov 2017

CHAPTER 1

The Point of Life

My understanding is that the point of our life, if anything, is to become Self-realised. This means that we see the ego, the movie of our life, is not who we are. When this is clearly seen, something profoundly changes.

The Point of Life

As we grow up in our family and society, we inevitably take on various conditionings, programmed modes of behaviour and habits that cover our true Being, the innocence we lived as children.

We feel disconnected and start to search again for that space we once knew. On the search, we have to see how we are conditioned and how our ideas about who we think we are create a kind of movie out of our life, a movie which we are usually totally identified with.

We perhaps have some spiritual experiences, which are actually moments of being with what is true.

Getting Started on the Spiritual Path

I have always been touched by the story of Gautama Buddha. Deeply yearning for Truth, he gave up the trappings and comforts of his given social status as the son of a king and went on a profound journey into himself. Finally arriving at the simplicity and totality of the present moment, he understood what Truth is. It was his burning priority that led him all the way from the start to the end of his spiritual path.

His teachings spread through most of Asia. He has had so many temples and statues built for him that 'Buddha' has become a general term for someone who becomes Self-realised.

There are only two mistakes one can make along the road to Truth: not going all the way and not starting.

Gautama Buddha

Dear John David,
I've been very much with myself for the last year and feel a strong longing for Truth. I never learnt about meditation but I find myself doing it naturally. I feel inside that I really want to start on the spiritual path seriously. Should I find a technique I like, or a teacher? Or what do you suggest?

If you really want Truth then you should take Buddha's advice: get started and don't stop. Unfortunately, many people do stop, so I would like to say something about starting and continuing the search.

Yesterday I was in Madrid, in Spain, and I was talking to a group of people. There was a woman asking me a question who had basically decided that she wanted Truth, pretty quickly, and she was hoping that in my pocket I had some special technique.

She was disappointed when I said that I unfortunately didn't have that. Then in our dialoguing together I found myself formulating what she, or anyone, could do to get started on the path.

The first thing you can do is to stop talking, or at least not talk very much. The second thing you can do is to cultivate a quiet mind. If you can stop talking that will help your mind to become quiet because unfortunately the more we talk the more we activate the mental part, and then it's very difficult to become quiet inside.

There are many spiritual techniques to help with this, in particular many kinds of meditation. Then there are active practices like yoga, qi gong and tai chi and a myriad of breathing techniques. From the enormous possibilities of spiritual techniques you can find the practices that best suit your particular situation.

When you start intensely practising your mind will naturally get quieter but two other important things are also likely to happen. Firstly, you'll start looking inside. Generally, when something strong happens to us our response is to blame something external, for example we say, 'He made me angry.' We don't own the anger or acknowledge its presence. When we start doing these spiritual practices we get this natural sense of going inside, looking inside, and, we start to develop self-awareness.

To be aware of the outside is relatively easy. We look at others and we have our sense about them, a feeling about what's going on with them. We are aware of what's going on in the world – the weather, the temperature – and by travelling between Spain and Germany in one day you can always be very aware of the different energies and cultures. Self-awareness is not as automatic, but it develops out of spiritual practice, and it requires present-moment awareness.

I would like to include here some powerful advice from Eckhart Tolle. Eckhart has become one of the most popular contemporary masters.

Realise deeply that the present moment is all you ever have.

Every day and all day long everyone refers to 'my life'. We've each become used to identifying with a movie in our head that has grown from the conditioning of our particular family and the culture of our country. It has been building up since birth and that's what we've become identified with. We relate with other people from the position of that movie. Our task now is to examine this automatic identification with 'me', this wrong identification that has built up inside all of us.

We are like a mouse with a piece of cheese in front of its nose. We're always chasing something. What is this something we're looking for? It's happiness. We're looking for love. We've been brought up with the idea that the way to feel like this is to go out and get something. It might be a new dress, a new car, a new partner. Or it might be money and power. We constantly chase what we think will bring us happiness and love.

This then becomes your life, but if you stop for a moment and turn your attention and awareness inside, you will soon discover that life is about whatever is happening right now. You will begin to experience that there is something inside which in itself can nourish you, can make you feel love and peace. In fact, you even discover another level where you understand that you are peace, that you are love. By completely accepting what's happening in any moment we become present for our life, we show up for our life. Very simple.

So, you start meditation or tai chi or whichever practice suits you. After you've gone quite a long way along the road there comes an inner decision that you want to come to Truth, you want to finish the journey, and if that is a clear inner decision then you will attract a teacher.

By spending time with him or her you then have to decide if this is the teacher for you. This is controversial in Europe because various countries like Germany and Spain, and of course Russia, had rather authoritarian bosses and therefore hesitate to take a teacher, to take somebody as an authority.

Many of us suffered at the hands of our family, particularly with Daddy because somehow he takes on the role of God in the family. Our resistances or our difficulties with our father can create all kinds of authority issues and so this can make it difficult to invite a teacher into your life. To get the most benefit from the teacher you need to spend time with him or her exposing yourself and developing an open heart. So this teacher is another step on the way to Truth. Of course, there are some slightly more advanced things that you can do.

Precisely what these are comes through the teacher. There isn't a common technique that will bring you to Truth. Everybody's needs are different and so if you have a true teacher then he or she will come to know you and will create some learning situations from which you can recognise those things that prevent you being free. I shouldn't say prevent you from being free because the Truth is we are already free, but because of our attachment to our conditioned mind, to the ego, we cannot be aware that we are free. Therefore one of the teacher's roles is to create situations where you yourself can see what is preventing you from being connected to your own freedom.

This is actually very, very beautiful. Once you get to this level you're not going to stop. Truth is close.

Exploring the Meaning of Life

I have two quotes tonight. The first is from Meister Eckhart. He was a Christian mystic who lived in the fourteenth century. He's a rather rare kind of person because there weren't so many mystics in the Christian tradition who still touch us today.

If anyone went on for a thousand years asking of life: 'Why are you living?' life, if it could answer, would only say: 'I live so that I may live.' That is because life lives out of its own ground and springs from its own source, and so it lives without asking why it is itself living.

Meister Eckhart

Dear John David,
I read this quote and could see that even though the concept that there is no point to life is familiar, I still believe on a deep level that there must be some point. It is very beautiful to allow the possibility that there is indeed no point to life and also to see how deeply we are conditioned to work in life for some great goal or point. Perhaps you can share something about this.

Looking around on this planet today, we see the results of an enormous evolution of life forms. It seems from my small understanding of science that life on this planet began in some kind of chemical soup billions of years ago.

If you look back at this kind of time scale, human life is a tiny little dot on one end of the history of evolution, but if I ask one of you what is the point of your life you probably wouldn't really consider this enormous time span.

We humans are unique because we have an ego. We have a sense of ourselves, some idea about a point to our lives. The fact that we might not have a point can be pretty scary. If there's no point to life then there's not really a reason to get out of bed in the morning. We have invented different points to life, points that are very much supported by education and by society.

As Meister Eckhart is suggesting, we don't really think much about it, but the people in this room are a bit different and don't just accept the usual points to life that society endorses.

Eckhart says, *'I live so that I may live'*, and you can feel in the whole of life the living element in which this is true. It's just life perpetuating itself. So when we human beings ask ourselves about the point of life, allowing Meister Eckhart's suggestion that there is indeed no point to life is a very beautiful possibility.

My guess is not many people would find that particularly beautiful. Most people spend a lot of effort to find some kind of point and then they dedicate most of their lives to satisfying that point. If there really is no point, then what? Then we're left very much with this moment, now, not knowing what the next moment will bring us, not much interested in the last moment and surrendering to the moment-by-moment development of our lives.

If there would be a point – or let's say the only point I could ever find that is somehow worthwhile – naturally it would be to know who you are. This is what we're all doing sitting in this room. I see there are some people watching on SatTV tonight so I would also include all of you. We have stumbled onto some possible point, this point being to know who we are, which is not a small job of course.

Here in our community we have known for some years that this does not reveal itself so easily. If we accept everything that happens in our lives with moment-to-moment presence, if we can surrender to this process of life – including all the so-called good things and so-called not so good things – our acceptance of our moment-by-moment experiences will lead to understanding and insight that give us the possibility of discovering who we are.

This means to see that the ego, the movie of our life, is not who we are. When this is clearly seen something changes. Suddenly there is a dynamic shift and inherent in that shift is a sense that everything is as it should be. This shift is called Self-realisation.

I have another beautiful quote that follows on from this rather well. It is about Self-enquiry and is from Annamalai Swami, who was Sri Ramana Maharshi's caretaker for many years and later the foreman for the construction of the ashram.

Sri Ramana Maharshi was one of India's most renowned *Advaita* masters. He spent most of his life at his ashram in Tiruvannamalai in South India. I consider him to be my master.

One day, after a playful hug from Sri Ramana, Annamalai Swami had an awakening. Soon after, he left the ashram and stayed close by, alone, for some forty years, never again visiting the ashram. I spent a wonderful afternoon being with him in his tiny ashram. He was tremendously surrendered to Sri Ramana.

The purpose of Self-enquiry is to make the 'I' thought move inwards, towards the Self. This will happen automatically as soon as you cease to be interested in any of your rising thoughts.
Annamalai Swami

And here is a second question:

> *Dear John David,*
> *It was actually this quote that brought me to this Indian retreat with you, but I wonder what I am really doing here, and what the point is of such a retreat if we are all already the Self.*

In the Indian tradition, the master is never important as a person or as a personality or character. What's important is what he or she is passing on. Each master will have their own personal attributes, their own way of communication and each will attract a certain kind of student. What's being communicated is nothing personal, it's not his or her teaching. Each master is only a vehicle for the ancient wisdom.

The roots of many of the main religions come back to India, disappearing there in the mists of time. The message that is passed down is the ancient wisdom of humanity and you can see that understanding this wisdom is not about anything personal, it's not a story. It's almost a scientific thread, which, when you access it, you can figure out for yourself. In fact you have to figure it out for yourself.

If you have an inner curiosity about what the hell's going on here, if you want to understand yourself, then this ancient wisdom gives some pointers, some clarity, and can offer some understanding that we can use to make the ultimate discovery for ourselves. This ultimate discovery is what we can call the Essence or consciousness or the Self, or God. There are many other words to describe it.

This retreat is an attempt to provoke you into this discovery. This is amazingly exciting and I hope it also gives you a glimpse into a possibility that is beyond the personal. It's very easy to enjoy sorting out the personal: 'My partner left me last year and I'm very sad, and can you help me, blah blah blah'. This is okay, but if your partner left you and you've been feeling very sad that is a wonderful trigger to really find out what's going on.

You probably had partners before who left you and you also felt sad so something must be going on because these things tend to repeat themselves. When you start to investigate you can quickly discover that this is not something the world is doing to you. If certain patterns are repeating themselves it has something to do with you and with your false identification, your false idea of who you think you are.

Sri Ramana says, '*Always keeping the mind fixed in Self alone is called Self-enquiry.*' As I was just saying, this is a teaching that has been passed down from the ancient times and Sri Ramana was a significant master in the last century. He built an ashram in the 1920s and for about thirty years he received travellers who visited him in the south of India. He became known particularly for this teaching of Self-enquiry.

Today I got an email all about Self-enquiry from another spiritual teacher, Paul Lowe. When he was with Osho he was accepted as his main disciple. He's an interesting character, now in his eighties, living in Australia, and every so often he sends out interesting reflections.

So he's reflecting on this question, 'Who am I?' I'd like to read this from him because it's a slightly different angle to how I explain it:

Who am I is a favourite technique for many who are seeking to expand their realisation of consciousness. Starts off fine or starts off easy: I'm a man, a woman, wife, husband, son, daughter, gardener, doctor. Then comes a realisation that the image of the self keeps changing, moment to moment. Just a stray thought and the image of the self is changed. And all that changing is uncomplicated when compared to another stage. Who is it who is asking the question? Who is it who is asking who am I?

Later on the process becomes even more confusing, you can't identify to a self at all. It seems as if the self is everywhere, in everything and everybody. Nothing is separate. In the presence of one's person there is an experience of being one person, then the presence of another person, again change.

Then there is the dog and mosquito and trees … and then, is there actually a separation at all? One with everybody and everything. When it happens, it cannot adequately be explained in other words, even to the self, whatever that is. Something does happen. What we call time does stand still, then disappears altogether. Just 'is' ness. When the question disappears, so does the questioner.

Yet, there is still more of a sense of something than ever before. Magnificent. And at the same time, less time. Nothing changes. Thou art That and always have been. As an experiment, consider it is a game – we forget who we are in order to have fun with the experience of remembering again. Happy remembering. And don't be in too much of a hurry. Enjoy the ride. Because that may be what you have invented this dimension for: fun.

This is a nice provocation for why we have gathered here together: fun. When I started to engage with Osho, now many years ago, I was kind of surprised because he always included jokes in his discourses. He always came with jokes written on a notepad. The rest of his talk was spontaneous. About two-thirds of the way through the discourse, when he saw everybody was sleeping, he paused and told some jokes and woke everybody up again. So for him the jokes were a device, you could say.

I was completely confronted in the beginning because, without realising it, I had been brought up as a Christian. I almost never went to church, I was completely not interested, my own family was not interested and I wasn't obviously a Christian, but I discovered when I was sitting with Osho that I had all kinds of Christian ideas. One of my ideas was that spiritual stuff should be serious. Osho was driving me a bit potty because everybody was laughing and rolling around.

I had this idea that it should be very serious, we should have very long faces, our noses should be a bit in the air and so on. This was my idea about spirituality. So I can say a big thank you to Osho because he completely confronted this idea.

It's ludicrous to think that consciousness has any particular intention that it will be there more strongly if you're serious than if you have fun. Or consciousness should be there stronger if you have your eyes closed. We have all kinds of ideas, but if we really investigate we see it can't be like that. So Osho liberated me from the idea that the important things in life are very serious.

Later, this helped me better understand for myself what life is about. Is it to pay my rent every month? Doesn't seem like a good enough reason so I guess that's not it. Is it to make a child? A lot of people are hot about that. Passing on your genes to another generation, is that what it's all about? It doesn't seem like a very good answer either. What's it all about then? Maybe it's not about anything? How about that? How about considering the possibility that it's not about anything? Maybe it's about the discovery of our essential nature.

The Conditioning of Our Mind

When Jiddu Krishnamurthi and his brother were young boys in India they were taken by the Theosophical Society to be brought up as world teachers. Unfortunately the brother died and it was then left solely to Jiddu. He turned down the responsibility but in his own way actually became a world teacher.

Jiddu Krishnamurti was introduced to me by Osho, who encouraged us to spend time with him. I joined one of his retreats in Brockwood Park School in England, one of his three schools. He had a strong presence and I enjoyed seeing him go for his afternoon walks with the headmistress and the school dogs.

Our minds are conditioned, that is an obvious fact. Conditioned by a particular culture or society. Influenced by family, government or religious conformity and so on. Our minds are trained to accept fear and to escape if we can from that fear, never being able to resolve the whole nature and structure of fear. So our first question is, can the mind, so heavily burdened, completely resolve its conditioning and also its fears because it is fear that makes us accept conditioning.

J. Krishnamurti

Dear John David,
I was born in England and although I lived there only until I was twenty, I obviously picked up the conditioning. I am not sure exactly how the English conditioning works in the sense of escaping from fear, as it is not as clear as some other countries like Germany and Russia. Does some work have to be done to face the fear and work with it?

We all accept that we are conditioned. This conditioning means that we have certain patterns of thinking and responding that repeat themselves and this creates a robotic way of functioning. When you get to understand this well enough you can use it to get the result you want from somebody. A lot of this conditioning is so well understood that there is no excuse not to be aware of how it works.

For example, I can remember many years ago being in a crowded Tube train in London early one morning and I found myself being pressed up against a rather big man. I couldn't help it but due to the crush of people I stood quite heavily on his shoe. And what happens? He says sorry! Because the English are very conditioned by this 'sorry'. In that situation if anybody should've been saying sorry it was me because I stood on his foot, but for English people this 'sorry' is very close to the surface. It is fed from the very common structure of 'I'm not good enough'.

English people are very concerned with 'I'm not good enough' because they are always looking at who is higher and who is lower. This comes out of the embedded hierarchical social structure in England and the enormous disparity of privilege this creates. Everybody is looking to see: 'Am I higher or am I lower? Where do I fit in?' Hence 'sorry' is always on the tip of the tongue.

A typical English person tends to lack confidence. They are a bit shy, a bit tentative. This is a deeply English conditioning and then of course whatever your particular family puts on top of that. Perhaps your family was one of the privileged families and sent you to one of England's elite schools and you easily grew up with the conditioning that you are rather special. You might be unlucky and your father might be bus driver, a perfectly good job, but well down on the social scale in England. There probably wouldn't have been enough money to send you to one of those elite schools, even though you might be very intelligent, and you would always have this feeling of being less than some others.

So, how to deal with this conditioning? Krishnamurti is raising the question: *'Can the mind, so heavily burdened, completely resolve its conditioning ...'* The first step is to see it, to be aware of it, but the one thing that will get you out of this conditioning, and only this one thing, is to find out about your 'I', because it's the 'I' that is conditioned, and each of us has a different 'I'.

Tonight we are translating into Russian and the conditioning of a Russian is very different from that of a German or an English person. It helps to know your conditioning. All our conditioned thinking, attachment and identification is directed to this 'I' and so if you resolve the problem of the 'I' the conditioning simply falls down, or at least gets much, much weaker.

I was born in England and I hardly ever say sorry as a conditioned response any more. It's no longer on the tip of my tongue. That's because the one that was 'not good enough' simply disappeared. There is no longer an attachment to this 'I', this fantasy 'I', and so the conditioning simply breaks down by itself without having to do anything.

I can remember very vividly in the months after this 'I' was resolved how different structures of the mind came back very strongly and suddenly there was nobody to receive it. There was a strong structure of not being good enough but suddenly there wasn't anybody who wasn't good enough and therefore the conditioning had nothing to bite onto. I noticed after some time that these structures simply evaporated because the 'I' didn't exist anymore and therefore the conditioning had nowhere to grip.

Rather than trying to resolve each of your many different conditionings – which could take a very long time, even if you could do it – you have to focus on the 'I'. When you clearly resolve the question of the 'I' then all these other things that cause trouble simply dissolve over time.

There is a nice quote from Sri Ramana Maharshi:

'You have to ask yourself the question, "Who am I?" This investigation will lead in the end to the discovery of something within you, which is behind the mind. Solve that great problem and you will solve all the other problems.'

This is the whole effort we are making in the Open Sky House Communities. We are taking whatever happens in our typical day and using this as an opportunity to see how everything is relating to the 'I'. Whether we are washing dishes, cooking lunch or cleaning the floor, we are always attached to the 'I'. We need to find out what this 'I' we are constantly referring to is. We behave as if this 'I' really exists, yet does it?

As you start to investigate it you discover very quickly that you can't find it. So the one who is supporting the whole thinking of the mind doesn't exist and when you clearly see that, the whole thing breaks down. This moment of clear seeing is often very strong and can come combined with a lot of laughter for example, or energy phenomena, which are not really important in themselves.

What is important is the clear seeing that this 'I' is our identification with a thought, created through conditioning, that has no substance in reality. It simply doesn't exist. This is the real work.

The Movie Called My Life

This quote is from Robert Adams. He recounts how he visited Sri Ramana Maharshi when he was young man. There is doubt if this visit happened as no one remembers him. At any rate he was very quiet, not asking any questions.

You look at the movie, and you see all sorts of horrible things going on. But then you catch yourself and you say, 'It's only a movie. It's not the Truth.' And so it is with life. You observe everything that is going on in life. You watch. You look. You see. Yet you never react. You're never for or against. You understand that this makes you free.

Robert Adams

Dear John David,
It is not easy for me to become involved with the life in my heart, the soul, and also to remain unattached. It's a fine line, I think, because the mind can easily become lazy after reading this quote from Robert Adams. How to find the balance between being involved and caring and not being attached?

It's not easy because we've been brought up to believe that everything we see and smell and hear around us has a particular meaning or reality attached to it. We have very little experience of really looking inside without this conditioning. So although we may understand in an intellectual way that we attach our own subjective reality to what we observe on the outside, we still carry on living our life as if it is an absolute reality. We're constantly getting emotionally caught up and we're still taking what happens around us seriously, even here in our communities.

We have a resident who's been working in our guesthouse for probably eight years, and along the way of these eight years he's come into an emotional combat with every person who's worked with him. This is rather funny to watch, but somehow we have to understand that this movie, whether it's emotional or mental or physical, is only running in our mind. When we go to the cinema we sit in front of the screen with our popcorn and Coca-Cola. We know we're in a cinema, but maybe five minutes into the film we've forgotten about our Coca-Cola and popcorn.

If it's a well-made film it takes us on a roller coaster of emotions. We've become completely identified with the action on the screen, and the emotions appear to be real. So after some time we've forgotten all about the cinema.

We're totally identified with one of the characters and at the end of the film it's rather shocking when suddenly the screen appears again. We see our popcorn all over the floor and our empty Coca-Cola cup and in a kind of drunken haze we stagger out into the street. We take a deep breath and we go, 'Ahhh! So nice to be back!' as if going out into the street is real and what was happening in the cinema was only a movie.

Robert is suggesting that when you observe this apparently real movie that's going on in the street, you never react. You just stay without any judgement for or against it because you know and you understand that, just like the movie on the screen, this also is not real. When you understand that and when you can actually live it in daily life, that makes you free. Robert was extremely clear about describing this situation. I can really recommend his book, *Silence of the Heart*.

The question, how to find the balance between being involved and caring and not being attached, is another one of those questions that is asked from a certain position. It is being asked by someone who is identifying with their 'I'. The questioner's understanding is that if he didn't take life seriously he would become lazy, and he feels the need of being involved and caring. But this is a wrong understanding, and he doesn't see that it comes from his conditioned mind.

Until you've really seen this fully for yourself it is very, very difficult to understand. It's extremely easy to be identified because of the way our upbringing has conditioned us. This movie of life was presented to us as real and naturally we accepted it.

That Which Never Changes

Hans is an extremely heartful, private, simple man. He lived in India more or less alone for many years. I interviewed him about his master, Papaji, but after that I could never get him to talk about himself again. I tried once. He was clearly somebody who understood, but unfortunately he understood so well he wasn't interested in talking about it.

Hans was one of Papaji's earliest western students. When they first met he lived in Germany and he would go to India, to Haridwar, for about three months at a time, often staying in a guesthouse with Papaji. They would share a room and go on long walks along the river, mostly in silence, which is where he asked Papaji this question.

Hans said to Papaji, 'You can stay in peace and stillness, I cannot. Why does it come and go with me? With you I see this strength, love and being perfectly at ease. My experiences pass.'

Papaji answered, 'Why do you say this moment comes and goes and not your other experiences?'

Then Hans says, 'I call my states of peace experiences because they are short, compared with the length of my usual life.'

But Papaji said, 'I don't call that experience. I call experience what comes and goes.'

Papaji wanted me to see this is your nature, it doesn't come and go. The other things that are adopted by culture, environment and whatever – he means other conditionings like the religion – are what come and go.

Hans from **Papaji Amazing Grace**

Dear John David,
I feel this is my life exactly, being caught up in all my experiences like being caught on a wheel, turning in the same way, over and over. I've been meditating for over four years now and notice I have become much quieter than

before but only extremely rarely do I directly experience my True Nature, let alone live from it. What needs to change in my life or in me that will allow me to always live from this space of peace that never changes?

This is a very beautiful question so I hope I can find a beautiful answer. This is one of the fundamental points that I'm trying to share. I have here an audience with different kinds of experience and maybe, like the questioner, some of you have your own knowing of your True Nature. I call this a glimpse because it's like looking through veils into your True Nature. Many of you can't really understand my answer, or the question, because you're listening from a certain position, the normal position for ninety-nine-point-nine per cent of humanity.

If you want to experience your True Nature, if you want to know who you really are, if you want to get the full human experience in your lifetime, then what's being discussed here is very very important. Many of you are spiritual seekers and occasionally you have this glimpse, and in this glimpse you feel very good. You tell your friend, 'I had a spiritual experience.'

Hans is also telling Papaji that he sometimes has an experience and Papaji says, 'No, no, not like that.' He says that your conditioned daily life with all your ideas, concepts, judgements, all these kinds of things stored in your conditioned mind, mean that you're constantly having different kinds of experiences. In fact very often we keep repeating the same experiences. We call it 'my life' and it's almost robotic. It's very difficult to see it's robotic, to get an insight, unless you're used to really looking inside or you have a friend who has some understanding and can act as a mirror for you.

What we are pointing to in this meeting is something that never changes and this that never changes is in fact your True Nature. Very few people live in full awareness of their True Nature. I've met forty or fifty people, including Papaji, who are living like that. They are like rare tigers that maybe you feel lucky to glimpse through the trees.

We all know the experience of eating chocolate. Chocolate tastes very good and so we look for it because we're pretty sure if we eat a piece we will have a good experience. We often keep chocolate for when we don't feel good. We pop in a piece and then we feel better and we can call that an experience: 'I feel much better. I had a very good experience eating that chocolate.' We are constantly looking for things like chocolate that can make us feel good, and we don't realise that our True Nature is chocolate. Did I say that? I'm joking of course.

Our True Nature can be described by words like love and peace. These words are pointing to something that never changes. We arrive on this planet, we leave this planet; our True Nature never changes. It's a constant. Papaji is pointing out to Hans that what Hans calls an experience of his True Nature shouldn't be called an experience because naturally experiences are always changing but your True Nature is a constant. So we might ask ourselves, 'Why don't I know that?' This is almost a tragic joke; it is a paradox of life.

When we arrive on the planet we are just our True Nature, in fact when we're very small we don't even feel separate from our mother. We experience ourselves as one with her, even one with everything. There's no separation. As we grow older Mummy says, 'Johnny, Mummy.' There's Mummy and Johnny: two. So Johnny starts to get a sense of separation that gradually increases as he grows up. It all happens very naturally. Without realising it we absorb all kinds of ideas – it should be like that and not like this – collecting more and more as we grow older.

When a little child arrives it's very spontaneous, acting out of innocence. As we grow up we act more and more out of the conditioned mind and lose touch with our innocence and spontaneity. So in any particular situation we have our answer ready, and this is actually a rather unconscious way of living.

The questioner is asking what he can do to always live from this space of peace that never changes. He's been meditating for four years and he's become much quieter. Meditation, like yoga, breathing exercises and mantra singing, is a spiritual practice. By doing it for a number of years we can get great value, mainly a quiet mind.

The other value is that we learn to turn our attention inside. The greatest change for any human being happens when we're not constantly looking outside. As soon as we change direction and start to bring our attention inside, inevitably our lives will start to change. It's not that 'I' change my life, it's simply that by looking inside things start to change. As soon as you start to look inside you've actually embarked on a great adventure. And by being vigilant you start to become familiar with certain patterns of thought that keep repeating, which is what our questioner calls '…*being caught on a wheel, turning in the same way, over and over*'.

So, how to get off this wheel? The only way to actually get off the wheel – and this is of course the biggest project – is to wake up to your True Nature. Here's an excerpt from my interview with Hans:

'In Papaji's presence, I found it easier and easier to be at peace.' And he said that after four or five years he felt pretty good. I asked him, 'When you say you were feeling so good, do you mean the mind was quiet and you were feeling clear and peaceful?' And his answer was, 'Not totally, but always relatively', and then I asked, 'When you were in Germany, could you still maintain this?' He replied, 'No. I couldn't do it continuously with Papaji nor when I was alone; not in Germany or India. I couldn't because I had the wrong idea of having to maintain it – as if it were something one has to hold onto with effort. Rather it comes in the moment when effort subsides. So this misunderstanding is what Papaji mainly helped me with.'

This is an extremely common misunderstanding because we've all been brought up to do something and so we assume in order to live from our True Nature we have to do something. Do you do anything to be a man? Do you do anything to be a woman? So why do you have to do something to be you, to be your True Nature? Extremely simple, you don't have to do anything. It's a given. Almost everyone who has some kind of glimpse is surprised because they thought they would have to do something: 'Oh, it just happened.' You don't have to do anything to be who you are. You don't realise it, but to maintain all these experiences you have to do a lot. You're constantly doing a lot, and all this 'lot' is keeping you from realising your True Nature.

Honesty On The Spiritual Path

Without me knowing it, Jesus was my first teacher. I was brought up in school with stories about Jesus, and being English I was involved in such things as celebrating his birth at Christmas and his death and resurrection at Easter. Much later I was interested to discover that he might have been part of a spiritual community, the Essene. More recently I found that his core teachings express the same Truth that we are discovering in this book.

Blessed are the meek, for they will inherit the Earth. The meek will inherit the land and enjoy peace and prosperity.

Jesus

Dear John David,
For me, this word 'meek' means that the ego within us that thinks it knows everything has to dissolve, and this feels like becoming humble. It often feels so challenging for me, but I can see that the reason it is so challenging is because my ego has such strong ideas about how it should be, and that when I am honest with myself and can see these ideas, then they start to dissolve. This leads to a sense of being more humble, of not knowing. Could you share something about what it is to become meek or humble?

One thing to consider in the beginning of this retreat is that I am a guide, a supporter, a reminder, but I can't do it for you. You will have to make an inner decision that you want to do this. Here in Ukraine particularly a lot of people have the wrong idea that the teacher should be some kind of magical God who will bestow wonderful things. That's a very childish idea about spiritual life. Unfortunately very often in Ukraine, when it gets to looking inside and dealing with the stuff you have accumulated, people don't want to look. They don't want to get involved.

Particularly I don't want to bestow wonderful things onto you. I want you to bestow wonderful things onto yourselves. Of course if I could give you this magic pill then I would have given it years ago because I would like very much for you to come to a wonderful space inside yourselves. But you have to step up and take the mature responsibility of making this a priority in your lives. Doing what the teacher points towards is always helpful.

This is a very unpopular message and I am very sorry to start with this. I can't do it for you but I hope you will empower yourselves from inside. I like very much to support that and to give some suggestions.

The other thing that is quite interesting to look at in the beginning of the retreat is how you hear what I am saying. Some of you have been listening to me for many years, so how is it that what I am saying doesn't engage with your box of tricks? I am not going to say anything different in these two weeks, so why didn't you hear it over the last few years? What I am saying is actually quite simple. You are taking the words and inside your mind you are evaluating them from some position. And what would that position be? This position is from your own movie.

Everything that comes in is processed, for example, against your beliefs, what you have been taught to believe. If what comes in doesn't fit with these, then what happens? You have a choice. You can put away your old beliefs and accept something new. Or you can simply reject it. If you keep rejecting this new information then of course nothing much is going to change because you are constantly choosing what is already known.

This is one of the things I have noticed is happening very strongly in Ukraine. Almost everyone comes with enormous expectations, with a lot of ideas around these expectations. When they are not met then a lot of them leave. They just go away instead of examining whether in fact they have some wrong expectations. Maybe their ideas are wrong; maybe the teacher is not wrong.

If your ideas are right why aren't you already awakened? Why is there a need to come to a teacher? If you come to a teacher you have to come to some kind of trust in that teacher. If you can't then basically you are wasting your time. Without trust you will judge the teacher and the new information through what you already believe. If you don't trust what he or she is saying you are very likely to refuse to take it and you will stay with what you already know.

It took me some years before I saw these patterns that are inherent in the culture here in Ukraine. There are three particularly strong ones. The first is to always postpone what you could do now. You do it later. Everybody does this constantly. The second is what I call the Ukrainian lie where basically nobody is honest. Nobody considers themselves dishonest because everybody does it. This dishonesty is normal behaviour. Of course this happens to some degree in most cultures.

Unfortunately, dishonesty does not help you in spiritual work. That is why I chose this simple quote from Jesus at the start. Meek means humble, and in order to awaken to your True Nature you need to be humble and to be honest.

Honesty is absolutely essential in spiritual work. You need to be able to look at what is going on inside you and reflect on it in an honest way, without judging whether it is good or not good. Sometimes what you discover inside will be very confronting and sometimes it won't. When it is confronting you can accept that it is confronting, without making a judgement and without taking it personally. If you are taking it personally you are going to resist and say no. These are popular Ukrainian structures.

This question of honesty is very important. The more honest we are the more benefit we get. We are often not honest because one idea we have grown up with is that we have to be nice to people. We have to tell them what they want to hear. One particular member of our community is an expert at this. She will always tell me the things that she thinks I would like to hear because she wants me to be happy. She generally doesn't like to give what she would consider something I don't want to hear.

I don't know if you begin to see, but both these things I am talking about – postponement and dishonesty – are focused on the personal.

The third thing is that we are so much affected by our personal movie. In millions of different ways we are completely supporting, liking and afraid to lose our personal movie ... the ego. We have grown up absolutely identified with this ego so unfortunately we believe the ego to be who we are.

If I believe my movie, the daily soap opera of 'my life', my ego, to be who I am, then of course I am going to resist any attempt to change that, or any suggestion that this may not be exactly what it seems to be.

When you take postponement, dishonesty and belief in ego together, you may begin to see why some of you have been sitting with me for many years and feel that nothing much has changed. This is one of the big problems in trying to share and teach, that in fact we are all living in our own little bubble. In this little bubble I have certain beliefs, certain ideas, certain things I know. I know this is right and I know this is wrong. If you examined these positions you would discover that they are not really your beliefs but that they have been given to you by your family, by your culture and by your religion. There are certain parts of this that are so fundamental that you can't even imagine that there is anything that needs to be looked at.

The Fear of Authority

I met Swami Dayananda during filming for my *Blueprints for Awakening* film. He had become the leading *Vedanta* master with two large ashrams in India and one in California. His master was Swami Chinmaya. Swami Dayananda was a powerful man who taught a three-year *Vedanta* course and had the financial muscle to offer one hundred students a free course. He became my favourite living master. He passed away in 2015.

People who are afraid of gurus have an authority problem, a problem centred on father, and they have to solve it; it is a psychological problem and it means that they are afraid of authority. The guru is not authority; the guru is one who makes you see that you are not any different from him. He doesn't say, 'I am the guru, you are nobody.' He says, 'You are the whole.' Not only does he say that, but he also makes you see that. He makes an honest attempt to make you see. Where is the authority in this?
Swami Dayananda

Dear John David,
Whenever I have to face the projected authority inside myself I make myself very small and it hurts. I feel like I am living under the eyes of some terrible monster who will judge me. I can see that this is my own inner judge and that projected authority is just a kind of old shadow from my childhood.

This fear of authority is just another result of conditioning. It can go something like this … From when you are very small your parents want to get you to behave in certain ways, and as a small child you don't really care about that. Let's take bedtime as an example. So there is the parent who is rather big and there is the active energy of the little child. How to manage this situation? Every parent does it in a different way. Maybe some parents don't care too much about the time and they wait until the child gets tired and then put him to bed. Another parent has a very clear idea about the time and they might even threaten punishment to get the child to do what they want.

If this is the case the child starts to get used to living in this kind of fear regime. The child is very small, the parent very big, and so gradually, over some years, this game of fear and big authority gets engraved in our psychology. As we become older this stays in our unconscious mind, or we can call it the inner child or the ego. We tend to live our lives from these programs.

Most of us are not aware of these programs because it just seems to be natural. When we see our school teachers, for example, we easily project onto them the authority which we used to experience with our parents. Later, when we take a job, we project the same authority onto our boss. The effect of this is that we disempower ourselves; it is quite rare to see someone not being disempowered by an authority.

There was a very nice moment on the television today. I was watching the Russian Grand Prix. It was won by an English guy, who has been the champion for the last year. He is about thirty, a very confident guy. After the race the first, second and third place drivers go into a special room where they prepare themselves for the presentation, have a drink of water, put on their sponsors' caps. Normally it is just the three drivers talking a bit together and getting ready for the presentation.

Today the TV showed President Putin waiting in this room. It was a kind of funny situation because the drivers are completely busy with relaxing after the race. They only have a few moments and President Putin is standing there looking as if he is expecting something. I wondered what was going to happen and the English guy who won the race very casually shook Putin's hand. Putin tried to hug him and he wasn't really interested in this hug.

You could feel that he was completely busy with his own situation and here was this great authority, the president of Russia, being treated very casually. I was very impressed by that. If you think about yourself in that situation, could you be as casual as this English guy was?

Very often we project onto the authority, we feel some kind of fear and then we treat the authority very carefully. My experience as a teacher is that people project a lot of things towards me. They have ideas about how I should behave, how I should be spending my time, how I should speak, what I should speak about, how I should treat them and so on. So we have lots of judgements towards authority.

Parents often have very particular ideas about how 'my children' should behave, and so this game of authority gets engraved deeply into our psychology. Very often the ultimate authority in the family is the father, not always of course, but usually. The father is a man, so most of us have a male authority issue. Thinking back to my own family, I can say my mother was rather easy going and if she felt we needed some kind of punishment she would always call in the big guns: my father. He always got the job of being the ultimate authority, and this role is passed down through generations.

I remember once sitting in a restaurant and a young family came in. The father called for the menu, he looked at it and then he ordered the food for the whole family. He made no attempt to ask the children what they would like. They weren't treated like little individuals. They were treated like 'my' kids.

At some point we leave the family, we leave the father, we go off alone into the world and in some ways we might even become our own authority, but we forget to deal with this conditioning and so even though we leave the parents, in a psychological way we take them with us. Their voice is still there and we project it out onto some other authority figure, like a teacher or a boss. Most of us never really examine or investigate that. It operates in our lives like a movie along with all kinds of other conditionings. All these subconscious voices are running along inside us and we call this 'me'. It is like a theatre script that we might act out in the theatre, but we act it out in our lives as if it is completely real.

There is no point in blaming our parents because anyway they were conditioned by their parents. This goes through the generations, it comes to us and we suffer. We feel pain in certain situations and that can be quite a good thing because pain helps us to investigate. If you feel some pain then you can start to look at where this pain comes from and how to be rid of it.

What can we do to drop this projection of authority? We can become aware of what is going on inside us; we can develop self-awareness. We are always projecting something such as: 'He did it to me', and while you project that somebody is doing it to you, you can't ever become really free of it. The first step is to see that actually it is happening inside of you from your conditioned psychology. It has become ingrained in your mind and in any particular situation you immediately project from that conditioned mind.

Effectively you are a prisoner of a fear that may have been real when you were small but once you grow up it is no longer sensible. That's why I was really impressed by this English racing driver when he suddenly had to meet President Putin. Mr Putin tends to project himself as a very strong authority.

We are constantly making the authority big and ourselves small, that is, not powerful. The reality is everybody is equally powerful but we can only access this natural power if we are not unconsciously caught up in this psychological game of projection. It would be very attractive if the teacher could give you some nice technique, which, if you apply it, gets rid of the projection, but it doesn't work like that. If you really want to get rid of this projection only you can do it, by becoming self-aware and bringing understanding into this game that is going on.

As you start to see yourself projecting out this authority issue, when you really see it, it just stops by itself because of the understanding that you have. It's not going to stop after you've seen it once or twice. You will have to see it many times. As you become self-aware enough, actually it will melt and disappear by itself. Other kinds of psychological conditioning and structures will also disappear with this process.

If you have a deep desire for freedom, to be really free of all these psychological conditionings, then you need to watch and ask yourself who is in this game of conditioned projection: Who am I? Who is this me? Surely this me is not psychological conditioned structures, but if these structures would all drop away, if it's possible, what would be left? This is a fundamental question and the understanding of it can bring us true freedom because the reality of every human being when we say 'me' is not all this conditioning.

'Me', the true 'me', is in fact my Being, and what is this Being? The Essence of who we really are is something that exists in this moment, not in the past, not in the future. It exists only now, present, spontaneous, perhaps also innocent. Innocent in the sense that we are not using our memory or our projections into the future. We are simply here, in the aura of innocence this brings. This innocence is something that we sense in small children because they haven't yet taken on lots of these conditioned structures.

What Holds Us Back from Truth

Tonight we have a quote from Robert Adams. As a teenager he had already made contact with Yogananda (author of the famous book *Autobiography of a Yogi*) in California. Then he seems to disappear for many years to reappear in Los Angeles in 1987, where he started holding meetings with small groups.

The only burden you ever had is your mind. There is no other burden. See if you could stop your mind for a few seconds and see how peaceful you are. Where there are no thoughts there are no worries. There are no fears. There are no anxieties. There are no desires. No wants, no greed, no hurt, no enemies. It is the mind, the thoughts, that cause these things to come to us. We actually create these conditions. We create our own reality.

Robert Adams

> Dear John David,
> I have experienced many challenges where life is somehow presenting me with situations, often involving more thinking and careful planning, where I feel I must step up. I've heard you talking about the movie of our lives that we believe so strongly and which holds us back from knowing who we really are.
>
> I meditate pretty often and feel quite a good flow in my life. I'm very often busy, but if I want to quieten my mind do I need to slow down on the outside? Is my life simply a movie that I should just let go of?

If you meditate regularly that creates a quiet mind. My suggestion is that you find a meditation that you like doing and then do it regularly, every day. Sometimes people have very strong experiences in their first meditation, but for most people with busy minds it requires patience. The benefits usually come slowly, but if you meditate for long enough you will certainly fall into moments of great silence where the thoughts actually just stop or where thoughts appear but you are not bothered by them, not identified with them.

In order to have fear or stress or jealousy you have to have thoughts. You only feel jealous when there is a thought, so falling into this deep silence is a relief and encourages you to continue the meditation. Having a quiet mind is not an awakening or Self-realisation, but this quiet mind, without a lot of busy thoughts, creates a clean place or clear field for a moment of clear seeing.

Identification with the 'I', the movie, is seen clearly so that it can fall away, giving you a taste of your True Nature. This taste gives you something truly beautiful: tremendous peace, tremendous love. Love in the sense of oneness with all. So by meditating regularly over some longer time, certainly some years, you will often fall into a deep silence, deep peace.

Robert Adams suggests to *'See if you could stop your mind for a few seconds and see how peaceful you are.'* Once you become an experienced meditator, then you will actually often come into this peace. When that starts happening it then becomes very attractive to meditate.

One thing I can say is that there are different types of mind, of thought. We're not very troubled by practical thoughts. We use the practical mind to solve a problem such as how to get to the airport, and when the problem is solved the thoughts stop. There is another kind of thinking that goes something like this: 'What might happen on the way to the airport? Maybe I don't have time. Maybe there are two entrances to the airport. Maybe we will have a crash on the way. There's a traffic jam.' These kinds of thoughts are generated by the thinking mind and when our thinking minds are not very quiet they can go round and round inside.

In order to live your life you need practical thoughts. In order to cook dinner you have to know where to get the groceries and how to use the stove, but thinking about a bad dinner last night and how you drank too much wine, this is a never-ending disturbance. These are the kind of thoughts that trouble us.

You're asking if you need to slow down in order to quieten your mind. We often think of a 'spiritual' environment as being very silent, very quiet. My own spiritual schooling was in an ashram in India. The guru understood that we westerners have busy minds, so he set it up in a way that kept us busy half the day and meditating the other half. In this busy-ness we gradually learnt how, despite being busy on the outside, we could keep quiet inside by not identifying with and hanging onto our thoughts.

Some years ago in our community, Open Sky House, we made a decision that we would like to be self-supporting. It's rather a powerful situation because it means that the community has its destiny in its own hands, you could say. From that decision we developed four businesses: a seminar business, a guesthouse, an art gallery and a publishing company.

Inevitably, that creates a busy, getting-things-done environment. We also have three periods of meditation each day, and then often in the evenings we have some meetings like we're having now. So there's a lot of impetus to be silent and at the same time there is a lot of busy-ness involved in running the businesses. But whatever we are doing, our focus is to investigate, without judgement or expectation, the reality of our inner life. We begin to see just how brilliant the mind is in creating worries, fears, anxiety and desires. As Robert says, *It is the mind, the thoughts, that cause these things to come to us. We actually create these conditions. We create our own reality.*

This creation is the story that we hold in our minds, a daily soap opera that goes on day by day throughout the whole year that we call 'my life'. You ask, *Is my life simply a movie that I should just let go of?* It is something that can't be let go of; it doesn't work that 'I' decide to let go. What is necessary is to see clearly that the 'I' doesn't exist, and therefore this movie or this ego also doesn't exist. So there is no question of letting it go. You can't let go of something that doesn't exist. It apparently exists, and we're apparently identified with this apparent existence. In the right moment, with a clear seeing, this will drop. It will drop without you doing anything.

Robert's words completely support this: '*The only burden you ever had is your mind. There is no other burden.*'

The Mistaken Search for Love

We're going to talk about love. We older boys remember Richard Alpert as the professor from Harvard who did all kinds of experiments in the 60s with LSD, and as the author of the spiritual bible *Be Here Now*. He became Ram Dass when he went to India looking for a teacher. He found a wonderful, incredible Indian guru, Neem Karoli Baba. This man was very old at the time and he was always wrapped in a blanket. He didn't really have any teachings, but in his presence you could feel tremendous love. This tremendous love, or you can call it an energy field, had the effect of a teaching. This quotation is from a new book by Ram Dass called *Be Love Now: The Path of the Heart*.

When we talk about the heart, it's easy to confuse the emotional heart and the spiritual heart, because, though they are both heart, they represent different levels of consciousness. There's the emotional heart we're all familiar with, the one that romance and poetry are usually about (except mystic poetry) ... It is laden with hooks that constantly create attachments and constantly affirm our egos ... Emotions come into being and are interpreted in our own mind, arising and dissipating. If we're angry, we feel anger in our mind. The emotional and external stimulus or internal impulse that triggers it (usually some frustration that leads to anger) comes into the mind and stirs the thoughts like a gust of wind passing through ... Love is actually a state of being, and a divine state at that, the state to which we all yearn to return. The outer love object stimulates a feeling of love, but the love is inside us. We interpret it as coming from outside us so we want to possess love, and we reach outside for something that is already inside us.

Ram Dass

Dear John David,
I'm very familiar with this topic as I have experienced a lot
of possessive love situations, full of jealousy, neediness and
insecurity, which all arose from this deep misunderstanding
that love comes from outside. Although I'm more experienced
in this now, and have a wider inner space and ground that
I can stay connected to and not get so caught up in the
storms, I still don't truly understand and live this Truth. I
am not fully convinced that the love is already inside me. It
is such an incredibly deep conditioning. Could you share a
little bit about where these misunderstandings come from?

This is the subject that creates more human suffering than anything else. Unfortunately we have come to understand that love comes from somebody, therefore most of humanity is rushing around looking for somebody who will love them. Once we've found somebody we want to make sure we don't lose them, hence the contract called marriage.

When I think about it, it's really lunacy, but I don't think about it very often. More important is to examine the misunderstanding that we think love comes from somebody when fundamentally this misunderstanding comes from our wrong understanding of who we are.

As we grow up we're conditioned to believe ourselves as separate from everybody else. We've heard Mummy and other close family members say 'I love you' very often, so gradually the conditioning builds up and it seems that somebody who is separate from me is loving me. Without much being spoken about love the child learns to understand that Mummy loves Daddy and Daddy loves Mummy.

This may not be explicit but it's certainly the experience of the child over many years. So with this wrong idea of who I am plus this daily theatre that Mummy and Daddy love each other and they also love me, naturally I come to understand that love comes from somebody. So when one of these close people walks towards me, comes close to me, perhaps I also feel love. My own experience suggests that love is coming from the outside.

It's only when you start to look inside through meditation or some spiritual practices that you come to an experience that makes you question this. I would call this experience a glimpse, a glimpse of our True Nature. When this happens, another understanding about love becomes possible. We fall into a space where there is no need to change anything, where everything is perfect as it is and we feel enormously nourished. We feel enormous love – divine love, unconditional love, true love, authentic love. All these words point to a type of love that is very different from romantic love.

Usually we experience love emotionally, which means we experience it in our minds. These ideas of love are supported by romantic stories told to us through pop songs and Hollywood movies. Many of these movies have to do with family dramas, very often ending up in a church where the woman is wearing a beautiful white dress and the man is wearing a very nice suit and looking very nervous. According to Hollywood the implication is that this is the beginning of a life of happiness, full of love, so it is very hard to really escape from this tremendous focus that we need to find somebody who will love us.

Very few look inside and discover their own love. It's not really correct when I say 'own' love because actually this love is universal. It is a fundamental energy of the universe and is experienced by everyone the same. It's not my love or your love; it's just, let's use the word 'authentic' love. This love is our Being. It doesn't come from the mind. It has a different quality that is not so familiar because very few of us really come deep enough inside to know this.

When we consider what love is we immediately conjure up ideas of romantic love. Very few can go straight to our divine inner Being. In your question you're saying that although you're more experienced with this now you still don't fully understand and live this Truth because of the incredibly deep conditioning.

Very often we experience love as being triggered by another

person, so it looks and maybe feels like the love is coming from the other. However, if you look deeper and you watch carefully you can discover for yourself that although somebody may be a trigger for this love, it is actually inside us. It's always inside us, always available. Unfortunately most of the time we're not able to connect to that love because we're always looking in another direction.

We're always busy with our attachments, which are the story of me, 'my life'. We're so busy with the movie of 'my life' that we can't break through and experience what is true.

CHAPTER 2

Our Conditioning

By looking at our structures and our conditioning, and shining light on them, we begin to be less affected by them. This is transformation, the movement to become more and more open and aware so that these old structures are no longer what we identify with. Then we have the opportunity to see who we really are.

Our Conditioning

We start to look inside at what is false in our lives, what is standing in the way of us simply being free and present in each moment, and we take steps to come out of the conditioning.

We may do practices such as yoga or meditation to quieten the mind, or we can choose to deeply change our lives, to break away from the known, follow our intuition, and to be in a more conscious and nourishing environment.

At a certain point we may also find a spiritual teacher, a guide to take us deeper within ourselves.

— ● ———————— ● —

Inner Work

More than anyone I have met, Papaji is simply the human being I have most loved and felt the most gratitude towards. When I arrived in Lucknow we met at his gate. He asked me where I was staying, where my bags were and if I needed his help. A day later I had lunch in his house. Three weeks later in his presence I came to know Truth.

I asked Papaji two weeks after I had an awakening whether there was a kind of process or cultivation of the switch that had occurred. He just joked and said, 'You don't want to be a farmer when there is nothing to cultivate.'

John David, from Papaji Amazing Grace

Dear John David,
I found this quote when I was reading your book Papaji Amazing Grace. *It touched me deeply and I could feel that all the work I do on the spiritual path is actually to dissolve all the things standing in the way of my True Nature, which is just there. Is this your understanding of it? How would you comment on this quote now in your life?*

You say that your work on the spiritual path is to dissolve all the things standing in the way of your True Nature. This is not how I see it. Of course it is very good to become self-aware about your mind structures, but the idea that as you see these mind structures you are clearing a path and somehow your True Nature is being revealed is not how I see it. The work is to realise how identified you are with an illusory ego or movie. We become so very identified that we actually believe ourselves to be that.

The spiritual work is to realise that you are not this ego or this movie. It is a little different from the way you are expressing it here. Yes, you have to dissolve all the things standing in the way of your True Nature, but actually it is only really one thing. It is the identification with all these different structures that must dissolve.

In our conditioned mind we have many kinds of thoughts and thought patterns that tend to repeat themselves. This repetitive nature helps us realise that this cannot be who we really are. Yes, it is good to be self-aware and with it you find the power of these structures becomes less.

In that sense you can say that you are dissolving all the things that are standing in the way of your True Nature, but it is not by getting rid of all these things that you finally get to your True Nature. This is a thinking that the mind easily does. We have to see how identified we are with something that is not true. That is the work. It may happen quickly or after years of self-awareness but when that is clearly seen it collapses in a moment, because we are no longer identified with the 'I' that holds all this stuff in our conditioned mind.

In my own case, when I had my moment with Papaji there was an enormous release of energy. Looking back on that from where I am now it is almost as if I was pulling sacks full of rocks and in a moment all these ropes were cut and there was a release of energy.

A week later I sat with Papaji. My heart was full of gratitude to him. There was still some kind of energy phenomenon going on inside, and because I was used to doing this work I must have asked him something about whether there was a process now. He was joking and asking me why I would want to be a farmer when there is nothing to cultivate. Looking back that was true and also not true. The one who wanted to do something seemingly disappeared. But the tendencies of the mind, old structures of the mind, they had their own momentum. They continued for some time, gradually melting away.

So I found myself watching these things. Not exactly to do something and certainly not to cultivate something, but there was a self-awareness operating, which continues even now twenty years later. In this self-awareness some of the old tendencies of the mind could be seen much more clearly than before the identification dropped. I immediately felt very free of all these old patterns, they had fallen away, but some of the more entrenched ones returned.

I remember that perhaps the funniest for me was 'I'm not going to survive.' This moment of awakening was exactly a moment I didn't survive – this 'I' simply didn't survive – so when the structure would come I always found it a bit funny. My mind managed to keep repeating this old structure of 'I'm not going to survive' while I clearly understood at that moment that 'I' hadn't survived!

This reinforced the sense that the structures of the mind were just fantasies – maybe illusions is a better word – because what could be a better example than 'I'm not going to survive?' I understood clearly I hadn't survived, was very happy about that and everything was very wonderful because of that, so why would I have fear about not surviving? As far as I could see there was no reality in this. This helped me enormously to clearly understand that these tendencies of the mind were illusions.

Reconnecting to Our Being

I have a beautiful quote tonight from Georges Gurdjieff. He was a mystic who had a very unique, fascinating and rather mysterious life. When he was a young man he started on an intense spiritual search, which led him around the world meeting spiritual leaders, unique personalities and religious cultures. These travels and adventures are brilliantly documented in the book *Meetings with Remarkable Men*.

I was very impressed by the strength and power of his character and his burning priority for Truth. I was even more impressed to find out that he founded a spiritual community near Paris in the 1920s, encouraging the same intensity of inner work and inner transformation that I am encouraging and supporting in the Open Sky House Communities.

You are in prison. If you wish to get out of prison, the first thing you must do is realise that you are in prison. If you think you are free, you can't escape. Life is real only then, when 'I am'.

Georges Gurdjieff

Dear John David,

My first master explained that when we are young we are connected to our deeper part of love, energy and intelligence. With this connection we are living in our Being. But then this connection, this field of energy, gets upset. We lose the connection and we start to look for it again on the outside. The external part doesn't give us the love because we never see ourselves as good enough. And we are trying to be better, to improve ourselves, because of the external life. He said that we have to pass through all these feelings of anguish, but is it really necessary?

We're very lucky this weekend. You saw already that we have two little beings here. They're only five weeks old and so they're completely living in the Being, as you were saying. When they go into a deep sleep then you can see 'God' is there, because nobody is there. It is very profound to feel this energy of nothing. As we grow up we're always taught to be somebody. As we get older we want to be more educated, more wise, more intelligent. We're always trying to be 'more'.

This takes us on a journey outside. We consume books, for example. We go to lectures, maybe we study, and we're looking for something. We have forgotten exactly what it is we're looking for and at the same time we have a memory of something, of some place or some feeling of wellbeing.

We have forgotten how to get there because in the process of growing up we've been conditioned to always engage in the world rather than engage inside. You came to some kind of crisis that led you to meet your first teacher who told you to go inside. He pointed out that you have certain structures in your mind, like 'I'm not good enough', or the feeling of anguish you mentioned. Each person's life experience and therefore structures are different – they may be emotional or they may be intellectual.

All these things create a barrier and keep us separate from this place you were talking about inside, our true Being. This is what Gurdjieff is referring to in his quote. We are in a prison within ourselves. We become separated from ourselves, and also we feel separate on the outside, separate from all the others. On some level we're trying to reconnect and very often we do this by relationship.

We are looking for another human being who will bring us what we've lost. We experiment with love affairs, but in the end, even if you keep trying with different partners, it's quite likely that you will never fill this deep sense of lost love through a partner.

Love is a difficult word but I'm using it in a different context from 'I love you'. You can say that love is the same as our true Being, and actually we don't have to do anything for that. So the Truth is actually very, very simple. When we stop doing, when we stop separating ourselves and we are simply just Being, we easily have a glimpse of this lost love.

I can see on your face that you've had this glimpse, and the things you were saying are absolutely true. You have a good understanding. You are asking if we have to go through the anguish, and the answer is a little bit subtle.

It depends on each person. We all have challenges, things we have to deal with. It seems we each arrive on this planet with a different journey ahead of us.

These two baby girls are five weeks old. At their birth they were already very different and those differences have amplified themselves over the five weeks. One of them is very relaxed. She doesn't cry very much and is happy just to lie and look around, experience the colours and the light. The other little girl, from the first moment, had difficulties. She couldn't feed easily and she's rather fragile and very sensitive, over-sensitive maybe. She has already spent four days in the hospital. She developed an infection and had needles in her head to give antibiotics.

So this little girl, who is anyway fragile, is already attracting a very different path to the other one. It doesn't mean that the one who seems to be relaxed and content maybe later in her life won't also have some difficulties. But clearly they are having very different life experiences. Would you call that anguish? I'm not sure because we also have to go through joyful experiences, all kinds of different experiences. They all show us something, and together they are creating this barrier that prevents us from simply Being.

This is what we've come together for this weekend, to support each other to come deeper inside and reconnect with our true Being. We need a moment where we realise the 'I am' that Gurdjieff is talking about.

I'm sure that almost everybody here has had some moment, perhaps a powerful moment, when you found yourself simply Being, and you recognised that. It was as if you met something that you always knew. Maybe you even laughed, a wild laugh because you realised you were searching for something that you always had.

This is a very common response and often this deep experience of true Being leaves a kind of smile. I can see it on our friend's face. It comes directly from this true Being and it's the same smile you sometimes find on statues or paintings of Buddha. If you think of Buddha not as a person but more as an energy then this smile represents this true Being. Buddha Nature.

It's not personal. This is also one of the beautiful things we will discover this weekend, that this True Nature is like a reservoir where we meet together. This is one of the strengths of coming together. Just by being together we support that space.

Choose a Conscious Life

Chögyam Trungpa was a legendary Tibetan Buddhist master who inspired the Naropa University in Boulder, Colorado. He was a free spirit who indulged his passions and was often drunk! He was his own person. I liked that.

The Sangha is a community of people who have the perfect right to cut through your trips and feed you with their wisdom, as well as the perfect right to demonstrate their own neurosis and be seen through by you. The companionship within the Sangha is a kind of clean friendship – without expectation, without demand, but at the same time, fulfilling. True Sangha is only possible within a container of love, intimacy and trust. It takes commitment, willingness, time and patience to create this much-needed environment.

Chögyam Trungpa

Dear John David,
I want to make a change in my life. All my friends and family around me are nice, but I see they are more unconscious than me and I feel it is not helping me to become clear. My question is: If I want to transform myself is it necessary to put myself into an environment where the people are more conscious than me?

I feel a bit unsure because I also want to walk away from all the stress of my life and spend time alone. I find it hard to decide between throwing myself into a supportive spiritual group and finding a place where I can become quiet and be alone.

This is a universal question, but there's not a really universal answer because at a certain level of understanding we are very different, each one. Everyone's path is unique, although actually there is no path. Even the idea of wanting to transform yourself is in fact a wrong idea. To transform yourself still contains the notion of the small self. Someone is here who can transform themselves. This is still within the personal.

We all need a different kind of situation. For the right person at the right time it's wonderful to spend time alone and it might be very good to go and be quiet in nature. For another it might be helpful to be in a supportive spiritual *Sangha*.

The danger of being alone for a long time is that you might not really know what you have to look for. In the Himalayas there are many famous caves where people have stayed for many years, and I'm sure they got their benefits. If you choose to live with other people around, in a community, then you have the advantage of constant energetic support and, as Chögyam Trungpa says, '... *a community of people who have the perfect right to cut through your trips and feed you with their wisdom.*' But equally, you're never really alone. So again it depends on what's going on in your life.

Our whole community has become quieter over the years and we've noticed that new people get the benefit of being able to jump into this pool of quietness. Both situations have their advantages, and probably both are essential at different times.

Silence is also possible in community. Perhaps sometimes in our community we don't have enough of that. How to judge it? Everybody has to find their own kind of naturalness about such things. What causes us stress? What causes us to not feel quiet? Almost certainly it is our conditioned mind. We have certain structures of thought and some of these disturb us.

Of course if you go and be alone then you could be sitting there quietly but with a whole pile of structures in your basement. You might go into the cave with a very busy mind but after thirty years there isn't much thinking left. But not everybody wants to spend their life in a cave. If you are someone who sees the benefit in getting support to see the structures of your mind then, as an alternative to a cave, I would suggest that spiritual community within society is quite a good option. Of course the whole effort is to come to silence.

A spiritual community provides the space and encouragement for you to become aware of the unconscious mind structures that govern your life. For example, if you have the idea 'I'm not intelligent enough' then in the workings of daily life you're confronted with this idea and encouraged to become aware of its affects.

By looking at these structures and shining light on them we begin to be less affected by them. This is the transformation that you're talking about. The movement is to become more and more open and aware so that these old structures are no longer what we identify with.

Most of us are wounded by our conditioning. We are molded into shape by our families and society and never really know who we are beneath or beyond our conditioning. It muddied the waters. Working together in community provides many mirrors that offer us the chance to see ourselves, to know who we are. Interactions with people who are also interested in knowing themselves provide a profound mirror in which we can see all the things we are not, which is not always comfortable. In this process, we then have the opportunity to see who we really are. This mirroring is one of the greatest values of community life.

Therapy: To Do or Not to Do

If you want to wake up, these traumas are not going to be a hindrance. You can still wake up. You can wake up right now; it takes only a moment. But if you want to live this awakening, if you want to live in freedom, then you are going to have to deal with them.

John David

> Dear John David,
> Some years ago I did therapy because I felt a deep emotional discomfort in my body-mind, which I could never face alone because it always got too intense. I did the therapy for about six months and there were some moments of releasing and seeing. But it took a long time and was very expensive. The basic feeling of not being okay is still there very strongly in me. Would continuing therapy be good to release this deep emotional pain, to see my blind spots? Or what would you recommend? What is your feeling about therapy?

I don't have so much feeling about therapy, but it's an important question. I would see that therapy, like meditation, is an important tool for you to understand your mind, and in fact to see yourself, to get to know yourself.

If you develop a regular meditation practice then inevitably you will come to see certain of your previously unconscious structures. Also, if you focus on some particular emotional difficulty you can gain some insight into what is happening on a deeper level.

We might have an emotional response that keeps repeating itself in similar situations, such as relationship. Everything is going along well for some time and then it comes to some kind of sudden ending. Then we feel abandoned – very painful. We often say, 'My partner abandoned me and it made me feel terrible.' Superficially that may be the situation, but if you would sit quietly, or have some therapy on this subject of feeling the pain of abandonment, you would quickly get in touch with deeper levels.

You were four years old and your parents separated. You stayed with one parent and the other left, maybe with a new partner, maybe not. In that moment you felt very abandoned by the parent who left.

Many years later your own relationship separates and you feel this same tremendous pain of abandonment. There's a good chance that in the subconscious mind – the basement, the inner child, the ego – something from earlier times is creating this strong emotion of painful abandonment. Your early conditioning and experiences will determine what's in your basement.

Things that are held there – we can call them structures of the mind – are waiting to appear as some kind of strong emotion. But we may not be really familiar with what's going on. It may be we don't really want to look. Perhaps we think it's much easier to blame the partner who left us: 'It's their fault. They did it to me.'

This attitude is rather immature because as soon as you spend some time looking inside, sometimes using therapy, sometimes using meditation, then you will inevitably begin to understand how the subconscious mind works with the conscious mind. We start to understand that whatever emotion we're feeling right now mostly comes from something from our past.

This is pretty much accepted by the world of psychology, the world of psychiatry. If you are somebody who is interested in freedom, spiritual freedom, then you will certainly at some point come in contact with these ideas because, maybe without ever looking, you're just throwing out emotions. You can be angry suddenly, and yet there doesn't seem to be any particular reason for it. You're angry because something's being touched in your subconscious mind.

Once we come to understand how this works then we have the possibility of seeing and understanding what's stored in our basement. Personally I would recommend starting with meditation. Through meditating regularly over some years you will come to understand that whatever is happening in this moment has its roots in a past moment, usually from when you were very young. It could be that most of them occur before we can even speak. Whatever happened it's waiting inside your subconscious, your basement. Then in our adult life something happens, like feeling abandoned in relationship, and it triggers this old memory. After this has happened several times it seems sensible to consider if it's because of something inside you, after all it's not likely that every partner has the same dynamic that creates the same structure.

Of course in relationship anyway there are some intrinsic issues that tend to create separation after some time. If you have a healthy meditation practice issues and structures that you were not aware of will naturally surface. If these particular structures cause you a lot of pain and suffering that continue over a longer time then therapy could well bring light onto that particular emotional story.

Over the last ten years of our Open Sky House Community we've had quite a lot of residents who in my opinion needed to have some therapy. If you consider the wider society, almost everybody needs therapy because unfortunately nearly everybody has some neurotic behaviour patterns. It's very rare to actually meet someone who is living a fulfilled, peaceful, happy life. Even such a person may still have some particular structures that create suffering sometimes.

However, how the therapy occurs is very important, because my experience is that some therapists – maybe we can call them conventional therapists – see their role as assisting better functioning in society. This kind of therapy can go on for many months or even years and you are in danger of a type of self-hypnosis: 'There's something wrong with me.'

The dynamic between the therapist and the patient gives lots of opportunities for projection. Perhaps you fall in love with your therapist, or you hate your therapist. These kind of strong emotions are projections onto an authority, like Mummy or Daddy, so it's important to find a therapist who is mature and takes a neutral position. If in addition to that you can find a therapist who has a spiritual understanding you have a better chance of not getting identified with the therapy itself.

Trauma is a structure that comes from some particular old situation that caused a great deal of suffering when it happened, maybe a shock. Out of this shock the whole mind-body organism has been frozen. This often happens in sexual abuse or domestic violence. The nervous system of the child simply can't deal with the powerful adult energies of that moment and it leaves a deep scar in the psyche.

In cases like this I would definitely say that therapy can be a support, can be useful for bringing understanding. These structures are a screen that prevents us connecting to our True Nature. However, if we really want to become free we need to find a balance between looking at old structures and simply being here in this moment, being present, having an open heart, being vulnerable, being available, so that we don't constantly retreat into our mind looking at the past.

In my many years of spiritual seeking I was involved for some time with Osho and his ashram. Many western people who came to Osho in the late 60s and 70s were kind of New Age therapists and he encouraged all the western people in the ashram to be involved with them. In the early days of the ashram roughly half of Osho's disciples were westerners and half were Indian.

Generally speaking it was the westerners doing the therapy and the Indians doing the meditation, and of course western people also did meditation. There were all kinds of workshops. Often people were carrying around teddy bears or Barbie dolls – lots of crazy stuff happened. It made for a very vibrant communal energy.

The therapists were gradually developed into an institute that later became the Osho Multiversity and they were forever inventing new workshops. Some people maybe had more money than sense and were constantly doing the latest workshops. The collective seemed to encourage that.

If we're always busy with therapy that accepts this ego – this 'I', this subconscious – as who we are, we don't really question fundamentally the situation of this movie, of who's doing the therapy, because we're just identified with it. Therapy that comes from a spiritual understanding has more the intention of keeping this fundamental question in mind while at the same time exploring some particular aspect of the psyche.

If you are relatively new to knowing yourself, meditation is an essential part of coming to a quiet mind. Along the way, that meditation can also give you insight into what's in your basement. Then as you progress you gain more self-awareness and eventually you take the full responsibility for what's happening emotionally. You don't project it onto the other person. If you then have some particularly difficult structures therapy can be very helpful. Once you've become more free of these inner structures and you've dealt with a lot of your emotional, neurotic issues, then therapy becomes less important. What is more important is to have an open heart and be simply present.

Then, when the structures appear like a rainstorm on the ocean, you already have the tools you need. You might well become identified with the rainstorm, but once it has passed you can see what has happened. It all depends really on your maturity as a seeker.

Resistance to the Flow of Life

Adyashanti is an American teacher living near San Fransisco and feels like a kindred spirit, even though I have as yet not met him. I like his direct, no-nonsense approach. His book, *The End of your World*, where he talks about the characteristics of awakening, has profoundly touched me as he finds words to explain things that I know but find hard to express.

A community is flowing and it moves and as soon as you don't move with it, something falls behind in you. The teaching weakens if it doesn't stay fresh. Your own realisation falls if you don't move with it. That's why I always suggest to live in a state of discovery. Not a state of discovery where you are looking for an ultimate conclusion for that's the greatest illusion of all. Live in a state of discovery because that's how the Truth lives.

Adyashanti

Dear John David,
When I feel resistance to the flow of the community I try to see what it is in me that doesn't want to move. Almost always I can see that I am angry with the way things are. I don't want to trust and let go into that. I am resistant to freshly approaching the new challenge.

I can see that the resistance doesn't really help me because I fall behind even though I really want to believe I have a good reason to be resistant. This quote from Adyashanti points to a possibility to live without long-lasting resistance building inside, to surrender more into the flow of what is. What do you suggest to do when resistance comes up and how to live without it?

This resistance that Adyashanti is talking about here is in the context of community living, but you can also take it as resistance to life itself. The world is anyway a big community and this same resistance can also be experienced in any family or relationship situation.

Adyashanti is suggesting that we live in the moment. One of the problems of a spiritual community is that we come together because we are interested in Self-realisation – some kind of big bang that will happen one day in the future. He calls that *'the greatest illusion of all'*.

We expect that something wonderful will happen in the future and he suggests that what is much more important is that you live in a state of discovery and not focused on this big bang. What if it doesn't happen? Better to live in the moment, and live in the moment with openness, because everything that happens in each moment contains the possibility to see or understand something. If you see the simple daily happenings as unimportant and are always waiting for this special something, you can miss your whole life.

The big bang idea is rather common in post-communist countries like Russia and Ukraine. There can be the idea that if I just hang around there will be a miracle; there'll be some kind of secret transmission and I will just pop. Unfortunately, this means that there is often a reluctance to take responsibilty for your own awakening, and part of that is not taking the advice of the teacher seriously.

I received a rather shocking email this morning. I'm going to read it because it describes many people's situation.

> *Dear John David,*
> *You are right. For a long time I haven't done spiritual work, no surrender. When the retreat is finished, I will go again to my habits. I know this. Heart opens only for a short moment. No responsibility, only using the master's love.*

This is from someone who's been visiting my retreats for almost three years and actually is quite surrendered to the community and the work of the community. But she says she doesn't do any spiritual work and she knows at the end of this three weeks, when she's been back in Ukraine for about a week, she will do all the stuff that she did before she came here. She can see she takes no responsibility inside herself. This is a difficult situation for the teacher because he doesn't want people dependent on him.

When you decide to take responsibility, then the guidance and support of the teacher can make everything go much better. The idea that you just come and spend time with the teacher so you get to feel good, your problems disappear, and you run around happy for a week or two and then the teacher leaves and everything crashes back to how it was before is almost completely useless.

A big part of the spiritual work is to examine your own bullshit, which is probably not your own bullshit but actually just 'the' bullshit. It's all in your own hands. We give enormous power to certain sectors of society, for example our governments and churches. Why do they get this enormous power? Because all of us are completely brainwashed. We don't even question what we've been told and taught.

At school we had a class called religious study. It wasn't religious study, it was a study of the Protestant Church, and actually it wasn't study at all. It was a deep conditioning, brainwashing. When I was a little boy in school of course I didn't know I was being brainwashed. We've all been brainwashed and we don't even know it; we've given away all our power. We don't even know we've given away our power because maybe we've never had any, so it seems natural not to have any.

To many of you who've been living with communism for many years under the Soviets, what you really want is your own self-centred life, but unfortunately it doesn't work here. Choosing to hold onto your ego, your personal movie, will block the flow of energy. You have to be ready to let this melt away.

You have a choice now: Do you continue to surrender to your ego, to your personal wants, or do you surrender to your higher Self, to conscious presence and to the community? Our minds are very clever, so we have very good ways of creating strategies to explain our resistance.

In the question I am asked, *'What do you suggest to do when resistance comes up and how to live without it?'* Very simple: surrender to the flow of life and then you'll never feel resistance. It's the same as surrendering to existence. Existence is a kind of intelligence that has organised perfect conditions for life on this planet. You don't have to do anything about that; it's a given. You just have an open heart and say yes and then life is unfolding from moment to moment. That's very simple, but not easy to do it of course. The resistance comes from our ego, from our ideas. My idea is different from the ideas of the people around me: 'I don't think we should paint that blue; much better if we paint it orange.'

By simply following these egoistic ideas you miss the opportunity to *'live in a state of discovery'*. You have to see what is going on with this resistance. Is this something old from your basement – your conditioned mind – or is this something fresh coming from the moment? If it is coming from the moment you can speak to the others and say: 'Hey guys, we need to meet about this; perhaps it would be better if we tried it like this …' Nothing wrong with that. The other resistance is: 'It's very important that I go to the dentist tomorrow. I have to go and I don't care what happens around me.' This kind of resistance is a constant sabotage of the energy of the community, and ultimately a sabotage of your own awakening.

The Role of the Master

Osho was my first spiritual master. He was a controversial character who attracted many people in the 70s and 80s through combining the eastern and western spiritual and material cultures and creating a powerful field and support for inner work and awakening.

I came to Osho's ashram in a very mysterious way, at a time in my life when I wasn't consciously thinking about being part of a spiritual community. Yet I remember that as soon as I walked through 'The Gateless Gate', as the main entrance is called, I felt an enormous sense of coming home, like I had come to a place where I really felt accepted and deeply nourished. My following fifteen years of coming and going there completely changed my life, both through the presence and power of Osho and also from the amazing transformational energy of the community.

With me illusions are bound to be shattered. I am here to shatter all illusions. Yes it will irritate you. It will annoy you. That's my way of functioning and working. I will sabotage you from your very roots. Unless you are totally destroyed as a mind there is no hope for you.

Osho

> Dear John David,
> *A lot of fear comes up when I hear this quote from Osho. It feels like I can say a lot of nice things about spirituality but when it really comes to it my ego doesn't want to go. It is quite clear to me that the master's role is to challenge the ego, to destroy the illusion. Did you experience this with your masters? And did this contribute to your awakening?*

It is very easy to become involved in spirituality because you have nice ideas about it. You are not so happy with your life and you look to something like spirituality as a way of making it better. In the beginning it is quite easy. You read books, watch a lot of videos and begin some spiritual practice.

This is the beginning of how we come into our interest in spirituality. The master can have a rather amusing, charismatic energy. In the beginning it is often like that. Then, as the student starts to actually hear what is being said, there grows more connection between them. You come to the meeting and you leave feeling good, energetically good. Maybe you feel peace for several days. Everything is fine.

As this process goes on something begins to change. You think you are listening and hearing, but almost certainly in the beginning you are not. As more understanding comes stronger energetic things are happening to you, so the whole connection between you and the master begins to shift. At the same time you start getting more in touch with your own movie. Not in the absolute sense, but, for example, as someone from Hamburg with a Jewish family and certain ideas, and so on. We identify with these different movies.

Gradually the master's role is to act as a mirror, reflecting back for you to see how you are identified with a certain kind of story. We have a friend here from Italy; his story of course includes pizza and spaghetti. We have here someone from Hamburg, his story probably includes lots of rain, and I don't know what else … hamburgers of course! There must be a lot of hamburgers around in Hamburg. Someone from Italy will have a totally different story. It depends on many different factors.

All this is going along quite nicely until one day the master says something about Jewish people. He is saying it in passing, to everybody, but actually there is a Jewish person from Hamburg sitting in the room and he takes this on board. 'Oh!' Suddenly something happens. Out of all the many things that have been spoken this thing is taken strongly because it touches some belief. This belief suddenly gets a shock, it gets challenged.

This is a strong moment, because as Osho says, '*Illusions are bound to be shattered. I am here to shatter all illusions. Yes it will irritate you. It will annoy you.*' This goes on and on. As you surrender more to the teacher, as you spend enough time with the teacher for him or her to really get to know you, then he or she will find all kinds of little devices to provoke you. If you get provoked then it almost certainly means the teacher can see a hook that needs looking at.

We all have many of these. I remember in my own case I had a typical English middle-class character, with all kinds of ideas about England, British people, European civilisation. Then I went off to Japan. In Japan, as you know, they have toilets that are just a little hole in the floor. They lie and sit on straw mats and eat their food with chopsticks. Can you imagine how primitive that seemed to a 'sophisticated' middle-class European? I was very defensive, but the longer I stayed the more effect they had on me and my initial stay of a few months went on for some years. At this time I had to really look at what my ideas were. This was very painful sometimes; it made me quite vulnerable.

At one time in Japan I was living alone in the middle of Tokyo in a small apartment. It was one box, one room; you could not even call it an apartment. It was on the roof of an office building. Some friends of mine had arranged that I could use it for free. I lived there for a few years. It was my cave.

Later when I went to Osho this process continued. In the beginning I was completely excited to be there, to see what was going on, to experience meditation for the first time. I was excited about so many people sitting together in silence in the big hall. I was totally touched by the master, arriving in a Rolls Royce, wearing beautiful clothes. This was very impressive. It was all great fun in the beginning.

But in the years that followed there were many very difficult moments, moments when I felt extremely vulnerable. I remember one workshop where I felt very good, really good, marvellous in fact. But apparently my behaviour had become quite strange and I was disturbing the workshop. I got to meet one of the organisers of the ashram who suggested I take a few days off the workshop, sit down by the river, go to the park, chill out a bit.

What was that about? Was that a great spiritual experience I had? Was that a glimpse of the Absolute? Probably if I was asked at that time I would have said yes. I would have not known what a glimpse of the Absolute was anyway. I felt absolutely wonderful. I didn't really care if I disturbed anything. Almost for sure if I look back at it, what had been going on that day, or for some days or weeks, had put me on overload. I couldn't handle it. It was too much. It was disturbing my ideas and my sense of myself too much. My identity had been challenged too much or too quickly. So I lost the plot for some days.

I remember some very strong moments. Everywhere birds were singing, the sun was shining, the garden itself was like a jungle around the meditation room. Nevertheless, I also remember many times sitting almost in desperation. Somehow I had become so challenged that I was left in shock, maybe, or deep vulnerability. Something like this. This went on and on, for several years even. In the end there was an awakening. It came through the challenges. Spiritual work involves your ego, your movie, how you identify with yourself. This has to gradually be worn away, worn down.

Unfortunately, if it happens too suddenly very often there is a reaction, a resistance, and people leave. They stop working with the teacher. They make the teacher wrong in some way. That convinces them that it's fine and they go off to find another teacher, or not find any teacher. Care is needed, because by going from teacher to teacher you are never really allowing yourself to be deeply challenged, and the identification you have with your false self is never ground down and then gradually polished away. This process is actually the real work. The problem we have is that we can't recognise the true Self. Why? Because we are identified with the false self, we believe ourselves to be the false self.

Unless we are challenged we don't understand what our false self is about, and we don't see that it is just an illusion, just a story. If we come from Italy it is a story that involves spaghetti and if we come from Hamburg it is a story that involves hamburgers! This is not a very crucial part of our identity. It's quite easy to give up on spaghetti or hamburgers. Nobody has real problems with these, but as things get closer and closer there can be a lot of resistance to really seeing and allowing things to slip away. So many good spiritual prospects are actually sabotaged by leaving the teacher.

It happens to almost everybody, we get super resistant – 'now I have to go … anyway this teacher is no good, he always says the wrong things … I don't like the colour of his beard.' When you come to this point, it is a great moment. That is not the moment to run away. It's exactly the moment to look inward and examine with brutal honesty what is going on. You can even share it with your teacher directly. People tell me all kinds of things you don't normally talk about, and I don't mind at all.

I remember many times in my early days trying to look inside, feeling something, but not getting in touch with what it was about. It took years before I was able to access what was going on and was able to express it. This is not something that happens so quickly for most people. Not for me anyway.

Did I answer the question? Yes, of course it is a funny situation with the ego. We are completely identified with something that we call ego, our identity, who we think we are, and yet the same ego is bringing us to the spiritual master and putting itself in this dangerous situation where the master's role is to challenge it. In the beginning the ego is a little bit ready to be challenged, but at a certain point it is definitely not ready to be challenged anymore. This is a very delicate tightrope walk. It is the razor's edge. This is something everybody experiences when they do spiritual work.

Did this contribute to my awakening? I would say that almost every day of the whole fifteen years I was active with Osho, and later with Papaji, I was being challenged. Through this challenge a great understanding happened and a lot of things dissolved and fell away.

Looking back, I see that by spending time with Osho, following his advice and teachings, my ego was grossly diminished by the time I got to Papaji. This work of grinding and polishing away the ego is an essential part of the spiritual work. When you get so uncomfortable that you have to go away, that is exactly the moment where there can be a big shift. So don't just run away.

Did you trust Osho from the beginning, or did you question him as a spiritual master?

I'd been introduced to him by a friend in Japan and I was completely not interested. Then later on, in a strange twist, I found myself in Mumbai and I remembered this friend who'd told me I was ready for an Indian master. I thought he might be staying at Osho's ashram and I went looking for him. That's how I ended up there. I wasn't consciously planning it.

I was one of these very mindy people: 'Why? Why do you think that? What's that about?' My mind was going crazy. I was questioning everything. So I would say I fell in love with the master slowly. It's a gradual thing for some people. At some point I decided to become a *sannyasin* and get a name from Osho. That was a big decision. Once I made that decision, once I received the name, there was tremendous euphoria. Not exactly surrender, but some kind of movement towards surrender. This was pretty important.

Is it important to be given a name by a master?

I don't think it's so important.

What is the reason then that you give names?

Well, I try to find a name that marks some kind of potential that I can see in that person. The name is to encourage that particular aspect of the person at that time.

Some people have had two or three names, but it's not so serious. It's a playful thing, but also I'm suggesting that if you take a name it means that you're accepting me as your teacher. So if somebody asks for a name they should be ready for that aspect as well. In that way it's a recognition of our connection.

The other thing that I would say is that you must have a living master rather than a dead master. You can project as much as you like onto a dead master, but if you have a living master of course he or she is almost certainly going to be in your face, saying things that you never expected them to say. That's one of the games the masters play. They try to drive you a bit crazy.

CHAPTER 3

The Mind

Everybody's mind wants things to stay the same. Mind has an investment in staying as it is and so it does not know much about letting go. It is important that we see how our minds will try and sabotage our transformation when we start the inner work.

The Mind

We become very used to behaving and functioning in a certain way, and when we get challenged on the spiritual journey, or begin to see things about ourselves that we may have previously avoided, it is vital to stay in this process and allow it to happen.

It is by facing our conditioned mind, our desires and judgements, our deeply-rooted fears and becoming aware of them, that we can truly start to become free.

Don't Go Back

Osho, known for most of his life as Bhagwan Shree Rajneesh, was a former philosophy professor. He talked more than six hundred books on many historic masters, reinterpreting their teachings for a contemporary audience. His time in Oregon, USA, was controversial and when he returned to Pune, India, he accused the American government of slowly poisoning him. He passed away aged fifty-eight in 1990.

Between the animal and the Buddha is where most people are. And that is where anxiety exists. Anxiety is tension. A part of you wants to go back to the animals. It goes on pulling you backwards. It says, 'Come back! It was so beautiful – where are you going?' But in some indirect way another part in you knows perfectly well that to be a Buddha is your destiny. The seed is there! And the seed goes on saying to you, 'Find the soil, right soil, and you will become a Buddha. Don't go back, go forward.'

Osho

Dear John David,
After deciding to join the Sangha *weekend I felt enormous energy and a sense of liberation. This weekend I think I got a taste of what it means to serve. And then suddenly today, in the meditation, I had a very tough insight into a pattern that has guided me mostly for the last forty years. So what to do?*

The whole point of the *Sangha* is to work on yourself. Deciding to make a commitment to this inner work is always going to be a strong time. It is a deep decision, which doesn't much involve the mind. We know there will be tough moments on that journey and then it is a tremendous support to feel a connection to other people in the *Sangha*, and for that we need an open heart.

There were so many moments when I felt from my heart that it is just the right step now in my life; there is nothing more to get from the outside.

When you come close to this kind of decision it is very good to watch what the mind is doing. It is not really personal but everybody's mind wants things to stay the same. Mind has a kind of investment in staying as it is and so it does not always give the best advice.

It was really not my plan when I came to Germany in May to come here. I wasn't forcing anything. This insight I had today touched me very deeply. It was painful at first, then I had an awful afternoon and now I am thankful I have seen it.

Well, this is a very mature position of course, to be able to see that it is not just about feeling good all the time. People come to the *Sangha* thinking it is like a big ice-cream you can come and nibble on and feel good.

Most people are happy to rearrange their mask a little, but what we are going for here is taking it off. Why do we want to take off the mask? We just want to be who we are. It is very simple and actually it is very lovely but unfortunately we have all kinds of structures that the mind can grab onto with the idea that by being who we are we will be some kind of monster.

In reality, when the mask falls off or dissolves we are all beautiful, spontaneous and innocent human beings. It is so beautiful to be able to live this authentic innocence. We can easily get tired of all the tricks and games, but for sure the idea of change brings out a lot of fear. To be able to see this fear means there is some chance to change it. So you've done very well I would say.

I start crying, sorry.

We don't mind you crying, it's nice. Why wouldn't it be okay to cry? If crying is the response of this moment then that is totally authentic. It is speaking in another way. In your tears you are communicating a deep frustration – apparently that where you are in your life with your work, family and friends does not allow you to be authentic. We have set up a society that divorces us from our authenticity. We are sophisticated robots or puppets and we have been conditioned in such a way that nobody needs to hold the strings; we do it ourselves.

Inside you may feel you want to cry, but we have been taught we shouldn't. Lots of men wouldn't cry in front of a group of people. If you want this split you are feeling to change, it is in your hands. Only *you* can say you are not doing this anymore and find a place where you can be authentic, where in any moment you can be who you are. That is not to suggest that it is easy.

Most people are very into playing their roles. They are not authentic and it hurts me a bit if I walk around and see this.

It should hurt you a lot. When you look at current society, one of the most authentic responses is just to cry. Really good people, basically decent, heartfelt, sensitive people have got themselves in a situation in western Europe, for example, where they are split against themselves – playing their roles instead of being themselves. In the end for what? For making more money? Having a bigger Mercedes? It doesn't make sense. If you went to these people and asked what they would prefer probably they would say to be authentic. But we set up a situation where it is very difficult to be authentic because all we know is how to play our role.

Whether you wear a funny little hat at McDonalds or you are an executive in a big company you have a certain role, and you know what that role is – even when it hasn't been spelled out. Once you realise that what is going on is not what you really want there will come opportunities. Life is very abundant. It will give you these opportunities. If you compromise with that you will surely end up the way that other people end up – split against yourself.

If it was up to me I would win a million dollars in the lottery.

If you want to win a million dollars in the lottery you want to rely on the world out there. It is a completely wrong idea.

I need a million dollars to buy a small apartment in the Canary Islands where I want to stay.

A million dollars and the Canary Islands just mean you are completely lost. You still believe in the outside world.

I often have the feeling that I am not right the way I am, that I should be different. I should be better somehow.

Unfortunately this is a very common human condition. It is a mad world where almost everybody is trying to be like somebody else. It doesn't make sense. Why couldn't everyone accept themselves as they are and just get on with their life? Many years ago, I was involved in the fashion business. At one point this involved going to the fashion shows in Paris. I even got to know a few models.

I found it very interesting that these women, who most people would consider to be extremely beautiful, have exactly the same judgements about themselves as any other woman. This was quite a good lesson for me. I realised that there can't be much reality in self-judgement. I think this is one of the beautiful things about the work we are doing, that it brings us into a deep acceptance of who we are. So you came to the right place.

I would like to be as I am, without the fear of not being loved, the fear of being rejected.

Everybody has different structures that prevent them being as they are.

But I can see since being involved in the Sangha group more and more trust comes to be as I am ... and to be loved.

Without this loving environment, which is a fertile environment for trust, it is not so easy. In the society there isn't support to become more trusting. In fact the energy is the other way. This is unfortunately why many people are very neurotic and desperately trying to be somebody else. It's a strange joke. If you take a hundred people at least ninety-nine are trying to be somebody else.

I would say the support of the Sangha *encourages me to see what is inside. Once I've seen something I can start showing this to myself and also to the others, which is not really accepted in 'normal' society.*

Honesty and being as you are go together. Also realising that we don't really have a choice. We are never going to be as somebody else is; we are always going to be as we are. So when we can accept this there is tremendous tolerance. Everybody is welcome.

Becoming the Witness

Siddartha Gautama was a man who became known as Gautama Buddha. He famously made his own journey to understand Truth, to go beyond the attachment to form and to his mind, and to wake up and then spread the message. His words echo down through the centuries and still have a profound resonance.

It is better to conquer yourself than to win a thousand battles. Then the victory is yours. It cannot be taken from you. Not by angels or by demons, heaven or hell. Peace comes from within. Do not seek it without.

Gautama Buddha

Dear John David,
I used to think this phrase 'conquer yourself', by Buddha, was pointing to some kind of action or doing. But now I see that it is more about a deep self-acceptance and the clear understanding that the things that make us suffer aren't real in the way we think. I would be interested for you to share what this phrase means to you.

I think by now we all see that trying to change things outside in the world doesn't work – it's a huge job. It's just not possible for human beings to achieve this level of control, but when you see what's going on inside, how you create your suffering, then you can stop it.

So for example, right now we feel okay. But if we think about what might happen in the next month then fear arises and then we don't feel okay. We start to suffer. If you can see that you've created this suffering then you can bring your attention to whatever this thought or this fear is and you can simply see that this is being created in your mind.

We don't know the future, it hasn't happened, but usually we're projecting something from the past into the future. We also spend a lot of time fighting with ourselves about the past: 'If only I'd given that girlfriend more flowers and chocolate she wouldn't have left me.' This again creates our suffering, but this suffering is only happening inside our little movie. Actually I shouldn't call it a little movie because it's rather an epic that goes on through our whole life. This is the ego at work, and it is possible to understand this mechanism. When you see how it works you immediately become empowered because you yourself are the master of your own situation.

Once you come to this victory, Buddha says that heaven or hell or angels or demons can't take it away from you. He says peace comes from within. This week during the Self-enquiry exercise many of us had an experience, only for a moment or two, of the peace that comes from inside when we are not projecting into the future or considering the past.

As destiny would have it, five minutes before I came down I got this letter from an old friend who is here with us tonight.

It seems that for the first time I clearly saw how suffering was created – by the projection of someone ('me') somewhere on the outside, out of the source, out of the stillness. This someone that's creating the suffering no longer felt part of the oneness. It seemed separated. There was a wordless internal understanding.

In that moment it was like complete understanding and complete peace. No question, no answer, nothing. That lasted for a while and then from this nothingness, images came. Seeing these images coming out of nothing was seeing the beginning of separation.

A picture appears, of something that seems to be on the outside, and from another part something somewhere longs for that. Separation starts. So in one moment there is peace and oneness and stillness, and at one point it is no longer.

So are you saying that the suffering is because you had left this calm and peaceful moment?

In that moment it seemed very clear.

The suffering came out of not being present. Your mind became active and took you into some pictures or thoughts.

I wouldn't say it that way. I just explained that these pictures arrived out of nothing.

Well, everything is coming from nothing. Usually we're focused on what comes out of the nothing. These pictures and thoughts create what I'm calling the movie, the epic that we call 'my life'. We try to move between the past and the future.

I know this, but today I really understood it – I felt it in every cell of the body.

That's a very wonderful experience. You got a glimpse of Truth in that moment. It's when we identify with the pictures and the thoughts that we create our suffering. As Buddha says, it's in your own hands and we can conquer it.

You've been to many meetings and heard these words many times. You interpreted them in your own way, and now, suddenly, you've got your own understanding, your own knowing. If you give it the space and you make it a priority it will become clearer and stronger inside you. You're on your way to conquering yourself.

It's shocking to see that our suffering is something we create ourselves. It's much more comfortable to say that somebody is doing something to me, or something in the world is happening and making me suffer.

We like to blame the outside. That makes us feel like it's got nothing to do with us. He made me jealous – some action he did made me jealous. It's uncomfortable to look inside and see that we have ideas about how others should behave and that if they don't behave accordingly, then we suffer. If we see that we suffer because of our idea then we can very quickly change it.

I remember many years ago I was in Leipzig. I met a woman who was a professor of Asian Studies. She told me that she'd never experienced the Self so I said, 'Well okay, if you'd like to come tomorrow we can see what happens.'

We ended up sitting in a completely empty room doing a guided enquiry. After about twenty minutes there were tears running down her face and I could feel that she was very touched. Everything was very lovely and nothing was really happening until suddenly her mobile phone rang. Not really a problem actually – we were just sitting in the room with the phone ringing – but in that moment she apologised for her phone ringing and immediately she was out of this space.

A bird could have sung, a car could have passed and they wouldn't have disturbed anything, but she identified and said 'my' phone! This was enough to put her back in her conditioned mind. If we're at the source nothing is disturbing.

Presence is the Key

I took the students from my annual Arunachala retreat to visit Swami Dayananda on several occasions and a strong connection was established. He was a very impressive man. He had published a whole shop-full of books and was the leading *Vedanta* master in India. He trained many teachers, even supporting them with financial help to set up their own ashrams. He represented India at international conferences and at the same time lived very simply.

The whole mind is full of desires, and if one of them is freedom, then perhaps now and then it gets some attention. But when one understands that this is exactly what one wants in life, and that desire to be free is very predominant, then all other desires become subservient and fall away. It is automatic. You don't have to do anything.

Swami Dayananda

> Dear John David,
> I have the feeling that I am holding onto something inside me, that I identify myself with a kind of longing that has been driving me onwards. I am a bit afraid of giving up this longing that seems part of me.

It depends a little on what this longing is. We are never really content. We think if we could just get this particular something then we would be happy, but of course this doesn't make us happy and then we want something else – a new car, new partner, lots more money. There is always a feeling of something lacking and that leads to more wanting.

Look at the very successful people in Hollywood. Famously beautiful, handsome or talented, they have lots of money, big houses, an amazing lifestyle of abundance. Are these people actually happy? If you read the gossip magazines they are clearly not happy.

Masters' Biographies

A - L

Robert Adams

1939 - 1997

John David's book selection
Silence of the Heart

Robert Adams was an American *Advaita* teacher impressed by Sri Ramana Maharshi. According to Robert, in his teenage years he spent time with Paramhansa Yogananda, who quickly felt that he would be better visiting Sri Ramana Maharshi in India.

He recounts how in his late teens he visited Sri Ramana Maharshi in Tiruvannamalai, India. It's unclear if this happened as no one remembers Robert being there.

Later in his life he held *Satsang* with a small group of devotees in California and later in Sedona where he passed away in 1997. Robert's teachings were not that well known in his lifetime but since his death they have been circulated amongst those investigating the philosophy of *Advaita*.

He is remembered for his stillness, and a beautiful book of his teachings, *Silence of the Heart: Dialogues with Robert Adams*, which was published in 1997.

www.robertadamsinfinityinstitute.org

Adyashanti

born Steven Gray in 1962

John David's book selection
The End of Your World

Adyashanti is an American spiritual teacher and author from the San Francisco Bay area who offers talks, online study courses and retreats in the United States and abroad.

In his 20s he studied Zen Buddhism and at age twenty-five he began experiencing a series of transformative spiritual awakenings. While sitting alone on his cushion he had a classic awakening experience in which he '...*penetrated to the emptiness of all things and realised that the Buddha I had been chasing was what I was.*'

For the next few years he continued his meditation practice, while also working at his father's machine shop. Finally, at thirty-one, he had an experience of awakening that put to rest all his questions and doubts. In 1996 he was invited to teach by his master Arvis Joen Justi. He first started giving talks to small gatherings, which grew over the years. He changed his name to Adyashanti, a Sanskrit term for primordial peace.

His talks focus on awakening and embodying awakening. He downplays any affiliation with Zen. '*The Truth I point to is not confined within any religious point of view, belief system, or doctrine, but is open to all and found within all.*'

He has authored several books: *Emptiness Dancing, My Secret is Silence, True Meditation* and *The End of Your World*, as well as producing audio and video recordings. Presently he lives in the Bay area with his wife Mukti. Together they founded the Open Gate Sangha, a non-profit organisation devoted to his teachings and meetings.

www.adyashanti.org

Anandamayi Ma

1896 - 1981

John David's book selection
*The Essential
Sri Anandamayi Ma*

Anandamayi Ma was born in Bangladesh in 1896 to religious and unusual parents. They often sang devotional songs intensely to *Krishna* and her father was often spiritually ecstatic in his behavior. She was married at a very young age, but behaved in such strange ways that her husband thought she was possessed. However, local religious figures made it clear that she was intoxicated by a spirit and that there was no 'cure'.

She travelled through India and soon gathered a following of people who could sense a particular serenity and aloofness associated with someone being free of ego and in touch with the divine. An ashram was built in her honour, but she left as soon as it was completed. She didn't have any formal religious training or an outer guru and she emphasised the importance of detachment from the world and of focussing towards religious devotion. She also encouraged her devotees to serve others. She did much travelling and wandering, at times refusing to stay at the ashrams her devotees provided for her. While her parents worshiped *Krishna*, she could not be placed in any definite tradition.

An ecstatic child of ecstatic parents, she became a famous saint who, like many other female Indian saints, stood on the edge of several religious traditions yet in the midst of none. She influenced the spirituality of thousands of people who came to see her throughout her long life. She died in 1981.

www.anandamayi.org

Annamalai Swami

1906–1995

John David's book selection
Final Talks

Annamalai Swami, a direct disciple of Sri Ramana Maharshi, realised the Self after practising Self-enquiry for decades. He went to Sri Ramana's ashram in the late 1920s as a young man and worked there for nearly ten years, first as Sri Ramana's personal attendant and later as the construction manager.

One day he was assisting Sri Ramana in the bathroom and asked him if the ecstasy that the *sadhus* feel when they smoke marijuana is the same as that of the Self. Sri Ramana then playfully mimicked the inebriated *sadhus*, running around the bathroom then hugging Annamalai. In this moment, Annamalai reported that he got awakened.

After this awakening experience he knew that his time at the ashram had come to an end, and he moved to a house near the ashram where he practised Self-enquiry for many years and eventually became permanently Self-realised. This small house became a little ashram, as both western and Indian seekers were drawn to him, his presence and his clarity. He died in 1995.

The experience of Self-realisation gave him first-hand knowledge of how to perform Self-enquiry successfully, making his advice especially valuable to seekers. His teachings, which he delivered in plain, direct language, have been recorded in the book *Final Talks*.

www.inner-quest.org/Annamalai_Self.htm

Gautama Buddha

6th Century B.C

John David's book selection
Anguttara Nikaya:
The Teachings of the Buddha

Born in Nepal as Siddartha Gautama in the 6th century BC, he became known as Buddha. He was a spiritual leader and teacher whose life serves as the foundation of the Buddhist religion.

According to the most widely known story of his life, he was a royal prince who left the comforts and luxury of his palace life to discover what true happiness was. After experimenting with different teachings for years, going through extreme practices and hardships and finding none of them acceptable, Gautama spent a fateful night in deep meditation. Here, all of the answers he had been seeking became clear and he achieved full awareness, thereby becoming Buddha.

After his enlightenment he went to Benares and shared his new understanding with five holy men. They understood immediately and became his disciples. This marked the beginning of the Buddhist community. For the next forty-five years, the Buddha and his disciples went from place to place in India spreading the *Dharma* – his teachings – and living a very simple life.

Where ever the Buddha went he won the hearts of the people because he dealt with their true feelings. He advised them not to accept his words on faith, but to decide for themselves whether his teachings were right or wrong before following them. He encouraged everyone to have compassion for each other and develop their own virtue.

www.aboutbuddha.org

Pema Chödrön

born 1936

John David's book selection
Living Beautifully: with Uncertainty and Change

Pema Chödrön was born Deirdre Blomfield-Brown in 1936 in New York City. After University she travelled to France where she met Lama Chime Rinpoche who set her on a path to studying and practising Tibetan Buddhism. Pema then studied under the meditation master Chögyam Trungpa Rinpoche, coming to a deep understanding and becoming an ordained disciple.

Pema Chödrön is a leading exponent of teachings on meditation and how they apply to everyday life. She is widely known for her charming and down-to-earth interpretation of Tibetan Buddhism for western audiences.

A central theme of her teaching is the principle of *shenpa*, or attachment, which she interprets as the moment one is hooked into a cycle of habitual negative or self-destructive thoughts and actions.

Pema is currently a resident teacher at Gampo Abbey, Cape Breton, Nova Scotia, the first Tibetan monastery for westerners. She has written several books: *The Wisdom of No Escape* and *When Things Fall Apart*.

Ram Dass

born 1931

John David's book selection
Be Here Now

Ram Dass was born Richard Alpert to a Jewish family in the USA. He became a prominent Harvard psychologist and psychedelic pioneer with Dr Timothy Leary, experimenting with LSD. He was fired from Harvard due to his dealings with psychedelic drugs and he travelled to India in search of a spiritual guru.

In 1967, by a strange stroke of luck or destiny he met his guru, Neem Karoli Baba, whom he became closely involved with. Everything changed then. Taking on the name Ram Dass, his intense *Dharmic* life started, and he became a pivotal influence on a culture that has reverberated with the words *Be Here Now* ever since. This is the title of the book he published when he returned to America in 1971.

He travelled in The States and worldwide, guiding and teaching, and notably set up the Seva Foundation, dedicated to helping to solve world problems.

Ram Dass's spirit has been a guiding light for three generations, carrying along millions on the journey, in his words '*...helping to free them from their bonds as I work through my own.*'

He now resides on Maui, where he shares his teachings through the Internet and through bi-yearly retreats. His work continues to be a path of inspiration to his old students and friends as well as young people who are just discovering the path of Being Here Now.

www.ramdass.org

Deepak Chopra

born 1947

John David's book selection

Seven Spiritual Laws of Success

An expert in the field of mind-body healing, Deepak Chopra is a world-renowned speaker and author on the subject of integrative medicine and is a prominent figure in the New Age movement. He was born in New Delhi, India, in 1947. After attending the All India Institute of Medical Sciences, he eventually ended up in Boston where he began his career as a doctor.

Despite his rising career he became disenchanted with western medicine. As his interest in integrative medicine deepened, so did his view on the limits of western medicine. He met Maharishi Mahesh Yogi in 1985 and became involved with Transcendental Meditation, and, with the Maharishi, he co-founded Maharishi Ayur-Veda Products International. In 1995, already a prolific author, he founded the Chopra Center for Well Being in Carlsbad, California.

Chopra's core message centres around the idea that the decadence of western life leads to a complicated reliance on a material world to find happiness. He believes that a person may attain 'perfect health', a condition 'that is free from disease, that never feels pain and that cannot age or die' as the body is essentially made up of energy, not of physical matter.

His first book, *Quantum Healing: Exploring the Frontiers of Mind/ Body Medicine*, published in 1989, sold well, but it was his 1993 release *Ageless Body, Timeless Mind* that made him well known.

www.deepakchopra.com

The 14th Dalai Lama of Tibet
born 1935

John David's book selection
How to Practice: The Way to a Meaningful Life

Tenzin Gyatso was born in Tibet as Lhamo Dhondup. At the age of two he was recognised as the reincarnation of the 13th Dalai Lama, Thubten Gyatso. He was a happy and bubbly young child. He assumed full political power as the Dalai Lama in 1950, at the age of fifteen. However, his governorship was short, because in October of that year, the People's Republic of China invaded Tibet to little resistance.

Despite going to Beijing for peace talks with Mao Zedong and other Chinese leaders in 1954, the Dalai Lama was forced to escape into exile in 1959, following the brutal suppression of the Tibetan national uprising in Lhasa by Chinese troops. Consequently, he and several thousand followers fled to Dharamshala in northern India and established an alternative government there. Since then Dharamsala has become a centre for the upholding and spreading of Tibetan tradition and religion, a centre of learning and meditation for thousands of Tibetans and people from all over the world.

The 14th Dalai Lama received the Nobel Peace Prize in 1989. In his long life in exile, he has travelled the world and has spoken about the welfare of Tibetans, environment, economics, women's rights, non-violence, interfaith dialogue and many other wide-ranging topics. In his talks he always exhibits a sense of lightness, humour, clarity and wisdom.

www.dalailama.com

Mahatma Gandhi

1869 - 1948

John David's book selection
Selected Works of Mahatma Gandhi (Set of 5 books)

Mohandas 'Mahatma' Gandhi began his activism as an Indian immigrant in South Africa in the early 1900s, and in the years following World War I became the leading figure in India's struggle to gain independence from Great Britain. He was the architect of a form of non-violent civil disobedience that would influence the world. He was known to his many followers as Mahatma, or 'the great-souled one'.

While fighting against British rule in India he always maintained his principles of truthfulness, peace and non-violence. In 1942 he launched the Quit India Movement to drive the British out of the country and gave the famous slogan of 'do or die' to his countrymen. Though the movement didn't prove to be an immediate success, the British had to grant India's independence in 1947. After this Mahatma Gandhi continued to work toward peace between Hindus and Muslims. He was shot dead in Delhi in January 1948 by a Hindu fundamentalist.

Known for his ascetic lifestyle, devout Hindu faith, and a great purity and resolve of spirit Mahatma Gandhi was imprisoned several times during his pursuit of non-cooperation and undertook a number of hunger strikes to protest many injustices, including the oppression of India's poorest classes.

The book *Selected Writings of Mahatma Gandhi* serves both as an introduction and in-depth exploration of Gandhi's life and teachings.

Georges Gurdjieff

1866 - 1949

John David's book selection
*In Search of the Miraculous
by Ouspensky*

Georges Gurdjieff was an influential early 20th century Russian mystic, philosopher, spiritual teacher and composer of Armenian and Greek descent. Gurdjieff taught that most humans do not possess a unified mind-body consciousness and thus live their lives in a state of hypnotic 'waking sleep', but that it is possible to transcend to a higher state of consciousness and achieve full human potential.

He was born in 1866 in Alexandropol (present-day Armenia). In early adulthood, according to his own account, his curiosity led him to travel in the East. It was on these journeys that he met many of the men and ancient teachings that would greatly influence him and form his later teachings. The only account of his wanderings appears in his famous book *Meetings with Remarkable Men*.

In 1922, after settling near Paris in France, he opened his Institute for the Harmonious Development of Man. There, he taught students to reintegrate their spiritual nature with their daily modern lives. Gurdjieff was putting into practice his teaching that people need to develop physically, emotionally and intellectually, hence the mixture of lectures, music, dance, and manual work. In the 1940s Gurdjieff suffered some severe car accidents, and died of related injuries near Paris in 1949.

One of his closest and most well known students was PD Ouspensky, who compiled two important books, *The Fourth Way* and *In Search of the Miraculous: Fragments of an Unknown Teaching*, considered the most valuable and reliable documentation of Gurdjieff's thoughts and universal view.

www.ggurdjieff.com

Jesus

c. 6BC - 33AD

John David's book selection

The Essential Teachings of Jesus Christ by Robert Powell

Jesus is a religious leader whose life and teachings are recorded in the Bible's New Testament. He is a central figure in Christianity and is emulated as the incarnation of God by many Christians all over the world.

Jesus Christ was born circa 6 BC in Bethlehem. Little is known about his early life, but according to the bible his teaching began after being baptised by John the Baptist. In his following years of teaching, Jesus' most controversial act was that he repeatedly claimed to be God, which was a direct violation of the Jewish law. Therefore the religious leaders asked the Roman government to execute him. He was crucified between 30-33 AD.

According to Christians, Jesus is considered the incarnation of God and his teachings are followed as an example for living a more spiritual life. Christians believe he died for the sins of all people and rose from the dead.

Recent discoveries, for example the Gospel of Thomas, shed a new light on his teachings, stripping away much of the preachings found in the bible and leaving a core essence far more in line with *Advaita* or non duality: *'Whoever discovers the interpretation of these sayings will not taste death.'*

www.realteachingsofjesus.com

Jiddu Krishnamurti

1895 – 1986

John David's book selection
*Krishnamurti to Himself:
His Last Journal*

Jiddu Krishnamurti was an Indian speaker and writer on matters that concerned humankind and spiritual awakening. In his early life he was groomed to be the new World Teacher of the Theosophist Society, but when he was twenty-seven he had a powerful spiritual awakening which changed his life completely. Soon after this he bravely and officially rejected the mantle of World Teacher saying *'Truth is a pathless land'* and withdrew from the organisation behind it.

After disassociating from the Theosophical movement, he said he had no allegiance to any nationality, caste, religion, or philosophy and spent the rest of his life travelling the world, speaking to large and small groups and individuals. He was dedicated to helping bring about a revolution of consciousness, and he setup alternative schools, which encouraged youth to adopt a more conscious and holistic form of education than the normal schools.

The subjects of his many talks and sharings included psychological revolution, the nature of mind and human relationships, meditation, inquiry, and encouraging a radical change in society. He constantly stressed the need for a deeper understanding in the psyche of every human being.

He wrote many books, among them *The First and Last Freedom, The Only Revolution*, and *Krishnamurti's Notebook*. Many of his talks and discussions have been published. Through his books and talks he comes across as clear, peaceful and as having a quiet and insistent power.

www.jkrishnamurti.org

Lao Tzu

6th Century BC

John David's book selection
Tao Te Ching

Lao Tzu was an ancient Chinese philosopher and writer. He is known as the reputed author of the *Tao Te Ching* and the founder of philosophical Taoism. Although a legendary figure, he is usually dated to around the 6th century BC and reckoned a contemporary of Confucius.

According to legend Lao Tzu was a simple, honest man, a keeper of the archives at the imperial court in China. When he was eighty years old he set out for the western border of China, toward what is now Tibet, saddened and disillusioned that men were unwilling to follow the path to natural goodness. At the border a guard, on the request of the Emperor, asked Lao Tzu to record his teachings before he left. He then composed the classic text *Tao Te Ching*, the Tao being the true Essence of the universe, the one constant thing which can also be called Truth.

He famously starts the *Tao Te Ching* with the words, 'Anything that can be written about the Tao, is not the Tao.' The book is important, especially in a modern world distracted by technology and focused on what seem to be constant, sudden, and severe changes. His words serve as a reminder of the importance of stillness, openness and discovering buried yet central parts of ourselves.

www.taoism.net

Paul Lowe
born 1933

John David's book selection
In Each Moment

Born in England, Paul became a therapist there and then travelled to India where he joined Osho's community in Pune. He became a *sannyasin* and later was Osho's chief disciple and therapist.

After his time with Osho he travelled the world sharing his understanding and experimenting with developing communities and finding his own niche in the modern spiritual movement. In his talks and workshops he addressed everyday issues like sexuality, relationships, parenting, communication, religion, health, finance, career and happiness. His view of the world and its future encourages people to go beyond what they normally think is possible or impossible.

In 2007 Paul stopped travelling and settled down in Australia. He now shares via email, audio and video, and through his website. The main theme of his sharing nowadays is the more abstract and indefinable aspects of consciousness. Paul shares his insights with clarity, caring and humour.

www.paullowe.org

They are completely caught in the story of desire. If you are very poor, if you have nothing, then you have small desires. These desires gradually increase. If you become a Hollywood legend, then what is left to desire? Nothing. This can create great suffering. The cycle of desire has to be seen. It is a hopeless scenario that never works.

When you use the word 'longing' it is a little bit different. Out of the hopelessness of desire there can be a longing to be free of all this. It may be there for many years but it is not to be given up. When you recognise that this is the one thing you want, when the desire to be free becomes your priority, then all other desires will disappear. This longing is the mechanism that will take you to Truth. It is very, very important and not to be given away. It will disappear when you attain Truth.

My longing is like the longing you are talking about. Maybe the key is to be more present.

The key is always to be present. You have to be attentive to the way you are hearing this. If you think 'Oh, that's another job for me. Now I have to give up desire. How am I going to give up desire?' then what you are really doing is supporting the ego. You are constantly supporting the separate me who will give up desire. By being present you give up the whole issue.

Be aware of your desires. Take it back and understand where your desires are coming from. Most desires come from a feeling of lack. If I had a better job I would then be happy. Life would be much better. So desire comes out of the feeling that right now something is lacking. You see this? By being really present there is no feeling of lack. There is just this wonderful energy.

One thing you could bring more into your life is Self-enquiry. It is not so easy in the beginning so you have to persevere. If you are still very attached to the world and you have all kinds of desires about how the world is going to give you happiness, love and lots of money, you won't get any value out of this enquiry. If you have the right priority and you really persevere with this long enough, you will come to a point when the mind starts to support this enquiry. It is like training the mind with a new trick, and the mind is a little stupid and doesn't realise this will lead to its own demise.

Thoughts arise from the source, from the Self, and almost instantaneously we take a thought and we make it 'mine'. We identify with these thoughts, with the desires: 'I'm hungry'. Actually it was just a thought about hunger and immediately, without any gap, the thought about hunger becomes *I'm* hungry. Then naturally there comes another thought: 'Where do I get food? I can't wait for lunch. Ah! In my bag I have a little bar of chocolate. Oh! What a pity, now it is melted – all over my bag! I'm going to have to spend some time now to clean this chocolate out of my bag.' This is how it normally goes.

If you can catch this first thought, or desire, you can ask immediately to whom it is arising, before it becomes attached to 'I'. It is very subtle of course and if you continue this with all the thoughts that arise then you find that the thoughts and desires gradually become less and less. There will be more space in your mind, more silence and emptiness.

If you understand rightly and you are patient and have the correct priority from the very beginning, then you will almost certainly come to Self-realisation. You will win the gold medal. You realise the Self. You realise you were never separate from the Self. You are the Self; it's your True Nature.

Stop Following the Thoughts

About two years after Osho had passed away I started to hear about Papaji. People I was acquainted with returned after visiting him with a glow about them. Then a close friend returned very touched and it was clear I would visit him. I spent nearly five years living in his *Sangha* in Lucknow. As for many people, this was the greatest luck in my life.

You are ripe for enlightenment when you want nothing else. In order to be born, you have to spend nine months getting bigger and bigger. For enlightenment, you have to get smaller and smaller, until you disappear completely.

Papaji

> *Dear John David,*
> *I started a spiritual search seriously about eight years ago, which for me meant inquiring into myself – meditating and putting myself into places and situations where people were like-minded and had a good energy.*
>
> *Then about four years ago I started to get very depressed. But I could feel that the spiritual journey was in fact opening me to this deeper layer inside myself. Since then, many deep emotions and psychological structures have been seen, and many have started to fade away.*
>
> *But now I feel a bit stuck. I definitely have a priority for Truth, but my desires and attachment to my ego are still strong. When the priority is there does it just need time, or is there something I can do to make this ego disappear completely?*

'You are ripe for enlightenment when you want nothing else.' Papaji would say that it has to be the last desire. Then he would explain that it's not really a desire like the other desires, it's like a deep longing that creates in you a very single-pointed priority, but then it's very easy for some old desire to pop up. We need to be constantly watching to see these desires.

I remember a friend of mine was sitting in Papaji's living room. Somebody came in and said to Papaji, 'Oh, I'm going shopping.' My friend immediately said, 'Oh, could you get something for me?' After this other person had left for shopping, Papaji smacked her: 'Look at you! Sitting there, apparently quiet, then somebody offers some chance of shopping and you immediately want a lollypop. You need to watch that.'

We do this all the time. If we're really honest then we can see that we constantly want something. Maybe most of our wanting is quite small but even if it's small it is making a statement. It's saying 'I'm not okay here as I am now. Maybe over there could be better. Maybe I could feel happier if I had a lollypop.' The mind is constantly working on this – it's constantly producing desires.

If we're constantly producing desires, we are constantly in the mind, in the ego, in the thinking mind. What Papaji is pointing to is that we need to be quiet. In fact, when we asked him what his teaching was, he used to say it was to 'be quiet'. This means not to raise up any thoughts.

This was also very clear in the daily life of Sri Ramana Maharshi and his ashram. In fact, he's famous for being the silent guru. He used to spend many hours a day sitting with his disciples in silence. He answered questions, but generally there wasn't so much talking. The whole effect of this group sitting in silence was a tremendous sense of inner peace. In this peace you're sitting in your True Nature, and your True Nature is completely at rest – no desire. As soon as this stillness is disturbed by some kind of desire we're activating the thinking mind, and we usually become quickly caught up in our movie, in our structures.

Recently we had a ten-day retreat here in Denia and some of the Hitdorf Open Sky House residents came. We are only a few minutes from a beautiful path along the edge of the Mediterranean where it's possible to walk or cycle. In our beautiful, tropical paradise of a garden we have a huge swimming pool. The garden itself is so big you can walk for hundreds of metres around it. There are a lot of possibilities for exercise. After two weeks, when the Hitdorf people were flying back, one woman in particular was very quiet. The next day she made a big drama. So, what was this drama about?

Well, she said she couldn't deal with sitting at her computer and she very strongly got the message that she needed exercise. Maybe it's natural after two weeks in the sunshine, but of course other people also came back and they didn't have this drama. She's been living in the community for three years and this is one of her pretty constant, repeating dramas. She's been conditioned to believe that if she had a lot of exercise she would be more happy. Her mother was a sports woman.

Papaji makes the point that Self-realisation happens in the moment when you disappear. What does that mean? It means when your ego is no longer in the driving seat, when you realise deeply inside that the thought – say 'I need exercise' – is simply a thought. It's not a thought that comes out of the reality of that moment, but a thought that comes out of the conditioned mind, probably originating many years before.

We're constantly caught up with these conditioned ideas. So, what to do? One thing you can do is to become self-aware. That means to look inside and to be aware about what's happening. For example, for this woman to be aware of the structure about exercise, to watch out for it and to understand that it is her own structure that was put there many years before by her sporty mother, and that she is completely identified with it.

The invitation is to look, to be self-aware, to shine some conscious light onto your ideas. If you keep focused on the inner world you will come to a point when you can catch the arising of this thought without getting attached to it – 'Ah, there is that idea about exercise and happiness again.' In order to catch that moment we need to be very willing and to become very quiet. It's difficult because we're so attached to certain structures that arise. They seem to be completely normal, in fact we call them 'me'.

As our questioner said, when he started to look deeply there seemed to be no end to the emotional and psychological structures that he saw, and now he finds himself stuck in a birth canal. That's not so easy. The first years in the community were rather difficult for him. There was definitely something depressive, or something we can say where he avoided really being here. He was a daydreamer, and some people got frustrated that he was very difficult to really meet. However, he's an attractive character.

Gradually the community was able to be a mirror and show him what was going on. So over the last two years things have changed in his daily life. The daydreaming got less, and the being here got more. He has some periods where he's very, very present and he still has periods where he's very not present.

But anyway, because he has a deep priority he doesn't give up. There is always a movement. This movement is possible because each time when he might have given up he realised that his inner priority wouldn't allow him to just fade away. Each time this happened there was a kind of step into a deeper understanding. His question comes out of his deeper understanding of eight years of priority. But he says, '… *my desires and attachment to my ego are still strong.*'

Of course there would be a feeling that it should happen quickly. I don't know how long it might take for this process; it's very much individual. Four years of serious looking is not very long. In our community we have several people who have been intensely looking for six years, eight years, ten years. In my own case – I was a very slow learner – it took me fifteen years. We can't tell really how quickly it will happen. We would all like to think it could happen tomorrow afternoon. But that's not very realistic.

It needs this strong priority where your mind is not disturbing you with some desire. It was very interesting spending time with Papaji because he was a teacher who was only for ripe souls. People came from all around the world for his meetings. A lot of these people had been looking for years. For many of them, something happened.

What happened? What did they do? Actually they didn't do anything. They had already done something. In fact Papaji himself would say that your job as a seeker is to find a teacher. Once you've found a teacher you stay with the teacher as much as you can, and then there's nothing more to do. Then it's up to the teacher.

This is rather attractive to the western mind. Actually, that's probably not what Papaji really meant. The image is riding your bicycle to the top of a steep hill and flying down the other side without any effort. Maybe this is an attractive image.

When you say, *'Is there something I can do to make this ego disappear completely?'* the simple answer is no. The simple answer is that at a certain point in the journey you can't really do anything – except be vigilant. With vigilance you become more and more sensitive to the moment when the thoughts arise and when the attachment happens. Once you come to this moment the challenge is to rest in the source of the thoughts – the Self, your True Nature. If we can come to our True Nature then that's it.

It's not quite it. The thoughts and structures may continue, in fact they almost certainly will continue, but suddenly there's nobody to be attached to them. They can be seen very easily, almost as if they're somebody else's structure. They fade away over time and one day you wake up and realise that you really didn't do anything but there is an inner emptiness, which feels like peace. No desire. This is of course a total revolution. This is the true revolution, because it's your own revolution. The fragrance of this revolution is very, very attractive and you find yourself in a situation where people want you to share with them.

I recently had the chance to watch an ultrasound of an eight-week-old foetus. It was very small, but still, amazingly, there was a form that you could instantly recognise as human. The really magical moment was to suddenly see the pulse.

Where does the pulse come from? That's my question, because this is a mystical moment. Existence has created a passing on, from mother to child, from generation to generation. I don't think we really know how this is possible or where this pulse springs from. The passing on of consciousness is equally magical. We could use the metaphor of an unlit candle coming close to a lighted candle and the flame is passed on.

Judgement and Surrender

Mahatma Gandhi is a central character in contemporary Indian culture. His name has become synonymous with non-violent protest and has inspired many freedom movements. In spite of the ruthless operation of the British Government, Gandhi insisted on gaining independence for India by non-violent means.

Surrender means living every moment as if God has given it to you. Whatever happens, with everything that's given to you in your life, live as if everything is given to you by God.
Mahatma Gandhi

Dear John David,
I almost always have strong clashes where my ego is resistant. It's like an immoveable force, and I don't want to give in. The ego is so big, and there is this feeling of being overwhelmed. I go through so many feelings afterwards, like amusement, and it doesn't seem at all serious. How can I surrender?

Well that's after the clashes, but when it's happening do you see what you just said? My sense is that you have a very low level of self worth, and that your ego is not like a big chunk of mountain but rather a sort of subtle ego that's somehow caught up with the idea that 'I'm not good enough' or 'I don't really make it', or something like that. This is a very strong message that you've bought and it's absolutely not true.

In fact I would say you shine as somebody who is incredibly competent and can do everything from putting the baby to bed and cooking the dinner to fixing the roof. You have a wide range of possibilities. You're a very competent person who's running around with the idea that you're not good enough.

So when a big immovable force turns up there is some sense

that you have to defend this little bump. You don't have to! You're a great big strong mountain. There's no need to defend anything. I think everybody who knows you would see you very differently to the way you see yourself. They don't share your self-judgement that you're a little bump, a little shit.

You've done all kinds of brilliant stuff here, which almost nobody else could have done. People can respect that, can love you for that and even want to be close to you because of that. Somehow you feel you have to defend. Against what actually?

It's strange because I know I can do this stuff. This is not the issue. It's in a way feeling that I don't have the time or I don't give or allow myself time to do the job in the way I would like.

That's not true because you tend to take quite a lot of time to do the job. If anything, we'd prefer you to take less time. So time is not the issue. It may be that you have an idea that there isn't enough time and you can't really do what you'd like to do, but actually the quality of the work you offer in the house as a handyman, I can tell you without any question, is better than anyone who's been the community handyman in the last six years. You're definitely the best handyman, and it's important that you see yourself like that. You don't have to go running around with a big flag 'I'm the best handyman that has ever been here.' It's not like that. But it's important for you to give yourself credit for what everyone else would like to give you credit for.

Yes, it's this feeling of being overwhelmed – like one job on top of the other on top of the other. I go into a panic situation and this is when I start to explode. It feels like a pressure cooker and there's more and more coming. I know that's how this house is set up.

It's not just the way this house is set up. Look at the way life is set up. Can you ever think of a time when you didn't have lots to do? Everybody's busy all the time.

Well, I don't know. People can complicate their lives or they can simplify their lives. Maybe I'd found an escape route by structuring my life so it was fairly simple. There were times when stress came in, but it was pretty relaxed. I enjoy doing the work, but not so much when there's so much pressure. And in a way I'm very grateful – I mean I appreciate it, but I'm a little confused why you should feel the need to create so much pressure.

It's quite simple really. One word: surrender.

This is a hard one.

I know. It's not about surrendering to John David or surrendering to somebody. It's not that kind of surrender. It's about surrendering to the flow of life itself. If you were really surrendered to the flow of life there would not be this sense of 'not enough time', because life itself would give you the time. It's just a flow happening.

I understand this theoretically, but practically it seems I'm often exhausted. My body gives me a lot of physical pain. I know I'm identifying with the body and if I didn't then it probably wouldn't suffer so much. But I do tend to roll into bed pretty exhausted most evenings and then can't sleep very well because the mind is working overtime.

If you see when you go to bed that your mind is busy working overtime, you could assume that it's doing the same thing all through the day.

Well, not when I'm in the flow. Today it changed three or four times, and sometimes it was so easy and then ten minutes later I'm having a complete breakdown and the body is giving up.

The thing that makes you feel exhausted at the end of the day is not necessarily that your body is particularly tired out from what you've been doing in the day – which may be the case sometimes because you're doing construction type things so of course sometimes you're going to be tired from that – but more the activity in the mind. What makes people tired is their own minds.

Yes, I know this one as well.

You know everything. You know that you know everything, but still you get caught up in many things.

Yes, very often.

There are two possibilities here: you can get more and more resistant, or you can get into a flow and surrender. This is what everyone who comes into the community faces at some time. The community is a kind of energy centrifuge, an energy device that throws you round and round and you either surrender and become one with the centrifuge and it becomes very easy, or you resist and the thing collapses and then you leave.

This has been going on since the beginning of the community in fact. Sometimes it may be that John David needs to give a final little push, but generally not. Generally it's automatic and it just happens through the energy here. To me that means it's a very successful community because we are not here to run a beautiful guesthouse or to do all the other things which we do here. We are here to come into a deep flow with life.

The whole idea of this community is for people to come together who really want to become free. So the first step is to decide if you really want to become free because if you don't, you're going to resist. If you do want to be free then you'll say to yourself, 'Okay, I'm here, I'm going to give this a go.' Resistance doesn't work here and for sure it isn't going to give you much value from the time you spend here.

Actually, in your case you need taking apart, like an old car. Take it all apart, oil it, put it back together and then it will all run fine. You have to decide: Do I really want that? Am I willing to surrender to that? When the surrender happens, my job with you would be to build up all these good bits, all the sparkling, very futuristic well-maintained bits. I won't need to challenge you by terrorising you – you're actually very good at terrorising yourself.

You do it through your immense ability to make judgements. Have you noticed this? You have many judgements and in the end what are they? Desperately hanging on to a sinking ship. You know it's going to sink but you say, 'They should have put on a new coat of paint before it sank.' The thing is nobody cares; nobody cares about your judgements. 'I just see now that this lamp is in the wrong place. Whoever put this lamp here didn't put it in the right place … now it's exactly in the right place. Very good. We've got to get these things really right. Isn't that lovely now? Absolutely in the right place.' To go on like that all day you just go bananas.

I do anyway.

I know! You go bananas.

It's still pretty bad but it's getting better now that I walk through the house and I just see stuff without looking too closely. If I do look more closely then I would go crazy.

You're already crazy. We're trying to make you less crazy. One way to become less crazy is to say, 'Well, there's a roof on the house, there are walls, there's a heating system that works, you know it's not so desperate. I get food three times a day, I've got clothes to wear. Life's not so bad.'

It doesn't really matter if this lamp is slightly in the wrong place. Who decides it's in the wrong place? Maybe it would look very nice over in this corner. Who decides? Look how nice that could be. You see? It could be over here and I could turn it all the way around so you could see the other side. You could go on like this for hours and who cares about it? I could drive you all crazy talking about this lamp.

I'm surprised that you can even get to your bed at night. I would expect you to collapse under the weight of all your judgements. You carry so many judgements that by the time you get to the staircase you just collapse in a pile on the bottom of the stairs. Just give yourself a break. We're all a bit worried, you know. Take it easy because you're actually already doing a good job. You're a very nice guy who thinks he's not a nice guy.

Okay.

Just breathe that in. What would you do if you were actually a nice guy and didn't have anything to judge? How terrible. Imagine that! What if all the lamps were already exactly in the right place? Then we could start on the flowers of course, because look she's put this yellow flower next to this red flower. And look at this vase, there's a green vase and having a green vase with green plants, that's not right. I have to change that. You see; it's just endless. Will there ever be a perfect world where you can just say 'Okay, that's fine'? Absolutely not. No chance at all.

Guided Through Difficult Times

In the 1980s Robert Adams developed Parkinson's disease. At this time he lived with his wife and daughter in Los Angeles and was the caretaker of an apartment building. He gave *Satsang* to small groups. As his disease progressed he moved to Sedona where he continued his meetings.

There's something within you that knows what to do. There is a power greater than you that knows how to take care of you without your help. All you've got to do is to surrender to it. Surrender your thoughts, your mind, your ego, to the current that knows the way. It will take care of you. It will take better care of you than you can ever imagine.

Robert Adams

Hello Svetlana,

It's nice that you are sitting here again. For the last eight months it's been difficult for you to be here. Two years ago you had a very big glimpse and your life changed. At that time you had a very good job as a geologist working for a mining company. Your boss loved you very much and didn't want you to leave.

Finally you decided you had to leave. You thought you would leave and come and live in the community, but when you got to the community that was also difficult. Suddenly you had no foundation. Was it something like this?

Yes, it's almost exactly how you tell it, but what I can say from my side is that it was not very difficult for me but for my ego. I was worried that my brain would just drop from so many big changes. Actually it was blown up.

Your brain blew up?

Maybe not completely. But now it's much more quiet.

One of the things that happens is a lot of fear about survival. I think that was a strong structure that came up for you.

Yes, but still I have this issue in my life.

When you're aware of it, it's less threatening. You can't stop it really, but you don't need to be so afraid about it anymore. About a year ago this fear of survival got so strong that it was present in every moment. Maybe you didn't have lunch every day, so there was some practical reality to your situation. So it's very good that you came back here. Does it seem more calm now, less threatening?

Now it's more calm and peaceful but actually I have to say that I really don't understand what I'm doing or how I came here.

You don't know why you're sitting here?

It's like I don't understand anything. I don't know anything.

Well I think you're here because you have to be here. You've gone through a strong and difficult transition, which may be still going on. This transition is not to John David or to the community; it is to your own Being. Like most people, your mind was full of all kinds of reasons for why and what you were doing in your life, but now you're moving towards something more truthful. That's not so easy. Can you believe that you're very powerful?

Something inside believes that I'm strong.

Right now you talk more like a young girl who's very insecure. When you had an important job you spoke very differently. You knew you were very good at this job and you had a lot of confidence, your power was there.

This is true and I felt that I could manage everything. It's also not only about the job but about everything, a lot of things. But now everything is different.

It's so different that you feel some vulnerability. You know one of those big snakes, like a python, they have a tremendous power, but when they shed their skin they become completely vulnerable. You're shedding your skin. It's a very beautiful process, but not easy. I'm happy you're here again. It appears you're here because of your connection to John David, but it's not really about that.

If you remember, when you came to your very first meeting at The Tea Club in Kiev, about four years ago, you came from a business meeting. You had on your business uniform; you had your business power. But something happened that evening that has changed your life.

Something was understood and you can't just throw it away. You saw something that was true. This touched something inside of you and now, four years later, you're still moving towards that. You're very intelligent so this is something that you could recognise. That's why you're here.

It is to synchronise with your Being, to be who you really are, not somebody your mother or father or society wanted you to be. This is a movement to your own Being, and in this process the false has to die. So it's a kind of death process. The things that you believed before, they won't fit your Being. You had become an expert in the world of business and geology and you had managed all that because you were motivated by some kind of old structures that you're not so clear about any more.

I also went through something similar. When I left college, when I was around twenty, I got my dream job. I started working and very quickly discovered that I didn't actually want it. This became very difficult. It was a dream job but at the same time I didn't want it. I became horrified at my situation. I didn't know what to do, where to go, how to change. I had no idea. So I took a first step.

I stopped working and went back to study a bit more, which gave me a sense of time and space. That didn't work either, but because of that movement existence picked me up. Big changes started happening. The first change was a physical one – from England to Japan. In Japan it got very difficult because I was confronted with so much bullshit within John David. I was confronted by my own conditioning. The weight of all this felt like sometimes it would kill me. I didn't know how to come out of it. You've heard this expression, 'dark night of the soul'. In my case it was three years.

It was very strong. Then existence took care of me. It took me to meet somebody who pointed me to an Indian ashram. I had no idea that what I needed was an Indian ashram. It was completely out of my life's reality. I never thought about having a spiritual teacher. When it happened, it became very difficult because my mother got upset. She was rather happy that I was embarking on one kind of life, but not with this new life, which she saw as sitting in the sun and doing nothing, wasting the money that she had spent on my education. This also became a big pressure, and it wasn't easy to know what to do with that. This again took some time.

I'm very happy that I left my job. But in the beginning it was not always joyful. After three or four months I realised that I was just happy that I left. Two months ago I was offered another job as the main geologist at a big company. They tried to convince me and I was telling them, 'Oh I just got rid of this opportunity and you offer me the same.' I realised that I don't want to work so much – my mind doesn't want so much activity – and how this kind of work distracted me from feeling myself and being with myself.

You can never go back.

It was this kind of job for sure.

This is also not always easy. When you were thinking about giving up your job, if you remember, I encouraged you.

Yes, I remember. I was even angry with you.

Yes, I'm sure you were. You're not the first person who's been angry with me. The husband or the wife gets upset with me because sometimes people decide to stop their relationship. A lot of people get upset with me; this is a part of my job I need to accept.

But now and for some time I am very grateful to you.

There are other people who leave and they never come back and they're never grateful. Why are you grateful? You're grateful because you realise now you're on a journey to your own nature, to you. This is the most beautiful adventure. Already from the beginning of this you've had a glimpse of the possibilities. Is that right? So now you know, and this knowing makes everything possible.

I have a feeling that when I left my job something was released and I became more free. And more silent.

This will continue.

But there were moments when I wanted to stop all my ideas about enlightenment and all the other spiritual stuff. I saw that I started to face the structures that cause a lot of pain, so some power was still working in me, and I'm here.

You're intelligent and powerful. This is a big help, even though you speak without your power. You might still be talking like a twelve year old in a week, but maybe not, because your power can come back easily.

I have no doubts about this. I want to say that I have some connection with this community, and because of this I'm not lost. And I'm here. But the first time I came this year it was very difficult.

You're still a bit angry with me. It's a difficult year, yes?

Yes, it is difficult. But I believe that everything that is done is done for our best, even if someone is doing something wrong.

As I was saying in the beginning, everything is always right. We're always in the right place, always doing the right thing, even if it's difficult. What's been happening in your life is the same for many people, including me.

I also had a good job and good prospects for the future. So my mother was very happy about that, but going off to an Indian ashram and sitting in the sun, that was very difficult for her. It was also difficult for me. I would get her letter and then I would think maybe I'm crazy. All kinds of doubts would come.

There is something inside guiding each of us. You can trust that completely. You can even say that it is the one thing that you can trust completely – your own connection to everything. You can trust it and it is always functioning.

CHAPTER 4

Perseverance

When you have a deep understanding that the identification with the ego is to be given up, then perseverance is crucial. Every spiritual seeker will come to moments where they can easily sabotage themselves and just fall back into the known.

Perseverance

There will be all kinds of situations that you would like to run away from, and the most common way we run away is through relationship. We fall in love. It is important to see that you are already love, and that your effort to get it from the outside can very easily sabotage your awakening.

It can also be from ideas that we are not good enough, from the ego being too challenged, or through taking on spiritual ideas to avoid looking deeper.

Hiding in Non Duality

I met Paul Lowe when he was Teertha, one of Osho's main disciples, in the ashram in 1978. I felt the immense love and lightness around him. Years later we met in Berlin when he had become Paul Lowe again and he had fallen out with and left Osho. He briefly had a community around him in northern Italy but he stopped it because he couldn't get the residents to turn off the lights!

We don't want to see the way it is. We want to see it the way we want to see it, the way we want it to be. So when we keep looking for the way we want it to be, we don't see the way it is.

Paul Lowe

Dear John David,
I started running from looking too much into myself by 'doing'. First in Russia I did a kind of therapy where you end up in a very nice space – love, open heart. I hung in that for some time. Then I met you and Advaita *and discovered, 'Oh! I am That. I am nothing', and again I didn't need to look at anything. I feel it doesn't go deeper.*

I am nothing. I don't need to look at anything. Yes, this is just a concept. It is a comfortable idea and this is a popular mistake that people have been making in the last years with *Satsang*, with non duality. 'Oh! I have been to two meetings. Now I understand. I am not who I thought I was. I am not somebody; I am not a person. I am nothing. Oh! Great! So I don't have to do anything because I am nothing.'

This can be a complete cop out. It is not wrong when you say 'Okay, I am nothing.' There is nothing wrong in that because that is maybe a better understanding than thinking you are a somebody, but it is not the whole truth either because these old structures are still working inside us. Even if we are going around saying, 'I am nothing, I am nothing.' When you start to see that these mechanisms are still working then you've come to the point now where you need to investigate. We can call this inner work.

I was watching the ice-skating last night. The gold medal was won by a seventeen-year-old Russian woman. It could have been Padma in her younger days. She had probably been practising every day for the last four years. She won something in the last Olympics I think, maybe the silver, so she kept going and now she's got the gold medal.

You are an interesting character, Padma, because since I met you six years ago you have always been interested in the gold medal. Is that right?

Yes.

You didn't quite realise what it takes, how much inner work is needed. What is coming up for you won't be easy. This is where a lot of people are tested. I myself was very strongly tested in this period when I really allowed the mud to bubble up. People get involved in spiritual life because they want drips of honey every day.

You want to have a little bit of extra sweetness in your life. You want to be a bit happier, a bit more loved; it should all be a bit nicer. But unfortunately in order to get to, I would say not drips of honey but the whole pot of honey, often you need to go through periods where there isn't much honey.

There is a kind of winter when the honey is not really available and in that period it is very easy to give up because we have this idea that we should get honey every day. I think pretty much anyone who really gets to the honey pot has gone through some difficult time when there wasn't much honey around, a dark night of the soul, where you are struggling to manage. You are struggling to get your head out of the mud, so to speak. You have to struggle with the false self in order to come to the true Self.

It seems that for most of the last few years you've managed not to come to that. Is that right? Or if you did come to it, you had some defence mechanism that didn't really allow it to touch you.

You had this really handsome, big, lovely, Danish boyfriend. Do you remember him?

Yes, of course. (Laughter!)

You were very tough on him. Very tough! Rather than looking at what was going on with you, you always looked at what was going on with him. So if you have this clear priority for Truth – which it could be you have – if you want to go for gold, then you have to start seeing what is going on inside you. This will bring up the possibility of the honey not dripping down and keeping you feeling good. You can easily not feel good. Probably you will need somebody who can help you to see those things.

It's important to realise that when things happen to us as children we have no choice. There is no personal blame. We are born into a certain situation and we get conditioned in a certain way. If we're lucky we get good treatment, if we're not lucky we don't get such good treatment. Whatever the treatment is, it's likely to create very strong inner structures and if we don't look at them we'll never be free of them. Also there is a fine line between too much engagement with the past and being so defended we never really look at it. So there is some balance needed.

Yes, I have to see what's going on. This is a big discovery for me.

You have an open heart and I think you have a genuine priority for the 24-carat gold. Maybe you won't make the 24-carat; maybe you'll only make the 18-carat. That's also quite good. Better than silver. Definitely better than bronze.

What I can see is that you are still running a huge story that you totally believe is necessary for your survival. Without this story you are not going to survive – it is not true. The belief in that story is exactly the thing that is preventing you from reaching the thing that you apparently most want, which is the Self. The only thing that keeps you from the Self is your own story, and if you can't see it then come and ask a teacher. That's exactly one of the reasons a spiritual teacher is needed – to help you see your story.

You can see everyone else's very easily but tremendous honesty and insight is needed to see your own story and your own attachments. The mind is telling you that you can do it yourself, but it is the mind that is the problem so how can the mind help you get rid of the mind? This is just nonsense, an illusion! Complete nonsense and even very mature spiritual seekers somehow believe in it. 'I will do it. I will go to one more *Satsang*; I will go to one more teacher. I will do it. I will take away my own ego.' This is a very nice trick of the mind. They have read all the spiritual books and been to all their favourite teachers, spent hours meditating and years at ashrams yet nothing has changed. They are not living in peace.

I often ask, 'If you can do it yourself, why haven't you done it?'

Perseverance on the Path

This quote about perseverance is from Sri Ramana Maharshi. When I was Osho's disciple in Pune I came across an old photograph in a pile of rubbish in some rooms I was renting in a Maharaja's palace. The man in the photograph was naked, except for a loincloth, and had wonderful light in his eyes. Gradually the photo worked its way into my heart. I gave it a gold frame and hung it on my wall. Later I discovered this was Sri Ramana Maharshi and I came to know his teachings.

In two weeks we will be on a plane to visit his ashram and to have our own retreat just down the road from there. Over the last twenty-five years I have been witness to the increasing numbers of western people who have been touched by his life and teachings.

No one succeeds without effort. Those who succeed owe their success to perseverance.

Sri Ramana Maharshi

Dear John David,

In the context of spiritual awakening, is this effort and perseverance that Sri Ramana is talking about the perseverance to come to a still mind through enquiry and difficult situations that one might usually choose to run away from? I ask this because surely there is no effort needed just to be the Self. The effort is to see more and more clearly what is in the way.

Sri Ramana had a spontaneous awakening when he was sixteen years old and then he left his home and came to Arunachala mountain, a well-known spiritual place, a beautiful place where he stayed the rest of his life. So it would seem perseverance was not necessary for him to attain awakening.

After he had this spontaneous awakening he then spent many

years pretty much alone, very much in silence. Wandering on the mountain. Sitting in caves. Avoiding being in the mass of the people.

Gradually people discovered him, came to spend time and visit him. Later they came to live with him and almost by itself an ashram was built, but all of that was very much in a flow, you could say, a destiny. He often talked about destiny.

He's not the right guy to be talking about perseverance really. But having said that, I can say that as far as I can see the most common way that people sabotage themselves is by not continuing.

We've had our community here for fourteen years. During this fourteen years something like a hundred plus people have lived here and the vast majority of them drifted off, or for some reason they came to a wall or limit of looking. Maybe it got a bit painful. They left.

There will be all kinds of situations that you would like to run away from. Perseverance means that you have a deep knowing that there is something to give up – the identification with the ego. To persevere means to keep going. This is not always going to be easy. So although this is a little surprising coming from Sri Ramana, it is also perfectly good advice that he must have given to a particular devotee who came to visit him.

We have our own case at the moment, a man sitting here in the back row of our meeting. I think he first visited our community about eight or ten years ago. He had many questions; he was quite a mindy character. He was the most persevering of all our community visitors. He lived about an hour's drive away and he would come every Monday and Friday to these meetings.

This was an enormous effort. Then about two years ago he came to live with us, and a few days ago he told me that he would leave in the spring. Basically, it seems that he gives up. The longer you do the inner work the more will get stirred up inside you, the more difficult it gets. We all have our ideas about how things should be and how everything should be wonderfully easy. It's not like that. You have to persevere. Otherwise, what could you get of great value?

Yes, the Self is always there – you are always the Self – and if you're living that beautiful presence there is not a question of persevering. But most people are not living in this beautiful presence because there are all kinds of old issues and structures coming from the family, from society, from the culture that get in the way. They are like a screen that's in the way.

I can say to you, Johannes, it is a pity that you're giving up now because it's only been eight years. Eight years is not long. I spent fifteen years with one teacher, persevering through many, many difficulties and many boring moments. Many financial difficulties, relationship troubles. All kinds of things came up. Fifteen years of struggling. Becoming all the time quieter and quieter, but maybe not realising that I was becoming quieter and quieter.

It's hard to know really how long it takes. When we first started this community fourteen years ago, I would have said five years, but actually, we have many people who have been here much longer than five years and they're not yet free of their baggage, of their dust, if you like. Maybe these people, over the years, have had glimpses. They've had moments when they understood, when they were absolutely present for some moments, some hours, some days.

Then the dust settles back and you have to keep going. And what's the hurry? Why is there a hurry? This is the mind. It is always creating some kind of goal, some kind of target, and when we don't reach it then our mind tells us that 'I'm not good enough' or 'it's too difficult' or 'I don't really want it anymore' or 'why should I bother?'

The mind might just come up with nice little sabotaging ideas. It's very important when this starts to happen that you allow yourself to fall deeply inside and reconnect to something that I'm sure everybody in this room knows. You have to feel your own inner power. You have to feel it happening by yourself, and then it's easy to continue.

All the people I can respect as spiritual teachers have spent many, many years persevering. And yes, it's certainly true that there is always a temptation to run away from things that don't fit your idea or things that seem to be uncomfortable. Sri Ramana is saying stop. Stay. Turn around and face whatever it is.

As soon as you do this, then almost immediately you get a new understanding. Something new is revealed and then you can easily continue for some time, until it gets difficult once again. During all this time you are becoming more and more free.

Getting Lost in a Relationship

Thuli Baba was an extremely unusual, traditionally-minded master. As a child he was completely absorbed in spiritual life. His father was a holy man and was Thuli Baba's master. Thuli Baba had had a family but when I met him he lived with his close disciples in a gorgeous ashram built by a western disciple. He became well known to a small group of westerners. He was a traditional master, so men and woman lived separately at the ashram. He had a wonderful chuckle and was uncompromising.

To realise the ultimate Truth you have to get rid of relationships, you have to get rid of worldly attachments. If you think that we can realise our True Nature by living in the world and enjoying this world, all the pleasures of this world, that is compared to sitting on a crocodile and trying to cross the river. Because the crocodile will kill you.

Thuli Baba

Dear John David,
For me it feels like there is a natural yearning to be close and intimate with other people. Thuli Baba is saying that you have to get rid of attachments, like relationship, and I find this confusing. I think perhaps I am just misunderstanding something, so could you please comment on this topic of relationships and Truth? Could it be that the relationships themselves are not the problem, rather it is the attachments and structures that then bind us within those relationships?

It's quite clear that for almost everybody this issue of intimacy with another human being is a strong structure, a strong issue. In the eastern traditions of Buddhism and Hinduism there is a deep understanding that if you seriously want to become a spiritual seeker you become celibate and stay alone.

When we go to India for the January retreat each year we often visit two ashrams: one is Thuli Baba's and the other is Swami Dayananda's. In Swami Dayananda's ashram they teach *Vedanta* and they completely adopt this tradition. It's completely accepted that men and women are separate. In Thuli Baba's ashram, which is rather small compared to Swami Dayananda's ashram, there are around twelve men and three women, a very small group of people. He also makes his position absolutely clear – the men and the women are completely separate. The main group of people in his ashram are young men who are called *brahmacharyas*, meaning they have made a decision to be celibate.

I asked Thuli Baba about this, making the point that in western countries it's rather common to have a relationship, and that we don't really have any tradition for deciding on celibacy. His response was that *karmic* destiny requires some people to live as householders – being in relationship, working to raise a family. Then when the children have grown and the family has been provided for there is a withdrawal from intimacy and a focus on spiritual life. You might even leave the family and go on your way as a spiritual seeker. And for Thuli Baba this is completely essential.

This is naturally quite hard for western people to deal with as we don't really have any culture that supports this notion. In fact it's the opposite. We're brought up with a strong conditioning to be in a couple, to be a married couple. Over the years of our community this has always been something of an issue. What kind of advice could I give? Gradually over these years, after lots of consideration, it always seems to me that it's case by case.

At the same time it became clear to me that people joining our community are joining an experiment in conscious living, probably for a limited time, because they want to become awakened, to become free and to live in this freedom. So then the best advice that I can give them is to stand on their own feet, and from this position to relate as spontaneously as possible and as intimately as possible with the other residents.

We have a lovely connection with an English tantra teacher who comes to our community every year, and gives energy encouraging this intimacy. My own advice to western people is that if you seriously want to become awakened, if you seriously want to be free, better to stay out of any fixed love story.

In the past it may have appeared that I was against marriage, against relationship and family and so on. This was always a misunderstanding; rather, I'm for awakening. This is something that very few people are going to choose in their lives. So for these few people my advice is to be intimate – I'm not against sexuality – but to stay out of a fixed, marriage-type relationship.

This advice is mostly ignored because actually it's very difficult for western people. Our conditioning around intimacy and relating is very, very strong, partly because we have funny ideas about love. In our culture love is something that comes from the other.

He loves me. She loves me. I love you. You love me. We're going to be saved! It doesn't work like that. This love is actually something that is inside us, and so expecting it from somewhere or someone else leads to tremendous misunderstandings. However much I might talk about this, people very quickly forget my advice when they get into a closed, conditional relationship.

So I thought tonight I would illustrate what I'm talking about. As far as I can see – over the last fourteen years of the community and probably another six years when I was teaching without a community – one of the things that sabotages people more than any other issue is getting attached to relationship.

When this happens you can see that actually Truth was never really the first priority. In fact the priority was to find a boyfriend or a girlfriend and get them under contract, knowing that then you could be happy forever because you had somebody to love you. In fact, this is just falling into the traditional, conditioned trap of relationship.

Right now we have a particularly good example of how this sabotages us. Jill has been here five years and has given a lot of support to the community. When she first came she told me a bit about her life. She exposed the fact that she was quite relaxed about having boyfriends and that she'd had quite a lot of relationships, but unfortunately they often finished in a difficult way.

She was tired from these waves of 'I love you' and then the breaking down of the relationship and all the sadness and might-have-beens and so on that came out of that. I suggested that here in the community it's a little bit different because the focus here is on yourself.

She appeared to be very sincere about doing things differently and wanting to find her own inner peace. As time passed I discovered that she was quite hotly involved with one guy in the community and gradually I discovered that actually this relationship was very dramatic with both of them doing everything they could to make the other one jealous. Anyway, it got to the point where they were actually having a physical fight and out of this fight it was decided that the relationship was not really healthy anymore. I recommended they carry on living in the community but leave each other alone. Which I think they more or less did, for a while.

Over the next months they gradually began tormenting each other again until Jill found another person, Pedro, to be with. And things went on. Another year passed and it became clear that now after two years there wasn't much sign of peace in Jill. In fact she became recognised as the biggest drama queen in the community. There were almost daily dramas, often fuelled by jealousy.

She could not see that she was very much attached to her separate 'me' and that this gave her strong feelings of being possessive of the other – 'my' boyfriend. This then led to jealousy if 'my' boyfriend was looking at or hugging some other person. Any woman who was friendly to 'her' boyfriend was seen as doing something terribly wrong and was treated very coldly.

Her obsessive behaviour continued, not bringing her any closer to what she had wanted when she first came. She was simply carrying on the same structures that had been in her life before joining the community. She ignored my advice that she should stay out of relationship and should look at what came up inside her and take responsibility for these strong feelings; try to understand that they came out of an idea of herself as a separate 'me'.

She continued to carry on with Pedro and after a big drama it was negotiated that they would absolutely leave each other alone and they would both stay in the community. But even then they didn't really accept that decision, and it was beginning to feel as if Jill wasn't making any progress at all with her inner work.

Everything came to a head a few months ago and it was decided that she would go to the retreat we have in Ukraine. She'd have a silence badge and she would stay quiet, stay with herself. To support the process, Pedro stayed in Germany.

Anyway, to cut a long story short, Jill spent the time torturing herself with fantasies about Pedro coming to the Ukraine community, meeting a woman, falling in love and having children with that woman. Now she's back from the retreat and continuing to create more illusions and fantasies that of course never have any reality.

Sitting quietly, meditation and Self-enquiry are all simple and obvious tools for calming the mind and developing self-awareness. Constantly engaging the mind with fantasies leaves no space for peace or self-knowledge.

Pedro has decided to go back to his old life and Jill will leave the community. I find this an extremely good example of how we sabotage ourselves. She came to the community with a very sincere wish to become peaceful and yet she fell into the regular patterns of her conditioned mind. Now, three and a half years later, she gives up and leaves the community and any efforts towards peace because she can't let her relationship structures go.

Postscript.
I understand that shortly after they left the community they chose to live together.

Love and Relationship

We have two quotes from Deepak Chopra and I find them very interesting because he is not particularly from an *Advaita* background. He was actually very close to the Maharishi Yogi, but of course Truth is one, so what he is saying about love is exactly what *Advaita* says about love. Deepak trained as a doctor and cared for the Maharishi intimately for a year. Since then he has become one of the world's best-known spiritual teachers.

Love is our Being, Being is existence, so love is existence. Your essential state is love. What distorts that is that we look outside for love not realising that the love we experience outside is a reflection of the love we have for our deepest self. When I say deepest self, I don't mean your ego, which is not yourself. The ego is a socially-induced hallucination. I mean your soul, which is beyond your self-image. It is your true Self. Your true Self is love.

Deepak Chopra

I must admit that I've been saying this myself for twenty years but never as beautifully as he says it. *'The ego is a socially-induced hallucination'*. These are beautiful words. I describe this ego as a movie that we are busy producing, starring in and watching. It comes from our conditioning as we grow up and so I love his words *'socially-induced hallucination.'*

'Love is our Being, Being is existence, so love is existence.' It means this flower is love, this candle is love, even this chair is love, even I am love! We are all love! Everything is love. This is so clear and beautiful. He doesn't say it here, but I can also add that the normal definition of love that you get in pop songs and romances is a chronic disease that almost everybody suffers from. Avoid this type of 'I love you' because this is already duality.

In an interview he was asked about relationships and his answer was:

The first secret to attract a profound lover or a soul mate into your life is to fully embrace, love and accept yourself just as you are. Loving you, with all your flaws and insecurities, turns you into a powerful manifesting magnet. By diving deep into self-acceptance you will find that it is much easier for everyone else to feel at peace when hanging out with you. When you are okay with all your parts, it is easy to open the door to intimacy with anyone.

> *Dear John David,*
> *When I was young, I developed quite a strong mechanism to control love. I became aware of this after relationships with women where I gave off a very good impression to begin with and all went very nicely, but after a short time the feeling of love and intimacy would deepen in me and I would close off from the person, ignoring them and treating them very badly. On the journey to come to freedom, is it good to face and challenge issues of relating, or better to simply stay away until something becomes more grounded in me? A deeper self-acceptance maybe. I feel a big struggle with this.*

Everybody has some problem with relationships and the problem gets stronger the more intimate a relationship is. I've been giving advice about relationships and love for twenty years but now I understand that no advice helps, because relationships are driven by very, very powerful conditioning.

We start off as a little child with our parents, before we even know the word relationship, and for many years we are brought up in the aura of our parents' love affair. Day by day, without anybody needing to talk about it, we are absolutely conditioned by this love affair.

When it comes to birthdays, Daddy buys presents for Mummy, maybe some flowers, whispering 'I love you,' and so on. So children grow up with this kind of love affair happening in front of them, conditioned with the idea that love comes from the other. I would guess that very few people ever come across the idea that love in fact is our very existence.

Love is something that somebody gives me and when they give it I feel good. When they give it to somebody else I definitely don't feel good. So everybody is looking for that perfect partner who will give them love. Even if the parents do not have a very loving relationship the children will still want to create something along the same lines, but better. As we grow up, of course, the hormones act as a strong magnet. If you are at the level of the hormones no advice is going to help, and, as I can observe, it doesn't make much difference how old you are. And remember that probably the most difficult thing to deal with in your daily life is relationships with other people, so it's going to be a strong issue for almost everyone.

When you are alone you only have to deal with your own stuff, but as soon as you have closer contact with another human being then it gets a bit more complicated. It can be anything from an acquaintance or a work colleague to something more intense and intimate like actually living together.

More intimate relationships between two people often lead us into a lot of suffering because the relationships usually serve the ego of each partner instead of being a shared, open, energetic connection.

Very often, of course, the relationship starts full of hope. We have had other partnerships and we think we've learnt our lessons and now something new is happening. It's a new beginning with a new partner and it's very exciting and wonderful ... and so on.

But little by little, it's very common to find that after some months, maybe after one or two years, things are less easy. This is usually because each person is attached to their particular story. When you live alone you're dealing with only one story – your own – and if you're a spiritual person you're trying to become clear of this one story. As soon as you enter an intimate relationship with another human being you're also dealing with that person's story.

So now there are two stories and if this intimate connection continues you also have a third story, which is the story of us. There are usually all kinds of conditioned, repeating structures operating inside these three stories. It can even be that you've chosen each other because you reflect certain of each other's structures, even if you're not conscious of that.

After some months or some years, very often this weight of stories – your story, my story and our story – starts to take a toll and more and more time is spent on sorting out misunderstandings, different opinions, different beliefs, different desires. Very often these relationships break down and people may just split and try new partnerships or they may persevere, getting some counselling help to deal with all the issues that come up between them.

To some extent we can find this useful. If we are starting out on a spiritual journey and we haven't had relationship experience then it can be very good to get caught up in some sort of sticky story. In this kind of situation you could learn a lot about yourself because one of the great things about partnership is that you end up as very strong mirrors for each other. Assuming you have a gutsy and energetic connection I'm sure your partner would be very happy to tell you all the things they find they have observed about you!

In that way relationships can be very useful because they can really help you to know yourself. If we haven't had much experience of living intimately with another person then we've also not really lived intimately with ourselves. What we can see by taking space from relationship and coming deeply to our Being is that actually we're all one. There aren't really two. There's not really you and me. We're all One.

It's hard to think of anybody who ever took my advice in this regard! Can't even think of one, but I keep trying. The guy asking the question at the start of this chapter has a problem. He is on the road to freedom and he wonders whether he should challenge the issues of relationship or simply stay away. He feels a big struggle with this.

When he gets into something more serious than the odd back staircase meeting in the night he finds things get more difficult. My advice to him, which I know he isn't likely to follow and he doesn't have to follow, but I'll tell him anyway, is first to become more grounded and then carefully test the water of relationship. This is very good advice but basically bullshit because it doesn't work like that. My true advice is to do the best you can, because anyway that's all you can do, and not only with the subject of intimacy but with everything you do in your life. You can only do the best you can do.

Any great idea of doing it perfectly at some point is all right but in this moment now you can only do what you can do. I like very much what Deepak said about that: '... *completely embrace, love and accept yourself just as you are and then the Self acts like an enormous magnet and attracts the right person or situation to you.*'

As you become more grounded and you become more clear that your very Being is love then you don't really need to be looking for your own partner. In the community there is enough connectedness and understanding about authentic love that for the last year most people have not been searching for a partner to have a love story with.

At the same time there has been a lot of intimacy happening, without much story attached to it. I must say I am very touched by this. I don't remember giving that advice but I am happy it is happening. This is very particular, very unusual. Have I answered your question?

This topic came up recently for me – not with an exclusive relationship as it used to be, but I had a deeper meeting with someone for sometime. The same behaviour came up, pushing that person away, ignoring, punishing.

After you gave me the advice to just do my best, this is now quite different. I had a talk with this person and I could see it. It's completely not comfortable.

To see the old patterns?

Yes, really clearly, and it was shocking. Pushing someone away just because they feel love towards me is a very strong thing. Before there would have been such a strong self-judgement but now there is more of a cool seeing and acceptance.

What you are describing is a particular structure of your conditioning and as you start to see it hopefully you start to accept yourself. It's you, and actually it would help your relationships if you were able to discuss that with your partners. Probably they also have a structure of 'I'm not good enough' so when you start reacting from your structure they probably immediately judge themselves from their structure and the whole thing gets highly complicated.

Once you clearly see this structure and you discuss it with your partner you are bringing them into a closer understanding of you and it can only help your intimacy. It can only help and you will feel better because you've been able to be more honest in your sharing. It may not stop your structure happening again but at least your partner doesn't have to take it so personally then and perhaps he or she is even able to give some support in seeing it. Then it becomes a valuable relationship because you are close enough and are able to give feedback to each other. It becomes an honest, open relationship. That kind of relating is rather valuable.

But take care not to get stuck in that kind of relationship story because other people can also give you insights about your structure from different angles. So once you become clear about a certain structure you have, then you actually don't need that regular partner to keep reminding you; everybody can remind you.

Years ago I used to publicly give the advice not to have a relationship if you are serious about your spiritual work. An Indian spiritual teacher doesn't even think of people in relationship. A master in India would just assume that all his students are completely in a one-on-one relationship with him and have no interest in intimate relationship.

Anyway, the advice I used to happily give out in all my public meetings wasn't wrong, but it was silly because the people I was talking to anyway hadn't achieved the level of spiritual work where having a relationship or not would make a difference. So it's not really about relationship, but for sure at a certain level in the spiritual work it makes a lot of sense to really focus on the priority to come to your own inner Being, to focus on love itself.

Then relationship and the other things in life are less important, because we don't have to do anything for this deeper love. It's our nature so it's very simple. Unfortunately, because of all the wrong information, very few people are looking inside for this love. They are nearly all looking outside for it. The more empty and destitute we feel inside, the more we're trying to pull somebody to give us love. Very tragic and completely common.

You don't have to do anything to get love. If you are doing something to get love, that is not really love. It is what everybody thinks love is, but it is not really love. Real love is just your Being. You are this love you are searching for. Similarly, we want to get enlightenment, not realising that we are already That. It is our very nature. The thing we are seeking is our very nature. There is nothing to find.

A Deeper Truth to Love

We've already met Eckhart Tolle, and I have a quote here where he talks beautifully about relationship from the standpoint of Truth.

A genuine relationship is one that is not dominated by the ego with its image making and self-seeking. In a genuine relationship, there is an outward flow of open, alert attention toward the other person in which there is no wanting whatsoever.

Eckhart Tolle

Dear John David,
When I realised my relationship was not bringing me the happiness I thought, I began to look inside for it. I started my spiritual journey, but my partner was not very accepting or encouraging of this, and now I am in a conflict with her about me and the direction I'm taking. I can feel this open love for her, but I don't think she really has it for me. Do you think it's possible to stay with my girlfriend even when she doesn't understand this inner journey?

In your case, if you have an authentic wish to do this investigation, I would definitely advise that you share this as much as possible with your partner. Explain to her that you have a dilemma because you love her, you love being with her, she is a part of your life, and at the same time your life is changing. You want to take her along on this exciting journey. Through the power of this intimacy and love you share you can introduce her to this journey. So I would strongly advise that approach – try to take your partner along with you. If for some reason she is absolutely not interested in meditation or looking inside or asking the kinds of questions that you've started to ask yourself, this is not going to be so easy. Maybe now in the beginning it's alright, but you may find some problems come later on.

What is this spiritual journey about? It's about examining why we are not able to be simply present. If you start to examine this you'll find it's because of all kinds of conditioning and identification. Let's say your partner is completely happy with her conditioned robotic lifestyle and you are busy questioning everything. I think she is going to get pissed off with you.

In a way it's funny. It's all about the present moment and most people, including my girlfriend, are not able to live in the present moment without worrying about safety or some security in the future. This is the thing that changed in my life. I am not interested in the future anymore and I am not interested in security because there is no security.

This is why it becomes difficult. If you are starting to feel the juice of living in the moment it becomes extremely difficult to be with people who are constantly talking about the future or the past. You just get a headache.

So if your partner is caught up in the normal kind of conditioning, as you get quieter and more present you are going to find it painful and also irrelevant because she'll be dreaming of how happy she will be next year when she is on a holiday with you and you will just be cutting the carrots for dinner. You'll find something doesn't really meet.

This issue with relationship is almost without a doubt the biggest sabotage of awakening. It is number one on the list of reasons why people don't awaken. I am not making any judgement about it; it's just my observation over twenty years. I see that very often people choose relationship rather than awakening. Why? Because deep down we are so conditioned with the idea of the other giving us love, and to discover your own love is not always easy.

You are planning to climb to the summit of Mt. Everest and then you meet a very nice woman at the third camp up the mountain. She is offering everything and you look up at the summit and you think, 'It's going to be a tough climb. I don't know what's going to happen. I might run out of oxygen or fall down a crevasse; anything could happen up there and she is right here, completely available.'

It's very tempting. In a way God has set it up like that; existence is like that.

Sometimes it's about not wanting to hurt anybody. When I'm talking about it she feels the space and the distance and she starts crying. Then I feel the inner explosion of hurt.

Yes, this is difficult. From the way you are talking you are available for her to come with you. You are not saying 'Go away, I am going to do this alone.' You are saying 'Let's go on the mountain together.' You can't take responsibility for her pain. If she doesn't want to come with you I think you have to make a decision.

It's true. Step by step.

Just be aware that this is one of the biggest sabotages.

I like the metaphor of climbing up Mt. Everest. It's really good.

Either you are going to lose her or you are going to lose Truth. You can't have them both. Truth is ruthless. If you really really want Truth then everything else has to go.

I found on my own journey that every so often there was a situation where I had to choose between something and Truth. In my case it was always easy to choose Truth. I would move on with Truth, letting go of my family, some friends, my wife, all kind of stuff along the way. Over years you could say, not all in one minute. Maybe this is also why the spiritual path takes years, because it takes time for us to adjust ourselves to our new understanding.

Polyamory

Osho was always brilliant when he talked about love, as he could combine the western and eastern experiences into one common stream. He wanted people to celebrate love, both between lovers and with existence itself, but not to confine love with our limitations. So I wanted to start with a beautiful quote from him.

If you love a flower, don't pick it up. Because if you pick it up, it dies. And it ceases to be what you love. So if you love a flower, let it be. Love is not about possession. Love is about appreciation.
Osho

Dear John David,
As I've understood that I am not separate I'm open to being intimate without needing to be possessive. But I'm not really sure how to navigate my way through that because there are such strong conditionings in me and around me that really don't make it easy. Can you expand on this topic and maybe point me in the right direction?

As you go deeper and deeper into the spiritual understanding – through your own experiences, from reading books, from listening to people – you discover for yourself the possibility that you're not separate, that actually you're one with everyone.

If you're one with everyone, how does it work to only love one person? If you go out into the garden there are so many types of flowers. You might particularly love roses, but I'm sure you also love other flowers. We don't think twice. We just love all these different flowers.

We love all the different types of dogs, birds, trees. There's a multitude of possibilities. It's kind of automatic to feel love for many different varieties. We have no problem with it until it comes to people. Perhaps the strongest, deepest conditioning we have is to automatically look for one intimate partner.

We've been told that if we find this one perfect partner and relate with them for our whole life, we will live in love. We will live in happiness. We will be fulfilled.

I want to offer you a word, which I didn't know until recently. This word is 'polyamory', the practice of loving more than one person at the same time, and it seems to me to be almost a natural expression of what's going to happen when we follow a spiritual journey. Because very quickly we discover that we are all one. We are not two; we are not many.

This is actually the meaning of *Advaita* – non duality, not two. So when you at least have the intellectual knowing of that, even if it's not your direct experience every day, it then becomes very, very hard to put yourself into a one-on-one relationship and to completely believe that this is the only way to create love in your life.

Our strong conditioning around this belief can break down because of our spiritual work, then we can positively play with this idea that we can love more than one. It seems to me that here in our community, without realising it, we have all become polyamorists.

Maybe one of the reasons why people avoid polyamory is that when you realise that love is already inside you and not something you get from over there, from outside, from the other, then you have to deal with the things that can come up for you: 'I'm not good enough', 'I never had enough love', 'I feel abandoned'. This is a bit uncomfortable of course so we avoid really investigating what's happening. It's easier to just take the conditioning that love comes from the other.

'I love you' is supposed to be the pinnacle of partnership, sweet words. If somebody says 'I love you' my advice is to tread carefully because this other person wants you to be in a relationship with them that is actually going to lead to possessiveness. They are trying to create you as the one who loves them.

Jealousy comes directly from the idea of 'mine', possessing somebody. You can't feel jealousy unless you have the idea that this person is mine. Then if they seem to be loving someone else of course you can feel jealousy, which is very damaging to any possibility of love. This is reflected in Osho's words, '*If you love a flower, let it be.*'

When we understand that love is already inside, that we are the source of love, in fact our Essence is love, then there is no question of getting love from the other, of the other loving us. This is a major misunderstanding. Once you discover this, it's very hard to go back to the idea that there is only one person who can love you. It doesn't make sense anymore.

Polyamory is suggesting that you can have a multi-personal relationship. However, if you come to these relationships with your old conditioning that you get love from the other then you will just multiply the drama and suffering. I am suggesting that you approach intimate relationships in a completely conscious way, with full awareness that you're the source of love.

When I was growing up the only way I could find a partner was to go to a social gathering, like a party or a dance. Social media has changed all that and now it is possible to find many partners very quickly and easily. It's a revolution that's happening now in human consciousness, and out of this revolution things are going to change. For people who are becoming spiritually conscious, it doesn't make sense to only love one. You can also choose to love only one, choosing it consciously and naturally, and not just because you're conditioned to that choice.

My reason for suggesting polyamory is to show that attitudes towards what love and relationship mean are changing, and perhaps it can suggest to you a more conscious and open way to live and love, and to more freely explore yourself.

CHAPTER 5

Surrender

If we want to live in a way of surrender then we need to understand that we have the ego, our personal movie running on and on, and we have something else, which we can call the Essence. If we want to live in a deep surrender then we want to surrender to the Essence, not to the ego.

Surrender

At a certain point on the spiritual path we come to see that our mind can't take us any further, and we learn what true surrender means. We learn to tap into and nourish our creative impulses, to come into our hearts and live from a deep trust of life instead of from the thinking and planning of our conditioned mind.

We come out of the habitual safety net of our ego and fall into something much deeper, a flow of life that happens despite us, not because of us.

Creativity

One of the most attractive aspects of Osho for me was how he included everything in the spiritual path he was putting out. It was nothing like the dry Zen Buddhism that had first attracted me to spirituality. Osho was encouraging us to love openly, to be intimate with many people, to explore our sexuality, to explore our creativity and celebration, and also our silence – to have fun and to be a complete being.

And that is the essence of wisdom – to be in harmony with nature, with the natural rhythm of the universe. And whenever you are in harmony with the natural rhythm of the universe, you are a poet, you are a painter, you are a musician, you are a dancer.

Osho

Dear John David,
Whenever I am involved in some kind of creativity I find myself in a beautiful space of peace and joy where there are not many thoughts. And yet when I'm not doing that I can see that my mind often creates suffering. Is it because of the creativity that I was present and at peace, or is it something else?

It's a beautiful day today. Maybe some of you went for a walk by the river. In the beginning you were probably very aware of whatever had been going on before: some problem in your life, an unpleasant meeting that had just happened.

As you went off on your walk your mind was probably very busy. Maybe this is often how you begin walks, but as you go along you become aware of the warmth of the sun, the slightly cool breeze, the beauty of the trees, the greenness of the grass, the sun dancing on the Rhine. You become more and more present.

Whatever problems your mind was busy with when you left the house began to fade away. Then at some point you became aware that you were just here. The mind was apparently not really busy anymore and you felt joy for no real reason.

You were in touch with your inner silence, a space in which the beauty of that moment, or any moment, is evident. Beauty doesn't have to have a special moment. Today's dance workshop may have been another example of this beauty being experienced. When the music begins you have an idea as to how you should respond to it. Maybe you're trying to dance very energetically or very 'spiritually'.

Somebody is there; somebody is dancing. There's a concept or idea and it's not very natural, but as you continue dancing you might come to a moment when nobody is dancing. And, rather like walking alongside a river, you're aware of this dance and you're aware of the presence, but you're not really aware of 'me'. When we're really present this character that we are very familiar with just dissolves.

It sounds like it ought to be very easy to be present, but if you know yourself a little bit you'll recognise that most of the time you're not present. In your mind there is a swarm of activity – mostly thoughts of things that have happened in the past. Some people are particularly interested in the future, but generally our minds are busy with the past.

Alternatively, you probably all know this moment when you're just present. For no obvious reason you feel tremendous peace inside. There's a feeling of well being, that everything is alright. You don't have to change anything, so there's no desire, just a tremendous acceptance of now.

If you want to taste that, then you can just meet Jane, our two-year-old visitor. She turned up this weekend to give you a chance to meet her. She is in that lovely moment when there's not much 'me'. She hasn't developed judgements about the people she meets. She's not thinking, 'Ah! I'm not interested in speaking with him.' You just get this beautiful smile and you realise you're looking at the divine. There was a time when you were just like that.

This is the smile of our True Nature, our Buddha nature, which we can also call inner silence, the Self, God. We have the idea that this is separate from us and maybe one day we'll get the bit that is missing. But I don't see it like that. We're all the divine and we just have to find this place inside us again.

Next week our film department will start making a film called *Art from Inner Stillness.* I want to talk a bit about creativity from this space because my sense is that there are different ways that art is created. In a simple way, we can say there is mindy art and art that comes from inner stillness. Most art actually comes from a busy mind, from a concept or an idea, and rarely from silence. When we first came to this house we saw the potential of having an art gallery inside the community – our living spaces would be our art gallery. Some people were a bit nervous about that, but anyway, ten years have passed and every year we've had three or four exhibitions.

Over the years we've been buying paintings from these exhibitions for the community and they are all hanging in this one room where we are now. We call this our Permanent Gallery. You may have already discovered the rest of the art gallery, which is spread throughout the house.

From the beginning, we only wanted to exhibit art that came from inner stillness – painting and sculpture, photography, graphic art and ceramic art. I had some sense of how that would look, but not really, and I had thought that probably it would be almost impossible to find much to exhibit.

Looking around this room we see some paintings by Peter Royen. He became a dear friend of our gallery. He managed to stay with us long enough to have a big retrospective exhibition and a huge goodbye party for his ninetieth birthday in Dusseldorf and be honoured by his fellow artists. A few days after his party he simply subsided.

When you look at this painting of his you'll see it's very, very simple. It's all white, and in fact, going to his studio, you could say all his paintings were rather similar to this one. Ninety per cent of his paint tubes were white.

This one is again white but it has a red stripe at the bottom. I think it took him about forty years to get to the red stripe. When you spend some time with these paintings you will discover that they don't start off a story inside you. They're probably touching something that we can call your True Nature. They touch a quiet place inside.

These next paintings are a little bit similar. They are by Dan Hepperle and are simply white stripes, and although both these paintings are white, they're not just white. Again, what happens is that they actually bring you out of any story. They bring you to some place deeper than just the mind.

Next are two paintings by Bettina Hachmann. She works in a beautiful old castle with a moat and the paintings show an abstracted view out of the window. Again, when you look at these two paintings they actually bring you out of any mindy story.

Christian, one of our artists, is here with us tonight. The painting over in the corner was bought from him six years ago, and as you see it has a black base with these bright colours coming through. His approach is very spontaneous and he lets the colours drip and flow on the canvas, giving space to something happening without being influenced by his mind. Whenever I look at this painting it always touches something very gentle and deep inside me.

It's not about whether I like this painting or whether I like that painting because actually I like just about any painting. But maybe you can begin to see that some art has this ability to take you deep inside, that art can help take you to this place that I'm talking about.

It boggles the mind to imagine how some of the world's great masterpieces could have been created. For example, in the Vatican there is a sculpture done by Michelangelo when he was only about twenty-two years old. It's called the Pieta and is in a small side-chapel of St Peter's Basilica. It is almost impossible to imagine the profound skill and vision that created such a masterpiece.

Van Gogh's Potato Eaters was painted in the eastern part of Belgium during a terrible famine. He stayed with the village people. It shows a family sitting around a table, and you can feel the whole scene of this famine in this one painting. You don't really see it; rather you just feel it in a deep place inside.

When he was in the south of France, just before he cut his ear off, he made two or three paintings of sunflowers. The energy that comes from these paintings is overwhelming. You probably know his story that in his lifetime he could not sell even one painting and now one of those sunflower paintings would be worth around a hundred million dollars.

The point I'm trying to make to you is the possibility of coming inside to that place of silence. Dance, music, painting and other creative pursuits are all vehicles for you to come to that place. By the way, if my little introduction to our art gallery is interesting, we have a website where you can see the paintings we've been exhibiting: www.flowfineart.com.

I invite you to come and dialogue about this theme of creativity, or maybe someone has a question about it. It's not really about creativity; it's really about this place inside us. It's taken us many years to find this inner silence as a community and it's very interesting for me to see that in the last three or four years many people have started to express their creativity.

Kabir, for example, seems to almost channel spontaneous poems. And his piano playing is really touching. Have you always played the piano Kabir?

Yes.

And here over the last three years has something changed with the way you play?

Well, there's definitely something about inspiration, which goes hand in hand with recognising that there's a lot more here than you think. Where do the spontaneous poems come from? And the piano music is also spontaneous; where is it coming from?

You don't play from sheet music, so are you suggesting that God is playing the piano?

In some sense, maybe yes. Not like how it might sound but...

So shall we have a poem about creativity?

> *My hands are bound behind my back,*
> *But I was not put off by the sirens*
> *As they winged their way around me.*
> *The chains were broken by the flames.*
> *Red-hot metal burned into my wrists,*
> *But I turned and looked upwards*
> *As the ground came to meet me.*
> *And I fell backwards.*
> *The chains are metal,*
> *But the soul is the substance*
> *That has no texture.*
> *It has no quality of the human*
> *Or the material.*
> *It is that which breathes through the open door*
> *As you sit and allow your body to open like a channel.*
> *It is the electricity moving through the wires,*
> *Giving light to the warehouse.*
> *It is just the pulse for life*
> *That floods through your body.*

That was really spontaneous? It came very quickly.

Yes. I had to start quickly otherwise it wouldn't come.

Could you feel how – I don't know the right word – spontaneous of course, but somehow very energetic. Did you all feel how energetic that was? It didn't really feel like Kabir. Of course, you don't know him as well as I do, but he won't mind me telling you that he's often very much busy with his mind.

His parents thought they were going to give him a good education by sending him to a boarding school and he never really recovered from that trauma. We often find him sitting in the office with his head on the desk, so when he does these spontaneous poems I'm very touched and I wonder who the hell is doing it. Where does it come from?

It's really like a channel opening. It's just a flood.

So can you see the possibility that all great art – or even not great art, or even just sweeping the floor or making a peanut butter sandwich – is not really personal? We become very attached to the idea that I'm making this peanut butter sandwich or I'm making this poem.

We just experienced that nobody made this spontaneous poem. We could probably thank his parents, actually, because by sending him to this boarding school he's got a great grasp of the English language. I'm sure he received a frightfully good education.

Frighteningly!

Kabir's life experience or his life journey is unique to him. But did Michelangelo make that Pieta? He'd been trained from an early age to be a mason so he was an expert at cutting marble. There would have been many expert masons in those days but when you stand in front of that sculpture something happens, something beyond anything that is personal. Would you like to comment on this? What is your well-educated perspective?

I can see how difficult it would be to even know that you can do something like that. I had no idea that I could create poems or that they could come through so effortlessly. Probably everyone can do something like that.

I would like to invite anyone with a self-judgement about your creativity – I can't dance, I can't sing, I can't paint – to challenge that. Because, of course, we can all do it, and I would suggest that you'd do it better when you're not there. Which may sound a little bit strange.

But that's how it is. That's definitely how it feels.

I think Michelangelo did something even more amazing than the Pieta. He was very skilled as a mason, but he wasn't a painter. He had a connection with the pope, and the pope said, 'Well, you see this chapel? You see this ceiling? There's a very high ceiling. I want it painted.' The pope was very keen to get this job done and he often came to see how it was going.

Michelangelo had to put up a scaffold and lie on his back to paint the ceiling. It's actually a three-dimensional painting requiring some very complex painting techniques. And it started with a disaster. He'd been working away for some time with the pope coming and telling him to hurry up and he discovered that he'd mixed the plaster wrong and it all fell off. Even Michelangelo had to learn a few things.

What was the spirit that created this amazing artwork? We can say that Michelangelo was a genius, but maybe he was somebody who was very good at 'not being there', and by not being there some other energy could take over.

Destiny

Nisargadatta Maharaj was a powerful and independent teacher of *Advaita* living in the red light district of Mumbai. He lived above his *beedi* (India cigarette) shop and met many western seekers in a small room, telling them to go once he felt they had reached their potential.

All that happens, happens in and to the mind, not to the source of the 'I am'. Once you realise that all happens by itself, (call it destiny, or the will of God or mere accident), you remain as witness only, understanding and enjoying, but not perturbed.

Nisargadatta Maharaj

Dear John David,
I have always been concerned with a very important question: Do I have free will or not? Is everything, every smallest thought, every smallest action really predetermined?
If so, I have not the slightest influence on my spiritual development.

Nothing happens here, in this Essence, in the source of the 'I am'. What comes out of this Essence, which then manifests through the mind, is what we call 'life' – 'my life'. Or perhaps more accurately 'the world'.

Unfortunately, we're usually very much attached to what we call the world and we can't really imagine how simply our life actually unfolds. Sri Ramana Maharshi said that if you want something to happen but it's not supposed to happen, it won't happen. And equally, if there's something you don't want to happen but it's supposed to happen, it will happen.

The reason I'm sitting here tonight, giving this talk in Open Sky House, is exactly because of destiny. When I was living in Australia I received a kind of inner message telling me it was time to leave.

I would come back to Europe, but where in Europe? Being English, I thought I would be going to England, but existence had other ideas and I ended up here in Germany. There were some little dances here and there and we ended up with this beautiful Open Sky House Community.

When I was a young man in my twenties I had the idea of being an architect, probably in London, making a small, private design office. This is something I was very much attracted to and had a lot of interest in. It seemed that that was my destiny.

There was a little tango, three steps here and two steps back, and I found myself in an ashram in India. Gradually my idea of becoming an architect disappeared and I found myself intensely involved in meditation. If I consider my situation, I would say that of all the masters I've been lucky to have had contact with, the one that had the most influence was Sri Ramana Maharshi.

Destiny introduced me to him, or, as Maharaj says, a *'mere accident'*. My accident was finding a photo of Sri Ramana in a pile of rubbish in the rooms I was renting in Pune, close to Osho's ashram. Later I went to see Papaji and on the wall behind him was exactly the same photo. So you can say my destiny, or my accident, brought me into contact with this great master, Sri Ramana. There was a deep surrender, and when I came from India, back to the West, I found myself being a messenger for his teachings. In fact his teachings were the essence of the ancient teachings of India.

Without any plan I ended up having my whole life change its direction. The question tonight was: *'Do I have free will?'* The answer is no. Sorry, but this is actually very, very beautiful because if you let go of your idea then life will show you where to go and what to do.

When you become quiet you can connect to this inner space, which we're calling the Self. It is your Essence; actually it is the Essence of everybody. This is your connection to the wisdom of the universe, and it will guide you, a little bit like your car's navigation system.

You can probably see how some small happening or decision has led to some big change of direction in your life. You meet somebody, you have dinner together, lunch together. You walk in the park. Over time you develop a deeper connection with this person and this leads to some new direction. This is happening to everybody, to all your friends.

Most people have the idea: 'I am doing my life.' The whole education system, all of society, is based on this idea. This is a false idea and gradually, as you fall deeper inside, you find yourself falling into the mystery of destiny.

Maharaj goes on to say, *'Once you realise that all happens by itself (call it destiny, or the will of God or mere accident), you remain as witness only, understanding and enjoying, but not perturbed.'*

This is an invitation to stay as the witness, to become quiet and stay as pure awareness. From this place we simply watch how things are unfolding and we can accept these things as they happen to us.

It is very easy to get caught up in our ideas and beliefs. We want something to be a certain way so we're constantly trying to push our life in that direction because we believe this will make us happy or bring us love.

The more you let go of these ideas the more you fall into the tremendous acceptance that everything is exactly as it should be and there is nothing to be changed. We are where we're supposed to be and what is supposed to happen is happening. There is nothing to be concerned about, nothing to be afraid of.

Would somebody like to come and talk about destiny? It seems you must be destined to come and speak here tonight – even if you didn't want to!

I have a problem with this word 'pre-destined'. It sounds as if there's something written somewhere and I am simply living it out.

It sounds like there's an enormous computer floating up and around the planet that's computing the life of billions of people. It's saying things like, 'Okay, today Barbara is going to wear this red scarf and black earrings.' But I think this view is a little bit childish. It doesn't work like that at all.

I find it difficult to express how I really feel about this. If I look at how I feel about my life now, it seems that when I step aside from all the ideas of how life can be then it just happens. So for example, if I don't know what to cook I just wait a bit and then suddenly clunk, clunk!

Yes. The voice is booming down on us: 'Steak for lunch!'

This is a small decision in life, and I think that it works the same with big decisions. It's only if we are very emotional about something that it is more difficult to step aside because something is in the way. When this happens I try just to be quiet and to connect to this still place. It's a bit like a question: What does this place say to this situation? It's like I can decide to connect to this place.

No, I don't think you can decide to connect to this place. I think we're always connected. It doesn't arise that we're not connected. Reality as I understand it is that everybody is connected always, and this is why this whole spiritual idea about enlightenment is not correct.

If you want to say it like that, everybody is always enlightened, but we are very busy with a kind of static – noise, interference. This is the noise of the conditioned mind, and it creates a false reality that we are very much identified with, but underneath our attachment to the false reality, the true Self is always operating and guiding and moving us through our life. Life is not working as we would like it to work.

Just this morning I read a very strong story in the newspaper. There was a quite well known comedian, married with a seven-year-old daughter. His wife was writing a novel based on a true story. It was about a man who had been raping and killing women, and this woman became very involved in the story.

She had the feeling that she could solve the mystery of who this person was. So she became a kind of detective. She was driving herself so hard that one day her husband said, 'You have a good sleep. I'll manage our daughter; I'll take her to school in the morning and you can have a good sleep-in. Okay?'

The next morning he took the daughter to school, came back, and his wife was breathing and sleeping normally, apparently normally. He went through a few emails, answered some messages, and just before lunch he went to wake her up. She had stopped breathing. She was dead. Things like this are happening every day, things completely against our ideas of how life should happen.

Destiny. We arrive. We leave. In between, we think we're doing our life. But this is only happening in the mind. When we understand this the attachment to the movie of the mind drops.

And at the same time, we cannot understand.

Well, you can understand on one level but fundamentally there is nobody to understand.

Service

As it's almost Christmas I thought we should consider some words from Jesus tonight. Perhaps I should say something about him, but he's so famous that there's not much I can add. Now that I have spent some forty plus years in the spiritual world I can say with no doubt that Jesus did not have a virgin birth, did not make a feast out of two small fish and some dried bread and it's pretty unlikely he walked on water. Try it!

Whoever wants to be first must be a servant of all, for even the Son of God did not come to be served but to serve and to give His life as a ransom for many.

Jesus

> *Dear John David,*
> *I always found this idea of serving to be very Christian, but actually I've come to see that it is intrinsic to the spiritual journey because it opens the heart and makes one humble. But I still recognise in me the Christian idea that I should serve and not enrich myself. Could you please comment a bit on this topic of service?*

If we're going to be in service, we have to decide who or what we are in service to. Generally, this time of the year, just before Christmas, we're all encouraged to focus on others and serve the poor, the suffering, the little children, the handicapped, and so on. This is the Christian idea of serving, but we have to be careful about the motivation for this kind of service. By helping the under privileged, for example, I can identify myself as 'a good person' and in a subtle way this serves the ego or the false self.

That's not the service that Jesus had in mind but it is very much exploited at this time of the year. The media and people running charities play on this part of people that makes them feel guilty for being successful or rich. It plays on their wrong ideas of service.

The right idea of service is service to Truth, or if you like to God – which can be a difficult word with many connotations, so I will say that we're serving existence itself.

We all have a destiny that unfolds throughout our lives, and yours might be serving the handicapped or the oppressed. If you're really present, if you're connected to your own Being, it will tell you clearly in any moment what that service is.

I would say that until about twenty-two years ago I was in service to my own ego. I was always thinking about what would be the best deal for John David. I was always looking around for what I could get that would make me a little more happy, a bit more 'full'. But it was always coming out of my own sense of lack – I was lacking something and therefore I was looking for something to make me feel complete or satisfied. Something like this.

Then something happened, and since that time I feel I haven't been so involved in my ego. I have an ego but I'm not so concerned about it, and by living more and more in the present moment I see that in fact everything in my life is service. This service is not to somebody exactly. It's in service to some kind of destiny that has been unfolding in the last years of my life.

When I sit here tonight I look at the residents of our beautiful community and I can think back to when our community started spontaneously. It happened a year after me coming to Europe from Australia. Actually I came from India because on the way from Australia I stayed in India for some time. Just before I was leaving India for Europe I was introduced to a man who lived in Germany. So I came to Germany.

That was not my plan, but that's what happened. So there was an acceptance that my trip was going to start in Germany and I would see what happened from there. Things did happen, and they happened and happened and suddenly I found myself in a community.

That was fourteen years ago and along the way there have been a few times when I might have decided to leave the community, to escape. But actually there was never a really serious attempt to escape because this would have been serving my own ego, my own sense of self. It's always been clear that I'm supposed to have this community, so I surrender to that. And by surrendering to that I'm in service, partly to the community and partly to the people who make up the community.

Actually I'm in service to a bigger picture that this community is part of. We are a small experiment that has developed through fourteen years and I see there is a value in this. I don't exactly know what this value is in terms of a bigger picture but this community is attracting very sincere people who together are creating something quite extraordinary.

They're creating a loving energy field. This is one of the most important aspects, but we're also creating a mechanism, a small experiment in an alternative lifestyle for human beings. As the years progress I'm very often touched by the alternative of this greater family.

We have in our community twin baby girls. Right now they are being cared for by at least half-a-dozen loving, responsible adults, in addition to their biological parents. Naturally their mother has been with them for the whole eighteen months, every single day, every single minute, twenty-four hours a day. The connection between the mother and the child is a completely natural genetic connection.

It is not so obvious, but that connection is also there between the father and the child. I was rather surprised to discover that some kind of genetic implant exploded on the birth of the children and left me feeling very much committed to raising and caring for them.

I realise now that there is no way I can escape from that. It's just part of nature, a beautiful mechanism to make sure that children are nourished and cared for and looked after. But also I can see that anyone who is ready to put their energy and love towards these children also has a role to play.

One of the things I always find difficult is to witness parents creating an egoic bond with their child. The child becomes 'my' child and very often you can feel how the parents are using the child for their own egoic needs. It is much better if mature, self-aware people can approach parenting with an attitude of service. Children are cared for and protected against injury but with as little interference as possible as they get on with the job of being kids.

I find it very lovely that these babies are being cared for by half-a-dozen close carers, all of whom have different characters. Hopefully the dominating influences of the mother and father are going to be moderated and enhanced by the different characters who are also serving these two little girls. You can see from their smiles how they enjoy all these close, caring people.

Of course, caring for children is only one direction in which our service can flow. You can look inside and find your own intuition, your own Being. You can get in touch with this, find out what your role is, what your destiny is, and then you can be in service to that destiny.

As the questioner suggests, the beauty is that it has the effect of opening your heart. Caring or being in service to raising children is a wonderful way to open our hearts. In that sense, service is absolutely part of spiritual life or the spiritual journey because the heart has to open. But this service is not the service the Christians are talking about. For me, it is a different sense of service – service free from ego.

Compassion

I haven't met the Dalai Lama, but he seems to me to personify compassion. He is a very unusual human being. At the age of two he was already marked out to become the 14th Dalai Lama and this meant that from a very early age he was in the company of the wisest of the Tibetan lamas. If I remember rightly, when he was a young child he used to sleep at the feet of one of the greatest lamas.

Tibetan Buddhists are some of the most heartful and compassionate people on the planet. As a young man the Dalai Lama had to leave Tibet during the 1959 Tibetan uprising and as far as I can sense he has devoted his life to bringing the best of Tibetan culture into the wider world, mostly into the West. So now there is a whole network of communities and organisations and travelling lamas and in this way they maintain the best of Tibetan culture.

During this same period the Chinese government has chosen to persecute the Tibetans. I watched a video of the Dalai Lama talking about this political situation in Tibet – completely relaxed and even laughing at this terrible situation. When he laughs or smiles you can feel the energy and compassion from the depth of his Being.

Compassion is not religious business. It is human business. It is not luxury. It is essential for our own peace and mental stability. It is essential for human survival.
Tenzin Gyatso, the 14th Dalai Lama

Dear John David,
In my spiritual search I have been focused on the way of knowledge and enquiry, trying to find out about who I am. I wonder about this word compassion and what it really means as I hear it a lot in the spiritual world. What is your take on compassion and what is its role in becoming Self-realised?

This is a beautiful topic. Compassion comes naturally out of an honest and open heart. What do we mean by compassion? Humans as a species are profoundly interdependent on each other and because of this our need for love is essential for our survival. A lack of love leads to suffering – both physical and mental – and the purpose of compassion is to alleviate this suffering. It is not an emotional response. Rather it requires a true feeling of responsibility and real concern for the wellbeing of others.

Compassion deepens and endures especially when things take a turn for the worse, for example the disappointment partners might experience as they come to know each other's real characters.

Within Buddhism, a *Bodhisattva* is somebody who becomes enlightened and then doesn't just leave to another realm but stays around here to bring other human beings to this enlightenment – an example of deep compassion. True compassion seems to me to be a natural way of life for somebody who has achieved a truly open heart.

There are individuals and organisations that ooze compassion. Martin Luther King comes to mind. He basically gave his life in order to create more justice for African Americans. It is easy for us to forget the great courage this required. Mahatma Gandhi is another. Almost single-handedly he challenged the British government to political freedom for India. He chose to do that non-violently, and of course he also paid with his life. We've all been touched by the story of Jesus who was also very compassionate and also paid with his life.

Amnesty International is an organisation that defends and frees political prisoners. They help individuals but also hold governments to account. Some people express their compassion by caring for everything in this existence. Organisations like Green Peace campaign for our threatened and endangered species and for continuing life on this planet.

Just today I was reading about a man in Venezuela. He is a vet by profession and he basically puts all the money he gets as a vet into trying to save an amazing eagle that lives in South America. It has a wingspan of two metres and has the power to pluck monkeys off the tops of trees or baby dear off the ground. The eagles are very rare and he has had trouble to even find them. Along the way he hit on the idea of getting the local people who hunted these eagles to actually help him locate the nests and then to put chips on the chicks. And so over many years he has managed to support their continuing survival.

Almost every day in the news you can find examples of people devoting themselves to giving back something to existence. My first spiritual master, Osho, used to encourage his disciples to leave the planet a little more beautiful than when they arrived. I was always very touched by that. It motivates my own life.

Service is an integral part of compassion. Attachment to an independent, individual 'me' actually works towards inhibiting compassion, and true compassion can only be experienced when this has been resolved.

Compassion is a rare fruit of an open heart, particularly because once you are no longer in the personal this easily leads to compassion for your fellow humans and for all beings on this planet. The Dalai Lama is saying here that it is essential for human survival, an almost fundamental law of nature.

The questioner asks, '... *what is its role in becoming Self-realised?*' It is more the other way around ... the conscious cultivation of an open heart and a lack of attachment to the personal leads to Self-realisation. Compassion naturally follows.

During the last twenty years I've had the good luck of spending time with many awakened teachers. One of their common characteristics is an enormous compassion. So don't be too focused on the way of knowledge and enquiry. There is a way of the heart and it will lead you in the end to become compassionate.

Falling into Grace

Paramhansa Yogananda was one of the first Indian spiritual teachers to permanently live in the West, coming to America in the 1920s. He had a great influence, sharing the ancient teachings of India widely during his life. He developed two beautiful ashrams in California.

His book *Autobiography of a Yogi* touched me in my early years. He made spiritual life seem like an exciting adventure full of mystical moments. Later Osho made me see mystical adventures as less important, but I was well on my way by then.

Now much later as a wiser man I can see that Yogananda inspired many in his time, but in fact simple presence is most important.

There is no way to find God's love other than to surrender to Him.
Paramhansa Yogananda

> *Dear John David,*
> *I've been increasingly doing Self-enquiry as I can see that the ending of the illusion of a false self is the only way out of suffering. Fairly often, when doing Self-enquiry, the identification with the ego fades and there is just a beautiful peace and lightness. Grace is ever present. My understanding of the surrender is to see the false self clearly enough, and to see how, by identifying with it, we are always missing the grace. I'd be interested in your comment on grace and how to surrender to it.*

You start off well. You understand about the self, the false self, and you see that this is the one gate that will take you out of suffering. This is your experience when you do Self-enquiry and as you say you come to a beautiful peace and lightness.

Moments of it, yes; little breaths.

That's absolutely perfect. But the rest of it is not right. You say, *'My understanding of surrender is to see the false self clearly enough, and to see how, by identifying with it, we are always missing the grace.'*

I just thought it would make a good question.

This is mind. This is not surrender. Surrender is not something 'you' can do, and certainly you don't want to be so understanding about the false self and then see that you're identifying with it. This is all mind. Surrender is happening when you do Self-enquiry and you come, you say, to this beautiful peace and lightness, or as Yogananda says, when you *'find God's love'*.

This beautiful peace and lightness is the grace, you can say. Grace is a difficult word because we don't know really what it is, how it is going to manifest. We could even say that it's destiny. Some people seem to go through life and things seem to be easy; they're in a flow. Perhaps they were taken to an ashram or to a teacher, or they came to a community like this, for example, and you can see grace working very clearly. But grace is not picky – there's not good grace and bad grace.

One of the women living in our Ukraine community is planning to leave tomorrow. Almost exactly one year ago in India she had a very big glimpse or opening and was laughing about the craziness of life. She was very free, you could say, at that time. And now a year later she's become very closed down.

Probably there's a lot of fear working inside her. In the last two years she's gone from being a business woman in a town in the heartland of Ukraine to meeting the teachings, coming to India with me – where she had a good experience – and joining the Tripillya Open Sky House Community.

Now after four months in the community she has cut herself off from the other people there, from me and from her friends. She feels she can't go back to her old life, to the known, but this new situation in the community has brought up a lot of fear. So this is a very strong situation for her.

But this all must be grace, because grace does not choose. And what is grace? Grace is existence itself. She's surrendering to a grace that does not appear to be in her own interest at the moment. But who knows? At the same time, for example, you are finding moments of peace and lightness through Self-enquiry. This is also grace.

Self-enquiry consists of two questions that bring you into this lightness. It's nothing about surrendering because you see this or that. That's all mindy stuff.

What I meant is that if there's any surrender, it's not to identify with the ego.

If there's any surrender, you surrender to the lightness and peace, but this surrender just happens because the lightness and peace are very touching. It's not that 'I' surrender because of some reason the mind has come up with.

Yes, this is an idea. But surely there has to be a conscious decision to try and change before some change can happen. Or an awareness that it needs to change or that it can change.

Yes, but you don't choose to have that decision. You don't do anything because you don't exist.

This is what I'm trying to say. There's an idea here, that I can do it.

That's because you're identified with being somebody who can do all kinds of things. And that's the problem.

It's really funny!

What's really funny?

The joke of it...

Yes, of course. And yet we're all doing this. This is also part of the big joke – even this we are not doing.

In these moments it always just comes back to the same thing. It's so simple.

Why wouldn't it be simple?

It must be because of all this conditioning.

Before this meeting I was looking at a video from the first day of the Indian retreat. We did the Self-enquiry exercise where we ask each other, 'Who are you?' We do it for enough hours so that in the end you begin to see that everything you believe yourself to be can't really be true. At the end we have a sharing that goes on for quite a long time. I invite the people to come and sit with me and share something from now.

It's extremely touching because even after only a few hours of asking and looking and realising you're not who you think you are, people share such beautiful be-here-now moments. Often it's something along the lines of, 'I just feel touched.' Even some tears come. What have they been touched by? They've been touched by their own Being. So this 'own Being' is very, very close. It's not surprising it's simple.

But yes, it's not so easy because we're so much conditioned to always look into and identify with the false self. What you are explaining in your question is not wrong exactly. It's the right idea but surrender doesn't happen like that. Surrender happens when it just happens, not when somebody is surrendering.

The Divine Navigation System

Neem Karoli Baba is one of those incredible Indian gurus who does things that our western minds can't follow, like being in two different places at the same time. A group of American seekers, included Ram Dass, Krishna Das and shortly Steve Jobs, spent time with him in the 1970s.

The real contentment comes only through the grace of God. When you have full faith in Him, full reliance on Him, when you can surrender everything to Him, then that grace comes to you by itself – you do not have to ask for it or make any effort.
> *Neem Karoli Baba*

> Dear John David,
> *I have some confusion about the topic of surrender. I feel the pull of my desires and my ego wanting to decide what I do from moment to moment. I also feel a strong urge just to surrender, to give up the ego and just be authentic. I live alone, and I don't feel much interest in the outside world anymore. Can you please share your understanding of surrender and how it can be brought into daily life?*

This is a very good question. The simple answer is yes. The way of the heart, the way of trust, the way of surrender – which in Sanskrit is called *bhakti* – comes down to saying yes. In many situations we can easily say yes. If we want to live in this way of surrender then we need to understand that we have the ego – our personal movie running on and on – and we have something else, which we can call the Essence. We can call it our Being. In India, they call this the Self. This is something that never changes.

If we want to live in a deep surrender then we want to surrender to the Essence, not to the ego. If we are not able to distinguish between the two we'll be surrendering to our egos, to our movies, as this is our default situation. We're constantly living in this movie and saying yes to it, but *bhakti* (devotion) is different. If we become sufficiently quiet, and sufficiently self-aware, then we can allow ourselves to fall deeply inside. This happens automatically when the mind gets quieter.

When we have achieved the ability to come deeper inside, to our Being, then we can activate what I call the navigation system. This navigation system is a lot like the little app you can have on your phone, but instead of being focused on a satellite, it's focused on existence itself. It picks up the intelligence of the universe. If we become quiet enough to tune in we can take regular guidance from this navigation system.

If you walk slowly enough through your life you can stay connected to your navigation system. Then, when you say yes, you're saying yes to the directions of the navigation system and not yes to your programmed ego. This is the true surrender. In order to surrender in that way you have to trust your own ability to come into the navigation system. So surrender is very much connected to trust and heartful, devotional energy. When the heart is open, then the access to your Being begins. As you surrender deeper and deeper, as you surrender more routinely then everything gets easy – you live in a flow. This is the flow of your life and it is a wonderful way to live.

Of course, in order to stay in this yes, in this *bhakti*, we need to break our attachment to the ego. This comes out of our deeper understanding.

This word 'surrender' can be very misunderstood. We learn as we grow up that we have to surrender to Daddy. Then we meet our school teacher and we have to surrender to him; then the boss. We can slip into the idea that surrender means surrendering to somebody, therefore people are quite wary, but in the sense of spiritual Truth this is a completely wrong idea. It's never about a personal surrender.

Perhaps you've seen images of people bowing down to a teacher in India or a statue in Asia. As we are so attached to our own 'me', we assume that the person is bowing down to the 'me' of the teacher, or of the statue, but it's not like that. When somebody bows down to a teacher it has the meaning of bowing down to the Self of the teacher. This Self of the teacher, of course, is the same Self as the one who bows down. There's nothing personal, even though it appears to be personal.

The surrender that we're talking about is never to some kind of external authority. It is always to the internal authority, which is your Essence. You surrender to yourself, The Self. It's very, very important to always remember that, because if you forget it you can easily get caught up in the ego and surrendering to your ego. And then you say, 'Well that's what I want!' Then the question is, well what exactly is this 'I' that wants? This is not true surrender. This is mistaken surrender. This is surrender to the ego, to the 'me'. And *bhakti* means surrendering to the universal Essence.

Open Sky House Community

The other day I came across a quote by Thich Nhat Hanh, a Vietnamese monk who founded a spiritual community in the west of France, called Plum Village, in 1982. I have not personally visited, but I can sense that a loving and powerful community and energy field has developed there, which has the power to really support other people and the consciousness of humanity as a whole.

I have the same feeling and vision about the Open Sky House Community, that it is an experiment in an alternative way of living and a guiding light for spiritual seekers. In its fourteen years it has developed a strong and profound energy field, which touches and transforms many people, and I can see that it is not personal – it is not John David's Community, it is its own entity, a force to wake people up. This ties in perfectly to the quote from Thich Nhat Hanh.

It is possible that the next Buddha will not take the form of an individual. The next Buddha may take the form of a community, a community practising understanding and loving kindness, a community practising mindful living.

Thich Nhat Hanh

We never had any plan of how this community should develop. But now there's an amazing energy field here. It's not created really by anybody. It's a result of twenty people living together as honestly as they can, being ready to be mirrors for each other, to get rid of the nonsense, to allow the Truth to emerge.

People can meet their potential. They can become quiet. And what we've discovered is that when you become quiet enough, enormous creativity is released – music, singing, theatre, painting. We use theatre to play out our silly inner structures, we've created a beautiful painting studio and for the last ten years we've been running an art gallery in the house – Flow Fine Art. We exhibit painting, sculpture and photography that we call 'art from inner stillness'. It's an expression of stillness and Truth, an expression of peace.

About being yourself – of course we have to find out what that means. Who is myself? Who is the Self? When we sat together in silence at the beginning of this meeting perhaps you felt how we became one – we're all this same stillness. Very beautiful. When you're ready to do the work to get rid of the nonsense you can find out that your True Nature is this stillness – and it wants to express itself.

Recently, somebody from the Ukraine Community wrote to me saying, 'Now I understand about the community. It's an organism that's made up of everybody but it has its own existence. It has its own life separate from each individual.' You see? This is actually another way of saying that we're all one.

It doesn't matter that people do stuff you don't like. It doesn't even matter that they do stuff that you do like. All this is completely unimportant, except in the context that it is all material for developing self-knowledge and conscious awareness. When a group of people spends enough time to melt together a different kind of communication develops. It is not from thinking but rather from an open heart. It is less suspicious and more trusting.

I remember an art gallery opening when one of our gallery painters brought a friend who was a gallery owner, a business man. After some time the gallery owner asked his friend the painter, 'What's going on in this place? I feel something.' He didn't know what he was feeling but he could feel something unusual, something he just didn't recognise.

All of you can easily recognise it – it's love. It's just love. It is our Essence and we've almost become afraid to experience it. We've become almost afraid to express it, but that's what this gallery owner could feel when he came into our gallery. He felt love, and this was completely strange for him. This is not the 'I love you' kind of love. I'm talking about something much deeper, about the love that is our Essence as human beings. You don't have to do anything to get it. It's our Essence and it's just bubbling away. Actually you do have to do something – you have to get out of the way.

As Thich Nhat Hanh says,: *'The next Buddha may take the form of a community, a community practising understanding and loving kindness, a community practising mindful living.'* This is the essential inner work that we practise while at the same time being busy with our outer work to create an income for the community.

So there is some work to do. Once you learn how to get out of your own way you just discover that yes, there it is bubbling away and it's called love. It's really love. And as a human being you have the right to live this love. I never understood it when I was in my twenties. I would have to say it's taken me forty or fifty years to understand this, almost my whole adult life. This subtle, beautiful love is what our community is about. We call it Open Sky House. Love is completely open. Everybody's invited.

Recently we made a film, *The Great Misunderstanding*, that tries to explain more or less what I've just been saying. Along with the film we produced a book that sets out in a much deeper way what I am talking about tonight. This lovely book has my name on it but actually it was created by the whole community – there are wonderful jokes from the joke department, amazing graphics from the graphics department. One of our artists produced the exquisite symbols we use throughout the book. We have our own publishing company that produced the layout and took the whole project through to printing and distribution. The publishing company has published twenty-five books and six films with subtitles in many languages.

For some years we've run quite a big guesthouse. We have the art gallery and a seminar business. We are self supporting. So as you can imagine, we work a lot here. You'll find the residents rushing around all the time with things that need their attention, but what we're really doing here is an inner work that you can't really see. This inner work is getting rid of the rubbish that the mind has collected over years of conditioning.

Masters' Biographies

M - Z

Ma Souris

Unknown - 2005

John David's book selection
A Memory

It is not known when Ma Souris was born. Her father, Gudipati Venkata Chalam, was a well-known writer, artist and admirer of women who advocated for their freedom. He was a disciple of Sri Ramana Maharshi, later becoming a disciple of Ma Souris. Ma Souris came to know of Sri Ramana in May, 1938, through this connection of her father.

She was deeply touched to meet Sri Ramana and on his advice she intensely practised Self-enquiry. This was how her spiritual practice progressed greatly and she became Self-realised.

Ma Souris lived simply with a small group of devotees in the north of Andhra Pradesh. Her story can be found in her book, *A Memory*. She left the body in 2004 or 2005. Very little is known about her.

John David has made a beautiful interview (see below) with her in his book *Blueprints for Awakening - Indian Masters*, where she shares about her awakening process, spiritual practice, the nature of Truth, and how she experiences the world.

Meister Eckhart
c. 1260 – c. 1328

John David's book selection
*Meister Eckhart, from Whom
God Hid Nothing: Sermons,
Writings, and Sayings*

Meister Eckhart is one of the great Christian mystics and also an accomplished theologian and philosopher. He was born near Erfurt in Thuringia and in his distinguished career became a Parisian professor of Theology and took a leading pastoral and organisational role in the Dominican order. He founded and worked with the Friends of God, a religious, mystical group outside the authority of the church.

In the language of the Christian tradition Eckhart expounds the eternal mysteries in a style that is fresh and original in the best sense. Through the vividness of his use of imagery Eckhart paradoxically directs us to that which lies beyond image. He was concerned to guide his followers to understand the nature of God as simple goodness, and to re-educate them to the fact that knowing and connecting to God was absolutely possible, as God designed the soul perfectly so that it may know Him.

The depth and universality of Eckhart's teaching has drawn seekers of Truth, Christian and non-Christian alike. His radical and penetrating insight makes him a natural point of reference for a genuinely universal understanding.

He was accused of being a heretic by the Pope in his later life, and died before his trial was complete.

Neem Karoli Baba

1900 - 1973

John David's book selection
Miracle of Love
by Ram Dass

Neem Karoli Baba, also known to followers as Maharajji, was a Hindu guru, mystic and devotee of the Hindu deity Hanuman. He is known outside India for being the guru of a number of Americans who travelled to India in the 1960s and 70s, the most well known being the spiritual teachers Ram Dass and Bhagavan Das, and the musicians Krishna Das and Jai Uttal. His main ashram is in Kainchi, northern India.

Neem Karoli Baba left his home in 1958, around the time when his youngest child, a daughter, was eleven. Thereafter he wandered extensively throughout northern India as a *sadhu*. During this time he was known under many names including Miracle Baba because of the amazing things that were happening around him. During his life two main ashrams were built, the first at Vrindavan and later one at Kainchi, where he spent the summer months.

In his life Maharajji established at least one hundred and eight temples, fed millions of people, advised government and corporate leaders, performed what can be called miracles, influenced current American and Indian society, brought grace into the lives of countless suffering people, and all the while remained out of the 'public eye'. He was a lifelong adept of *bhakti yoga*, encouraging service to others as the highest form of unconditional devotion to God.

He has become renowned for his incredible mystic aura and the amazing, seemingly miraculous things that happened around him and to people who came into his life. These stories are beautifully collected by Ram Dass in the book, *Miracle of Love*.

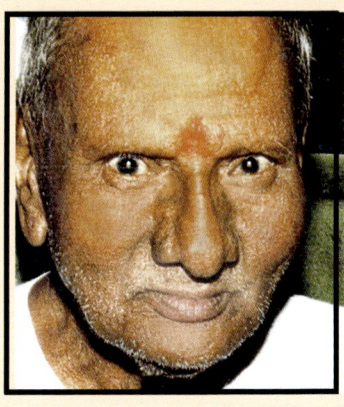

Nisargadatta Maharaj

1897 – 1981

John David's book selection
I Am That

Sri Nisargadatta Maharaj was born in March 1897. From birth he was called Maruti, in honour of Hanuman. After his father died, in 1915 he went to Bombay where he worked as a clerk and later selling hand-rolled cigarettes.

Through a friend, in 1933 he was brought to the guru Siddharameshwar Maharaj. Nisargadatta was moved and made his first steps to practise spirituality. After his guru passed away in 1936, Nisargadatta felt a strong sense of renunciation and lost interest in his worldly pursuits. But he stayed in Bombay and continued his life, meditating on 'I am', and becoming more and more rooted in That.

In 1951 he began taking disciples, and he would regularly give discourse in his house where he would answer their questions. These talks are summarised in the book *I Am That*. It has become a classic of *Advaita* philosophy, tying in to both the ancient *Upanishads* and contemporary teachers like Sri Ramana Maharshi. Sri Nisargadatta explained concepts in the simplest way, without any complex religious or spiritual terms.

OSHO
1931 - 1990

John David's book selection
The Book of Secrets: 112 Meditations to Discover the Mystery Within

Osho was a mystic, guru, and spiritual teacher, born in India. After an awakening at the age of twenty-one, he travelled throughout India in the 1960s as a public speaker and professor of philosophy. He was a critic of socialism, Mahatma Gandhi and institutionalised religions, and he controversially advocated a more open attitude towards human sexuality. In 1970, Osho settled for a time in Bombay, initiating disciples known as neo-*sannyasins* and expanded his spiritual teaching and work. In his discourses, he gave his original understanding and views on the writings of many religious traditions, mystics, and philosophers from around the world.

He moved to Pune in 1974, where his disciples established a foundation and an ashram for his presence and work, which also later moved to Oregon in the USA. In the ashrams a variety of transformational tools such as meditations and workshops was offered to the residents and visitors.

His ashram is today known as the Osho International Meditation Resort. His teachings emphasise the importance of meditation, awareness, love, celebration, courage, creativity and humour. Osho's teachings have had a notable impact on western New Age thought, and their popularity has increased markedly since his death.

www.osho.com

Papaji
1913 - 1997

John David's book selection
The Truth Is

HWL Poonja, lovingly referred to as Papaji, was born on October 13, 1913, in a part of the Punjab that is now in Pakistan. He had his first direct experience of the Self at the age of nine. In 1944, after many years of spiritual seeking for God on the outside, he met his master, Sri Ramana Maharshi the renowned Indian saint. Sri Ramana pointed him inwards to the Self instead of looking ouside for God. Shortly afterwards he realised the Self in the presence of Sri Ramana.

After some time he left the presence of Sri Ramana, but always remained devoted to him. He spent much of his life after his awakening managing a mining plant in south India.

As a disciple of Sri Ramana, Papaji offered to speak about what he had experienced with his teacher and what had become a living Truth for him. Hundreds of people from all over the world visited Papaji, especially in Lucknow, his home, during the last years of his life. Seekers of Truth from around the world visibly woke up in his presence. He had an extraordinary ability to seemingly transmit the experience of what has always been true and present.

He always remained a simple, ordinary, caring, unpretentious man, never declaring that he was on a 'mission'. He died on September 6, 1997.

Various books were made from the transcriptions of his *Satsangs*, notably *The Fire of Freedom*, *The Truth Is* and his biography, *Nothing Ever Happened*.

僧璨大師

Seng-ts'an
Third Zen Patriarch
died 606 AD

John David's book selection
Verses on the Faith Mind

The year and place of Seng-ts'an's birth are unknown, as is his family name. It is said that he was over forty years old when he first met his teacher Huike in 536 and that he stayed with him for six years. It was Huike who gave him the name Seng-ts'an (Gem Monk). After this time, Huike passed on the role of Patriarch, making him the Third Zen Patriarch.

Some accounts say that after giving Seng-ts'an *Dharma* transmission, Huike warned him to live in the mountains and 'Wait for the time when you can transmit the *Dharma* to someone else.' So Seng-ts'an lived in hiding in the mountains, wandering without a fixed abode for ten years.

At some point he met a novice monk, who, after being with Seng-ts'an for nine years, received the transmission as the new Zen Patriarch. Seng-ts'an died sitting under a tree before a *Dharma* assembly in 606. He is credited as the author of the text *Verses on the Faith Mind*, which famously begins:

> *The Great Way is not difficult*
> *for those who have no preferences.*
> *When love and hate are both absent*
> *everything becomes clear and undisguised.*
> *Make the smallest distinction, however,*
> *and heaven and earth are set infinitely apart.*

www.age-of-the-sage.org

Bhagavan Sri Ramana Maharshi

1879 -1950

John David's book selection
*Nan Yar published by
Open Sky Press*

Bhagavan Sri Ramana Maharshi is one of India's greatest modern saints. He was born in what is now Tiruchuli, Tamil Nadu, India. In 1895 an attraction to the holy hill Arunachala was aroused in him, and in 1896, at the age of sixteen, he had a 'death experience' in which he became aware of his true I or Self, which never dies.

This resulted in a state of spiritual awakening, which he didn't really understand at the beginning. Six weeks later he left his uncle's home in Madurai and journeyed to Arunachala, taking up the role of a *sannyasin*. He remained there for the rest of his life.

He soon attracted devotees and in later years an ashram grew up around him where visitors received spiritual instruction by sitting silently in his company and raising their concerns and questions.

Since the 1930s his teachings have been popularised in the West, resulting in worldwide recognition as an enlightened being. He gave his approval to a variety of paths and practices, but recommended Self-enquiry as the principal means to Self-realisation, together with *bhakti* (devotion) or surrender to the Self.

The Ramana Ashram and others have published many books from his talks and about his life and teachings, such as *Talks with Sri Ramana, Nan Yar – Who Am I?* (Ashram publication) and *Arunachala Shiva* (Open Sky Press publications).

Swami Dayananda

1930 - 2015

John David's book selection
Introduction to Vedanta

Swami Dayananda Saraswati was a monk of the Hindu monastic order, a distinguished, traditional teacher of *Vedanta* and founder of the Arsha Vidya Gurukulam. He became interested in *Vedanta* after listening to the public talks of Swami Chinmayananda in 1953. He became actively involved with the then newly formed Chinmaya Mission, and in time became a teacher himself.

His depth of understanding and nuanced appreciation of western culture made him that rare teacher who communicated the vision of non duality to modern listeners. He was able to make one see, with immediacy, the Truth of oneself as the whole.

Swami Dayananda taught *Vedanta* in India for more than four decades, and around the world since 1976. In his public talks abroad he spoke at many of the most prestigious American universities and addressed international conventions, UNESCO and the United Nations, where he participated in the Millennium Peace Summit.

A teacher of teachers, Swami Dayananda designed and taught seven residential in-depth *Vedanta* courses, each spanning thirty to thirty-six months. He also authored many authoritative books on his beloved *Vedanta*.

www.dayananda.org

Thich Nhat Hanh
born 1926

John David's book selection
The Art of Living: Peace and Freedom in the Here and Now

Thich Nhat Hanh is a global spiritual leader, poet and peace activist, revered throughout the world for his powerful teachings and bestselling writings on mindfulness and peace.

Born in central Vietnam in 1926, Thich Nhat Hanh entered a temple as a novice monk at the age of sixteen. When war came to Vietnam, he was one of those monks who chose to do both social service and spiritual practice, and in doing so founded the Engaged Buddhism movement, coining the term in his book *Vietnam: Lotus in a Sea of Fire*.

His life since has been devoted to helping people worldwide through spreading messages of Buddhism such as love and compassion, community, meditation and gentleness.

He currently resides at the mindfulness practice centre and spiritual community of Plum Village in France. Although his health is weak, he continues to offer his peaceful, serene and valiant presence to his community and visitors.

He has been a pioneer in bringing Buddhism to the West, founding six monasteries and dozens of practice centres in America and Europe, as well as over one thousand local mindfulness practice communities, known as *Sanghas*.

www.plumvillage.org

Thuli Baba
1930 - 2016

John David's book selection
*Blueprints for Awakening
Indian Masters - Vol 2*

Thuli Baba was born in 1930 in Tirumandiram Nagar, south India. As a child, he was completely absorbed in spiritual life. His father, Sri Vadivel Swami (Sri Gurudev), destroyed the bond of attachment and sense of 'me' and 'mine' in childhood and later went on to become his *satguru*.

When Thuli Baba was sixteen years old he followed the instructions of Sri Gurudev and never used the words 'I' or 'mine' or implied personal identification when referring to himself, but rather used 'This', 'we', 'our' or 'us'.

Thuli Baba was a highly traditional guru, working closely with a few devotees, but also travelling in India sharing *Satsang*. Until his death in 2016 he lived with his devotees and gave *Satsangs* in his Anbin Kudil ashram near Idappadi in Tamil Nadu.

His chuckles and dreadlocks made him sound and look like a wizard. Almost naked, wearing only a loincloth, he managed to appear like a child and a wise man at the same time. His core teaching was to drop the attachment to the world, the body and mind, and to realise the Truth is inside, to attain Self-realisation.

www.conscious-websites.com/blueprints

Eckhart Tolle

born 1948

John David's book selection
The Power of Now

Eckhart Tolle was born in Germany and educated at the Universities of London and Cambridge. At twenty-nine, he says a profound inner transformation, radically changed the course of his life. He spent the next few years devoted to understanding, integrating and deepening that transformation, which he says marked the beginning of an intense inward journey.

While in London, he also began to work with individuals and small groups as a counsellor and spiritual teacher. Since 1995 he has lived in Vancouver, Canada. His bestselling book *The Power of Now* made its American debut in 1999 and has since been translated into thirty-three languages.

Eckhart is not aligned with any particular religion or tradition. Through his writing and seminars, his simple yet profound teachings have already helped countless people throughout the world find inner peace and greater fulfillment in their lives.

At the core of his teachings lies the transformation of consciousness – a spiritual awakening that he sees as the next step in human evolution. An essential aspect of this awakening consists of transcending our ego-based state of consciousness. This, he says, is a prerequisite not only for personal happiness but also for the ending of violent conflict endemic on our planet. A sought-after public speaker and teacher, Eckhart travels throughout the world.

www.eckharttolle.com

Chögyam Trungpa

1939 - 1987

John David's book selection
Cutting Through Spiritual Materialism

Chögyam Trungpa was a Buddhist meditation master, scholar, teacher, poet, artist and originator of a radical re-presentation of Buddhist teachings to the West.

He was exiled to India from Tibet at a young age. In 1963, Chögyam Trungpa moved to England to study at Oxford University. In 1967 he moved to Scotland where he founded the first Tibetan Buddhist practice centre in the West. In his first steps as a teacher in 1969, he published *Meditation in Action*, the first of fourteen books on the spiritual path.

The following year he married and moved to the United States, where he established his first North American meditation centre, Tail of the Tiger in Barnet, Vermont, and various others were founded in North America throughout the rest of his life.

At these centres students were introduced to the possibility of integrating meditation practice and study into their everyday lives. He passed away in 1987, likely as a result of heavy drinking and smoking habits, which contributed to his reputation as a teacher of 'crazy-wisdom', often drinking in his spiritual meetings.

Recognised by Tibetan Buddhists and by other spiritual practitioners and scholars as a preeminent teacher of Tibetan Buddhism, he was a major, albeit controversial, figure in the dissemination of Tibetan Buddhism to the West.

www.chogyamtrungpa.com

Irina Tweedie

1907 – 1999

John David's book selection
The Chasm of Fire

Irina Tweedie was born in Russia and studied in Vienna and Paris. After the Second World War she married a British naval officer whose death in 1954 led her on a spiritual quest. Little did she know that her trip to India in 1959, at the age of fifty-two, would mysteriously lead her to a Sufi master. This meeting set her upon a journey to the 'heart of hearts', the Sufi path of Self-realisation.

Her teacher's first request of her was to keep a diary of her spiritual training which became the book *Daughter of Fire, the Diary of a Training with a Sufi Master*. This diary spans five years, making up an amazing record of spiritual transformation. From a psychological viewpoint, the diary maps the process of ego dissolution, gradually unveiling the openness and love that reside beneath the surface of the personality.

In her own words: *'I hoped to get instruction in yoga, expected wonderful teachings, but what the teacher did was mainly to force me to face the darkness within myself and it almost killed me ... I was beaten down in every sense until I had to come to terms with that in me which I kept rejecting all my life.'*

After her teacher's death in 1966 she returned to England where she started a Sufi meditation group in North London. Gradually groups spread throughout Europe and North America. She passed away in 1999.

Paramhansa Yogananda

1893–1952

John David's book selection
Autobiography of a Yogi

Paramhansa Yogananda was an Indian *yogi* and guru who introduced millions of westerners to the teachings of meditation and *Kriya Yoga*. In his youth he sought out many of India's Hindu sages and saints, hoping to find an illuminated teacher to guide him in his spiritual quest. His seeking after various saints mostly ended when he met his guru, Swami Yukteswar Giri, in 1910, at the age of seventeen. He describes his first meeting with Yukteswar as a rekindling of a relationship that had lasted for many lifetimes.

Paramhansa Yogananda was the first yoga master of India to take up permanent residence in the West. He arrived in America in 1920 and proceeded to travel throughout The United States on what he called his spiritual campaigns. Hundreds of thousands filled the largest halls in major American cities to see the yoga master from India. Yogananda continued to lecture and write up to his passing in 1952. His message was non-sectarian and universal.

Yogananda's initial impact on the western culture was truly impressive. But his lasting spiritual legacy has been even greater. His book *Autobiography of a Yogi*, first published in 1946, helped launch a spiritual revolution in the West. Translated into more than a dozen languages, it remains a best-selling spiritual classic to this day.

www.paramhansayogananda.com

CHAPTER 6

Self-Enquiry

The first thing really is to examine this illusory 'me', for which Self-enquiry is a profound tool. When you really become clear and you realise for yourself there is no separate somebody, that we're all actually one consciousnes, when this becomes your Truth, then surrender just happens. It happens in that moment.

Self-Enquiry

Longing to be permanently grounded in the Self, we become quiet, turning our attention more intensely to ourselves, and we become more aware of how often we need to look outside for attention or love.

Along with this more profound self-awareness we can practise Self-enquiry, questioning the reality of our sense of a separate 'I', and returning to our nature as the source.

We keep our focus on the Self, on that which never changes, our true Essence, being as we are, and allowing our ego and sense of doer-ship to dissolve into the flow of life.

Coming Out of a Love Bubble

We have a lovely example right now in the community of a normal love-relationship situation with the great twist that the people involved are actually trying and succeeding to consciously break through the bubble and come to what is true. These two young people have very kindly agreed to come and dialogue with me about this, but first I wanted to start with a quote from Lao Tzu, which illustrates nicely the situation we are in when we are dealing with our desires.

Lao Tzu is famous for authoring the *Tao Te Ching* (The Way) around 2500 years ago, and speaks very clearly in this text about how the attachment to thoughts and desires is the only thing really standing in our way of Truth. I find it very touching how such an ancient text, from a great mystic, thousands of years ago, can be so insightful and helpful today.

We should always be without desire if we want to recognise the deep mystery, but if desire is always within us we shall only see the outer edges.

Lao Tzu

So with that in mind let's turn to our couple in question, and we'll start with Rose! So, Rose, you're a bit familiar with romantic love?

Yes. I have an expectation that something will happen with certain guys I meet. In the beginning it is always very easy, very nice, and then it becomes more difficult. There's this pressure inside me about it and it becomes like an attachment. Last weekend we had a tantra retreat and things became very clear for me.

I could clearly see that I was searching for a guy who I thought would make me happy. In my imagination that means somebody who loves me and who I can potentially have a house with, have a kid with, the whole story. These are not really my wishes but this is subconsciously driving me.

Did your mother ever say things to you like, 'Find the right man and your life will be full of joy'?

I think she was more like an example because my parents were always together and they stayed together. That was really important for them. After my mother died I saw that as soon as my dad was alone he right away began searching for another woman in his life.

There's nothing wrong with it. I respect it, but the example I had is that in order to be happy you have to be with somebody. And then I also realised that I could not fully stand on my own two feet because I was searching for somebody to be one with, to be whole with, instead of being whole myself.

So you've been wandering around since you were a teenager being half, desperately looking for the other half.

I had been in a long relationship and it was really nice in the beginning. But after a couple of years, even though it was not really nice anymore, we stayed together because that's how it was supposed to be in my head. I was very unhappy and then we separated. I remember being happy after the separation and really in my power but then a couple of years later I started searching again.

But after the tantra weekend I felt this enormous space to just be. I actually stood really on own my feet. I really want to be aware of it. I don't want to fall into this clinging or wanting or needing somebody, because it's really nice standing on my own feet.

It gets nicer and nicer because it's not just about love. It's also about power, because very often in the dynamics of couples one of the two is not really empowered.

In order for the couple thing to function one accepts that they are following the other. Or maybe they both don't accept that and they're fighting to see who gets to be the top dog. But very often there's a compromise and people are disempowered.

Yes, my parents called it giving and taking.

We are very much conditioned by the experience of being in the family. We witness our parents and their friends talking a lot about love: I love you, I love you, I love you.

You can't really discover what love is until you discover who this 'I' is. When you know what is here, then you also discover what love is. You also discover an enormous power, which you're absolutely a part of. It's a universal intelligence, wisdom. This authentic love, or our True Nature, isn't easy to talk about but it's very familiar, instantly recognised. So it's not something new that has been acquired from the outside. It has always been there, inside.

I'm not sure I really experienced this kind of love before I started meditating.

First we need to find out what's here, and in order to do that we have to become aware that we have been conditioned with the wrong habits. One of those wrong habits is that we need to get something. We are conditioned to believe that right here I am lacking something and I need to get this thing that I'm lacking. Maybe we start with some ice-cream and some chocolate. But quite soon we're really looking for someone to give us love. Most of us experience ourselves as lacking love.

How is it possible that we're constantly experiencing ourselves lacking love if it's really true that we are love? This is simply because we're looking in the wrong direction. We're caught up in our movie. We put in a lot of energy to keep our daily movie running.

While we're attached to our daily movie we're certainly not looking deeper inside. When we start to investigate, when we're about to realise that we have been living with a misunderstanding, then there's some opportunity to see what's really happening. This is also very empowering, and it's rather lovely that this weekend helped you to experience this.

Often when I see myself looking outside I also see there is something inside that I'm avoiding. Like there's something troubling me that comes between my own love and feeling it. So now I try to be aware of when I get this need of wanting something – anything from a chocolate to attention – just to stop and actually look inside.

Yes. The way out of this situation is greater awareness. But it's not so easy because we're so conditioned.

Paying attention to my thoughts. In the email you sent today you wrote about a meditation for increasing awareness. It was very strong.

Did you try it?

Yes. You can actually do it every moment of the day. I can do it now.

You can explain to everybody about this new technique.

When you have a thought and you realise you're having the thought then you're in this awareness. You have brought your attention to what is actually happening. You can do it with anything. For example, I'm aware that I'm sitting here. I'm aware of my breath. And that creates a kind of distance; it's like you're looking into yourself. It's funny when you start seeing yourself doing things and then catching yourself.

We become a witness to ourselves. Most of us are very good at witnessing somebody else but maybe not so aware of ourselves.

So now I'd like to invite Rose's prince on the white horse, who may not be any particular prince but just one of many princes she discovered riding white horses around. Welcome. What Rose is saying is something you could also say. Is that right?

Yes. When I first came here you were always talking about the ultimate illusion and of thinking that love comes from the outside. And I was like, 'Uh-hmm, uh-hmm, that's lovely', but the real learning and understanding can only happen through experience. There was one very strong relationship situation that was a complete mess. For the first time it really confronted this strong need that Rose was talking about.

Life knows exactly which moment to challenge us. There's always something happening, something exactly right. And so the situation has actually got more intense. But as I experience more expansion inside and less attachment to the mind structures and to me, it can be dealt with in some way. It can be seen, and the next thing appears.

Existence, or universal intelligence, creates exactly the kind of experience we need at any particular time. It may not be what we want. It's not something separate from us. We are also the universal intelligence. In partnership we're creating what we need in every moment, and it's usually not what we think we need.

Another layer of this is that it also doesn't matter what you want, because what you want is coming from your mind. For example, I like writing poetry. I always romanticised it. I dreamed of being a writer with all the space I needed to write. And actually life created this – not how I wanted it, but much better – in the most unknowable or mysterious way. I see now that 'having what I want' is also just a thought. It's anyway happening as it should.

A lot of this desiring comes from the idea that I lack something.

This is still an issue for me.

For some months now you have a new understanding.

That was another perfect situation. It was right in the hot moment of a relationship when the honeymoon period turned and I realised, 'Oh. I'm really in a contract here.'

I remember exactly when it was revealed. We were having a weekend tantra retreat and it appeared as though you'd had a very good weekend. Then in the sharing, right at the end of the weekend, you told us you'd spent the entire weekend being very, very jealous of your 'girlfriend'. Even more surprising was the fact that she then revealed that she too had spent the whole weekend being jealous of you. The result of your love story was that you were both becoming completely possessive of the other.

Well, I'm glad you're laughing because often this is not so funny. If you fall into possessive love you're just heading for a lot of suffering. If your partner does something like go and love somebody else, it is likely to spark off jealousy and lots of pain. Even without your partner doing anything you can create this jealousy within your own mind. You get some idea about your partner and then when they don't quite respond in the way you think they should you can get very upset.

This is what was happening – basically the whole time thinking about her. It's really disempowering and it's very hard to step out of it. I can see it pretty clearly when it's happening but still this incredible sadness is just overbearing; this unbearable feeling of jealousy.

When you say 'my' wife or 'my' girlfriend, as soon as you add 'my', then you immediately start being possessive and protective and then it leads to suffering.

Yes, I've given up on the deep psychological analysis. I feel it like she's mine. There's a feeling of ownership.

Anyway, after this moment I was lost, and I really wanted to recover from it. There was support from you. There was this book to develop. The cartoon book was starting, and I basically just said, 'Okay. That happened and don't judge it so strongly. You fell into a story again. Just pour your energy into this book. Just pour your energy into your own power.'

Into your own power and into your own creativity.

The manifestation of love and creativity.

You did some cartoons that people really liked. So from your own effort you got people giving you love or attention and you started to feel satisfaction from what you created. You made completely original cartoons and I'm sure you had an experience of love and a deep satisfaction that replaced the feeling of lacking something.

This feeling of lacking is a very deep part of my psyche. It's still there, but many moments in this last year there's just this feeling of an open heart and power. Without this need for love from the outside they are given a much bigger space. There's a much bigger ground in me now, although it's not really a personal sense of me. It's more like Being-ness.

There are other reasons why we want to be intimate with somebody. It's not just because we want to get love.

I also don't want to make a decision to cut off from intimacy. That would just be an idea. I want to stay in connection with that. Things happen and I say the wrong thing, then there's this part of me that's not clear, not empowered. There's a space to go with that and acknowledge it and also be with it.

Basically I can see you are cooler to play the prince and hotter to allow your own creativity. As this goes on you'll find that it gets more solid inside you.

And more expressions. I see how I don't need to force things so much. There's so much for me to play with. I started learning Chinese again. This is enormously satisfying and when I'm doing it I don't feel like now I want a hug or something like this, because there's an inner nourishment.

This inner nourishment is clearly from yourself, so gradually you can realise that you're okay, that you have your own deep supply of love that can nourish you. You don't need to depend on anybody. This will remove a lot of the emotions that led to the suffering you used to feel.

Ten years ago, when I was talking about relationship, I was calling it the ultimate illusion and I was suggesting that nobody should do it, but I came to realise that it was completely silly advice because we're all full of different chemicals.

These chemicals take us into love stories. I don't think I have done this for many years. Probably if I let the clouds part I remember when I was pretty young, wanting to have sex with somebody and then saying to this woman, 'I love you', as if I should say it just because we had sex – we had sex therefore 'I love you'. But it's a long time now since I told anybody I love them.

My mum said that last week!

I think that you discovered your own creativity. That's very important. The alternative to a love story is to allow or open to or support your own creativity expressing itself, and then, of course, you feel the power of that. A deep inner satisfaction. So this feeling of lacking is disappearing.

It was not the whole structure that blew away but rather this deep hope that there will be someone who will just fill me up with beautiful love.

Whenever you wanted it, of course. It's no good having a lover who's not there providing it exactly when you want it! So you definitely have to go with, what does Amazon call it? Prime Service. You need Prime Service. She's got to be there at the time when you need it.

When this hope goes – which can feel like something's dying – then other things can come up. All the reasons why we want to have this hope and the reasons why we search so strongly for love from the outside, there's a reason for that. It's not just conditioning.

It's because we're terrified of being alone. Even though we are one and there's all this nice spiritual stuff, we're terrified of this moment where we have no hope anymore. Which is actually a beautiful moment when something else can change. This is what's happening for me this year. It's not easy, but there's a power in acknowledging the Truth.

It's one of the very tragic jokes, isn't it? That almost everybody in society is rushing around looking for love from somebody and never realising that all the time there's massive amounts of love just right here. So this is really tragic-comic.

The Power of Awareness

Jiddu Krishnamurti would again and again come back in his talks to the profound power of awareness and how just by being aware of our minds and identifications they can begin to lose their strength to hold us. He spoke very beautifully about awareness.

Awareness is not a commitment to something. Awareness is an observation, both outer and inner, in which direction has stopped. You are aware, but the thing of which you are aware is not encouraged or nourished. Awareness is not concentration on something.

J. Krishnamurti

Dear John David,
I've had some moments when there came over me a beautiful feeling. And I didn't do anything for this. It seems I have no control over what will happen in my life or how I feel in any moment. How to recognise awareness without concentrating, and why is it so rare that moments of pure awareness really happen?

We can say that in our Essence we are pure awareness, but of course when we come to this pure awareness we can't say it's my awareness. It's simply awareness. Pure awareness manifests when the personal disappears. It's an absence of somebody. We sink down deeper inside and we come to pure awareness, which we could also call Being.

Before we come to this pure awareness we will have an experience of awareness. In this experience I'm being aware. I am aware of it being night time and dark outside. I am aware of the world, and so on. This awareness is not like concentration. It doesn't effect what I'm observing. There is a me observing something, aware of something. I can be equally aware of the inside – feelings, thoughts, bodily sensation. All this kind of awareness is bringing us towards our own Being.

In this way we use the mind to become the witness of both our inner and outer worlds. Initially, somebody is being the witness, but in the moment of Self-realisation the connection to the personal melts away and leaves pure awareness or pure witnessing. There is a melting together of what is being witnessed with the one who is doing the witnessing. We call this merging Self-realisation.

It's not so easy to be self-aware, to be present, and only you can know what your pace is. Almost for sure in the beginning you have to move slowly. I remember one of Osho's many stories. When he was a university student he used to walk around with wooden shoes, and on the stone floors these shoes would go, 'tap tap tap', probably driving everyone crazy, but he did it consciously; he chose to do that because he used the sound of those shoes to keep himself aware. He didn't want to be robotic, unconscious. He chose that device for bringing him to presence.

Of course everyone is different and will need something slightly different, but basically we all need, at the beginning, quite a big effort. After some time it can happen by itself and nobody's doing it, but to shift years of robotic living into conscious living, that transition is not so easy.

The paradox is that when a deep shift in awareness happens, which we call Self-realisation, it takes no time at all. There is nothing to do. There is nothing to know. You could wake up now. You just have to see that everything you believe, everything you are, this whole story of 'my life', is simply a fairy tale that's only playing in one cinema – your own head. It's never going to go on general release. When you give up this fantasy you call 'my life' it's just paradise. There's not even anything spiritual about it. Now is the best time. It's actually the only moment. There is no reason to postpone. Next week won't be a better time.

When you first go to sleep at night there are probably some thoughts left over from the day. You see pictures and you have feelings in a dream-like way. And then you go into a deep sleep.

207

Then what happens? There are no more dreams, no thoughts. In fact, there is nothing. When you wake up in the morning you feel very nourished. You don't remember anything. For around six hours you completely disappear. Then in the morning you're right back again.

What is happening in deep sleep? The heart is beating, the lungs are breathing, the body is functioning, but there's nobody home. The question is: Has there ever been anybody home and is this whole story of 'me' just a story? My own experience is that when I investigate this 'I', I can't find it. If I investigate where the thoughts come from I find out that they come from nothing, which you can also call emptiness. Or peacefulness. You can even call it God, or the eternal Self, or the Beloved. There are many, many different words and they are all trying to describe something that you can't actually describe, but you know it. It's the closest thing. It's so close that you're not in any way separate. In fact, this is 'me'. I am that emptiness.

My emptiness is the same as your emptiness. It's just one emptiness and we're all part of it. We seem to be running around as separate bodies, all kinds of sizes and shapes, but essentially we're all one. If it seems a bit crazy or outrageous then think of the ocean. There's a lot of water and on the surface a few waves. Each of those waves thinks they're separate from the other waves. Some of them are great big lovely waves, and some are little cute waves; some a little bit sexy, and so on. They all think they're separate from all the other waves. In fact, they're always part of the ocean. It's similar with us.

When you use words like 'emptiness' or 'nothingness' it may not be so comfortable. Then you could try 'the Beloved'. But essentially this is something that is beyond the mind. The mind, in fact, is manifesting from this Beloved. The world, in fact, is the mind. The world is coming out of this emptiness. When the world is there, this emptiness is not there. When we're in our thoughts we don't experience this emptiness. When we're identified with some body sensation, then again we don't experience this emptiness.

When we're absolutely there in the Beloved, the world disappears.

In the knowing of pure awareness everything that you touch has a different quality because you're always focused on that Truth, and that Truth is manifesting in different ways.

Through the Fire With a Teacher

Irina Tweedie spent the last years of her life in London as a Sufi master. She wrote a beautiful, very powerful book *The Chasm of Fire, A Woman's Experience of Liberation through the Teachings of a Sufi Master.* It's a very thick book.

She was a very unusual woman. She had a lot of power and a lot of interest in freedom, and so she met an Indian Sufi. Actually he was a Muslim Sufi master living in north India, not far from Lucknow. She would leave England with some money and go and live close by this master. He would work with her and the book she wrote is a spiritual daily diary of the things that happened to her. I find it a very inspiring book for anybody who really wants to be free. It is not about a spiritual life; it is about what it takes to be free.

This master put her through hell, with the result that she really lost her ego. She must have been a very strong lady because she came back time and time again, even after being treated really toughly.

I hoped to get instruction in yoga. I expected wonderful teachings, but what the teacher mainly did was force me to face the darkness within myself, and it almost killed me. I was beaten down in every sense and so I had to come to terms with that in me which I kept rejecting all my life.

Irina Tweedie

> *Dear John David,*
> *This quote from Irina Tweedie is unlike many other comments you read out about people being with their teacher. Yet it seems this is the most real and accurate account of the work between the student and the teacher – if the student really wants to become free. Of course, it all depends on the student. Could you comment on the work between the teacher and student?*

Usually there is a gradual process that begins when the student recognises an interest in freedom. Perhaps this interest has been there for some time but a difficult situation starts to activate it. You might find yourself dissatisfied with some aspect of your life and you want to investigate some other alternative, or you might be suffering and looking for some kind of healing.

Often people begin by looking for information and understanding in books or on the Internet. If this leads to a bigger 'yes' inside for continuing the journey then they might watch videos of teachers talking about Truth. From their own energies they may start to meditate or join a yoga group. Then, progressing to retreats and workshops, they develop a deeper connection to their longing for freedom.

After some time the buzz of the mind's thinking gets quieter and quieter, and through some kind of intense spiritual practise there may be small glimpses of something that is very beautiful. At this point we may be ready to have a spiritual teacher or a spiritual master. In a way that is hard to understand, when we're really ready we will come in contact with such a teacher or master. Then we have to make a choice.

It may be that this particular teacher is not what we really wanted or what we were looking for, but inside we feel a deeper connection and we recognise the teacher as being a true teacher. Then slowly some kind of relationship begins between the student and the teacher.

In the beginning the teacher does not demand much from the student. He knows that for him to be able to really work with the student, the student needs to come to trust the teacher. A deep love, a devotional love, is needed for this, and of course it takes time to establish. The teacher is patient and he can see the progress the student is making.

Later, the teacher might make some tests to see what's really happening with the student. This won't be in the form of a spiritual practice but rather something that you can't really imagine.

There's a very famous story that happened between Gurdjieff

and Ouspensky. Ouspensky was a remarkable human being. He had met Gurdjieff in Moscow in about 1917, at the same time as the communist revolution, and he'd become a devoted student. Much later, Ouspensky went to England and Gurdjieff also went, but the British government thought that Gurdjieff was a bit suspect and they wouldn't give him a visa to stay longer. Some years later he was living in Armenia and he sent a message to Ouspensky: 'Please come here and meet me.'

This was extremely difficult because there was a war going on and it was almost impossible to travel through Europe. Ouspensky was a very devoted disciple, so he made the trip. When he got there Gurdjieff said something like, 'Hello! You can go now!' This is about surrender. It's not an every-day kind of story but rather for situations where the student really wants to become free. I'm talking about someone who really, really wants to be free.

What does it mean to be free? Well, it means to be free of this conditioned mind. If something happens in any moment, you respond from that moment. You don't react from the past. You don't react from some story inside your mind. True freedom is living in the moment, which usually means a certain degree of innocence and spontaneity. This is very, very rare. When a child is very small you can say they're living in freedom. Of course this is an unconscious freedom.

The connection between the disciple and the master develops over some years, and as the master sees that the student is ready he will work more strongly with the student. As the student advances part of the master's work is to grind the ego.

This is never comfortable. When I first started teaching I didn't really know how to talk to the people and I had the silly idea that everybody who came to my meetings was interested in freedom. So in my inexperience I used to do major heart surgery every night, and of course at the end of the meeting my students ran down the corridors with blood everywhere. Most of them I never saw again. I was always a bit surprised at that, but as the years passed I gradually understood that almost nobody is interested in freedom.

If you offer a spiritual meeting most people are just happy with a bit of spiritual entertainment. I save the true teaching for those people who come closer to me. I'm an unusual teacher because I live in three communities. These residents have made a tremendous commitment so they get the full grinding that's available!

While I was in Lucknow with Papaji I met an American woman called Prema. She had been involved in the sixties hippy movement in San Francisco and then she developed an interest in workshops and spiritual practices. She got to the point where she decided that she wanted to go to India. When she arrived she had a series of meetings with different spiritual masters.

Her first master was Sai Baba and quite early on she became a *sadhu*. This is very unusual for a western person but she made an inner decision that she never wanted to go back to America and that she would live the rest of her life in India.

When you become a *sadhu* you renounce the world – wearing simple orange clothes, eating only what is donated to you and never carrying money. Many times she begged for her food in the streets, which of course for a western woman was very unusual. Anyway, she came to Papaji in Lucknow and when she arrived Papaji greeted her very warmly.

He was very impressed that she was a *sadhu*. He knew that she didn't carry money so he arranged for her to get a room in somebody's guesthouse. He invited her to eat at his house. She would go in the morning, have breakfast, and after the meetings go back for lunch and be there also in the evening. Naturally she became a part of a family around Papaji.

This is a reading from the book *Papaji Amazing Grace* where I compiled interviews with people who had visited Papaji in Lucknow:

Prema, how did Papaji work with you?

Almost his first words to me were 'You're attached to nirvana, isn't it?' In retrospect, it's clear that much of his work with me was simply to dissolve that very strong, deep-rooted attachment.

213

Papaji immediately recognised that she was on an enlightenment trip. She had been going from master to master in India looking for enlightenment in the future, like many other western visitors to India. Papaji, in his wisdom, understood that this was false and so he immediately saw that one of the works was to bring her into the now. Then she said something to Papaji, which she shouldn't have said, perhaps:

> *A day or two later I could speak to him directly and said, 'Master, please destroy this mind and ego, every speck, so there is nothing left to reincarnate.' I asked for it, and he began to give it to me! Outwardly he was mostly harsh with me. Afterwards people would come up to me and say, 'You know, when he was shouting at you, I felt that he was speaking to me. I couldn't have taken it. I felt he was using you to speak to me.'*

When she went to his house for food he would wait until she'd eaten and then he would scream at her again: *'Go and sit in the garden!'* He'd throw her out of the house every day, for months on end.

Sometimes he would send somebody outside to hassle her. She didn't have much choice; she could either leave or accept this behaviour. She had a lot of respect for Papaji and he actually had a lot of respect for her too, but he treated her so badly that people around couldn't understand.

She is a rather small American woman who had already considered herself awakened and had come, if you like, for the final polishing. The people who observed this behaviour completely couldn't understand it because she was such a nice woman and behaved so well that they could only imagine she'd done something terrible that they didn't know about.

This is exactly what happened to Irina Tweedie, on a pretty much daily basis. She expected something quite nice but very often she would go and see her master and he would tell her to wait outside! Meanwhile, he would allow other people to come inside. It was a very, very hot and dusty place and she was a western woman living alone. All the other students were Indian. When she arrived from England, he would take her money and then give it back to her week by week, as a kind of allowance. If you have a serious interest in being free you'd do well to read her book and then reassess if that's really what you want.

In *Arunachala Shiva* I interviewed Ram, an American teacher. At the end of the interview we were discussing his life and he talked about somebody being qualified for freedom. So I asked him what he meant by qualified.

> *Qualified means you do not expect the world to give you one more thing. You're absolutely fed up. You're not looking for anything in this world. You don't want love, you don't want another girlfriend or a nice job. You're absolutely convinced that none of that's going to do it for you. That's the basic qualification, and if you've got that, and you really desire to be free, that'll do it for you.*
>
> *So if you have a strong desire for freedom you should be dispassionate towards things in the world. And you will be. In other words, you continue to act and do things but you're being indifferent to the results of your actions. The world is a tricky place. Everything looks very juicy, sexy and tasty. And you just want to grab at it.*
>
> *But inside all those good, tasty things there's a little fishhook that's ready to grab you. And you better have good discrimination or you'll get yourself caught up. I think we all know the truth of that.*

I've been living with roughly twenty students for the last twelve years and as the devotional connection has become deeper and stronger I increased my grinding. Most of them are now being polished. This grinding and polishing process is probably outside of your idea of spiritual work. But actually, everything else is a preparation for this last work.

The master is trying to show you that you are the same as he is, and to do that he has to get rid of all the nonsense. At that level, the master is ready to do anything he can spontaneously dream up, any kind of situation he can take advantage of, to do the necessary grinding and polishing.

I have to say, this is not for everybody. I never really planned it – I must have been a diamond grinder in my last life. Somehow I've taken up this role of grinder and polisher, which is actually very, very beautiful work because as the grinding and polishing continues, the love arises. I have devoted my life to it now. I don't really have any choice; it happened.

It's a very delicate game between the student and the teacher. I've seen when the grinding has been too much and suddenly suitcases get packed and the person disappears. This is particularly likely if a strong ego is combined with trauma. In this case at some point your self-reflection is likely to come to something that I call 'ego-wall'.

You're moving along nicely and you come to the ego-wall – something particularly uncomfortable, an old memory from your life that you want to avoid. The fear becomes too much and rather than looking at the issue you go away. This is very, very common. I would say this is on the list of the most common reasons why people don't become free.

The work between the student and the teacher is going to bring you, probably, to this ego-wall. This means that the teacher will bring you to face something that you don't really want to face. It might take quite a long time to get to this point because it will be something that has been denied inside.

Irina Tweedie said that the teacher mainly forced her to face the darkness within herself. We all want to be happy, but if you want freedom, which you could call true happiness, you will need to be brought to this ego-wall. You will need to face your worst demon.

The teacher's first job is to make you aware of what you're avoiding and then to encourage you to face it and to deal with it. This can be very confronting, and in over twenty years of sharing

I've learnt that you can't do heart transplant operations just like that. You have to prepare the ground. You need an assistant or a couple of people to hold the student down. I'm joking of course.

It's not quite that tough. But anyway, over the last twelve years there's been a number of people who've worked with me with the idea of becoming free but who came to realise the point that I now call the ego-wall. They definitely got benefits, but it's as if that's the limit. For whatever reason, they can't really go further. That often feels like a really big pity, so sometimes I've found it very, very difficult to let go of somebody I've been working with for quite a few years.

When the person doesn't want to really look they are almost certainly going to run away. When I talk about this almost everyone says 'No! I would never do that!' But actually they do it. Not everybody of course. A lot of trust is needed. Irina Tweedie's teacher treated her very tough for years. But it must have worked because in the end she became quite a well-known Sufi teacher in London.

She looked magnificent with long flowing white hair – like a goddess. She's somebody I would have loved to meet. She was a rare human being. And I must say, I've been very fortunate to meet a few people like her. They contained for me the essence of humanity, and of course they would have had masters who ground and polished them. This is how the Truth is passed on from generation to generation. I look forward to some of my students also passing this on. It's a very beautiful process.

Love is important in order to build up the necessary level of trust, which I think takes time. There has to be love. There has to be a connection. It can't work without this connection.

This connection appears differently with different teachers. Osho, for example, would arrive at his meetings in a Rolls Royce. After the meetings he would get in the car and be taken back a few metres to where he lived. Except for a few people – maybe the person in charge of the ashram, his doctor, sometimes his dentist and his household people that lived with him – the other hundreds and thousands of people who came to the ashram had no direct contact with him.

We never knew if he put his finger in his nose and we couldn't even imagine if he went to the toilet! It was very easy to create him into a godlike person.

My approach is rather different. I'm around doing ordinary stuff, and you may have seen me put my finger up my nose, or some other such thing. Therefore you can easily make judgements, some of which can affect your trust. It's not so easy to be with a teacher who's very available.

I spent fifteen years with Osho and I had one or two meetings here or there. I never had daily contact with him. Then I came to Papaji and I could go to his house whenever I wanted. So it was a bit shocking. In the beginning I thought this was great and then one day, sitting with him, I thought, well this is a bit dangerous. He's inviting me for lunch but maybe because he's planning to cut off my head.

As I got closer to him his behaviour was much stronger, as it had been with Prema. He had a great respect for Prema and a very deep insight into how she functioned. Out of that respect and understanding he gave her a very strong time, but if you meet this woman now you'll just feel tremendous love. Every time she opens her mouth you feel this glow of love – unconditional love. She's lived in India for thirty-forty years, with no money at all. Even now.

If you read the biographies of different spiritual masters you'll find that almost all of them have been through some kind of strong grinding process, because for most people the ego doesn't just suddenly give up. If you want freedom, you have to give up your identification with the ego, and that's not an easy process.

You can talk to Uta. She's been through many tough moments, but she still sits here, even after twelve years. When I met her she wasn't doing so well. She couldn't make a phone call; driving a car was impossible. If you talk to her now she'll tell you the amazing benefits she's had, but she's still not free. So we've still got a little more to do even though she's doing very well. Completely amazing how Lisa, Uta and Anna have managed the food for the whole retreat in a beautiful flow; you could almost miss it. No complaining when all the plans suddenly change, and there's the same kind of easy flow with the tech guys. Everything is taken care of no matter what the situation.

It's not really horrible to be ground and polished. It actually is very, very beautiful. I've been talking about it in a way that makes it sound quite tough. It works because you feel the love that the teacher has. The teacher is going to reflect whatever is needed to show you what you need to see. This is unique to everybody. There are no techniques. I don't even think about it, it's spontaneous, and sometimes it's very strong.

The teacher feels amazingly touched when somebody decides to come and join him. For the teacher it's one of the most beautiful things because, of course, the teacher understands the almost impossibility of such a surrender.

The love the student has for the teacher is not a personal love. It is an impersonal love for what the teacher represents. Even if the student has a genuine, deep, longing to be free, this love is needed to keep them with the teacher through the tough times.

A natural diamond doesn't actually look like much. You have to grind it and polish it. Then it shines. This is part of the work of a spiritual master.

Be Quiet

Tonight I have a quotation from Adyashanti who expresses very clearly in his books the core misunderstanding that causes us to feel separate and to suffer.

We realise often quite suddenly that our sense of self, which is being formed and constructed out of our ideas, beliefs and images, is not really who we are. It doesn't define us. It has no centre.

Adyashanti

> Dear John David,
> What is the best way to make this happen? Is it just about being quiet and looking at what is false until the Truth becomes so clear? Is this all we can do?

This is the complete focus of one of my books, *The Great Misunderstanding*. It is the whole crux of our problem because unfortunately, as Adyashanti says in this quote, we're completely identified with the false self, which is built from our conditioning. We believe our identification to be true.

Actually it is very, very simple, but somehow we can't see it. I recently watched again the first film we made here in the community, *Blueprints for Awakening*, where one of the old Indian masters likens this situation to being under a magic spell. You're under a spell – the spell of the false self – but you don't know it. One day the magic spiritual teacher comes along and waves his magic wand and away goes the spell. Suddenly you wake up and realise, 'Wow! I've been under a spell! It was all an illusion.'

It's that simple, but it's terribly easy to get caught up in ideas of spiritual practice: I have to do something; I have to work hard. Perhaps you think you have to analyse all your structures, or you let your mind take over constantly, examining everything, but you just have to see that this identification has caught you, has grabbed you.

You have to get round the corner. How to do that? Well, it depends where you are. It depends on your understanding.

If you have no understanding at all then the first thing you can do is to stop talking, or talk much less. This is the first step. Talk as little as you can, and don't think. Talking and thinking, they go together. It sounds very simple but it's very difficult to not talk. Maybe you've never heard that this is a spiritual practice, but actually it is, and quite a demanding one because we're completely conditioned to talk and talk. Endlessly talking.

Mostly we're talking in stories. 'Yesterday I went to a party and I met this guy. He's a very interesting man. He's been playing the saxophone nearly all his life …' We get completely identified with these stories. They're old movies, all past. It's like watching Charlie Chaplin movies. Nonsense. Rubbish. No point. Just stop the stories.

If you have to talk then say things like, 'Could you pass the salt?' This is not so bad because you give your quick message and then you shut up. But these stories: 'Yesterday I went to the football. It was very cold, but the match was really wonderful.' It goes on and on and on; old stories that you have to leave out of your life. If you do, then suddenly the mind gets less busy because you're not keeping the mental part activated and so the thoughts get less.

We want to become quiet. My own teacher, Papaji, he used to give simple messages. When asked what his teachings were, he would say, 'Be quiet!' You see? Be quiet.

This is perhaps the greatest spiritual teaching. Be quiet. So why would that be the greatest spiritual teaching? Surely there must be some incredible, complicated, drawn-out spiritual practice that I could do at four o'clock in the morning after a cold shower. Surely there must be some tough stuff. Stop talking. Stop thinking. Be quiet. Difficult, yes?

What happens when we are quiet? Everything becomes slower, we have a chance to see what's going on. It's called self-awareness; awareness of the self. We start by becoming aware of the false self.

Deepak Chopra said, '*The false-self is a socially-induced hallucination.*' I really love that – socially-induced hallucination – just three words that describe this terrible misunderstanding. When we are quiet we start to become aware of this hallucination. We become aware of the movie of 'my life', and of the constant thoughts that drive it. We see they are not good thoughts or bad thoughts – they are all just thoughts. They're old movies and we don't need them at all.

They won't stop completely. They will still appear, but not so much. Already this creates a profound silence where, without the noise of unconscious thoughts and judgements, we have a chance to look and to catch the thoughts that do still come. Catch the thoughts. Be self-aware. Be aware of the thoughts and also the feelings and body sensations. You will see that emotions are just another aspect of the mind and you will begin to see which aspect of the mind you are most identified with.

All of this is the dust covering the shining, sparkling diamond of our Being. There's nothing to do. There's nobody to do it. Even the idea that I can do something that will take the dust off is just another part of the hallucination. Actually there is no dust and there is no diamond.

I have a friend who's been living around the back of the mountain Arunachala for many years in a small cottage. I met him when I was with Papaji. Quite a lovely man. I gave him a copy of my first book and he was saying to me, 'What do you teach them? Why do we need another book?'

I was a bit shocked. What does he mean? In those days I saw a lot of stuff I could teach. I've been doing it for twenty years, but now I see clearly that there is nothing to teach. Now I've got the guts to sit here and tell you that there is nothing to teach. There is nothing to learn. Just shut up. Very simple. Be quiet. Deeply watch. Deeply look. And in order to deeply look we must become deeply quiet.

It's very easy to recognise if somebody has been doing spiritual work. They may tell you, 'Oh yes! I'm meditating. I do all kinds of things. I do yoga. I meditate every day.' You can see immediately if this is really true because if somebody has really done this 'be quiet' then immediately you can feel it. They have trouble talking; they don't want to talk; they don't like to talk; they don't like to listen to stories.

For me, after many years now, it's painful. I have to go away from people who want to tell me their stories. I have to avoid even putting myself in the situation where they have a chance to tell me. It's actually physically painful. So I avoid the situation. Of course, little stories are okay. Not much pain from those, but I would never put myself in a bar, for example. I avoid bars. Because there I know I would be caught in all kinds of stories. I might go by myself and sit in a quiet corner but I would never go with friends.

When we asked Papaji what we could do to come to Truth, he used to tell us, *'Be careful who you spend your time with.'* Across the road from where Papaji had his meetings was the local rubbish place. Everybody put their rubbish there, exactly opposite our meetings. On one side of the road there were meetings on Truth and on the other side was garbage. Pigs would come to rummage through the garbage for whatever little goodies they could find. Papaji used to say, *'Don't join the swine.'*

Be careful who you spend your time with. Choose to be with conscious people. This is not a spiritual practice; it is being intelligent. This is happening beautifully in this community. For twelve years now we've been choosing to spend our time with people who are trying to be conscious. Maybe they didn't make it but maybe they are making it, and they sincerely have the goal of becoming conscious. This is very beautiful and very rare. It almost doesn't exist – groups of people coming together to become conscious.

Watch the effect it has on you. Develop self-awareness. Develop the ability to see the thoughts arising. Look at where they're arising from. Where do they come from? We're not interested in the content of the thoughts. We're only interested in where they come from because they arise in our very Being, in consciousness. If we keep our awareness there, in some magic way we will suddenly see, 'Wow! I'm not this socially-induced hallucination.' Then we might laugh … like crazy … for days on end.

Or we might cry of course because it's a bit tragic to suddenly wake up and realise we've been asleep all our lives. So we could cry, but if we're spiritual seekers then we're more likely to laugh because we've probably taken on another kind of conditioning … a kind of spiritual conditioning that says we should eat tofu, not meat. We should meditate. We should do this. We should do that. We should do the other. If we do all of that then we will get something we don't have now.

We'll never get something we don't have now. We're complete. Perfect in every moment. We're just looking in the wrong direction. There's nothing to get. Rather we have to lose stuff. We have to lose the nonsense, the stories. It's that simple, you see? It's that simple. And finally, we have to lose the identification with the false self, the 'socially induced hallucination'. It's magic. It just happens.

The answer to this question is yes, it *is* just about being quiet and looking at what is false until the Truth becomes clear.

Self-Enquiry

Sri Ramana Maharshi spent his adult life living on the holy mountain Arunachala, which is considered to be *Shiva*. His daily life was very simple. For many years he was the main cook for the ashram. He would sit with his disciples and answer questions brought by his visitors. He died in 1950. In recent years he has become an emblem of Indian spirituality.

It is the higher power which does everything. And the man is only a tool. If he accepts that position, he is free from troubles, otherwise he invites them.

Sri Ramana Maharshi

Dear John David,
We all have many structures which are very strong and which operate in us automatically. It is a huge work to come out of this identification and perhaps then it is possible to just accept that the higher power does everything because then there is nothing in the way anymore. But until this point what does it look like in daily life to totally accept that the higher power does everything?

Of course this question comes from somebody who is identified with the sense of being a separate somebody. From the point of view of a separate somebody, 'me', it seems to be a great task to deal with all these many structures going on in the conditioned mind.

By becoming self-aware you can see what is happening in your mind. It is like you get to know yourself, but the self you are getting to know is not your true Self – it is a false self; the false self being the sense of 'I'. Or we can call it the ego, the ego-self. If we are looking at this situation from the point of view of the false self we can see many structures and we can see that they come automatically many times every day. It seems a completely hopeless task to become free of them in one lifetime.

Sri Ramana has another interesting quotation. He says, '*You have to ask yourself, "Who am I?" This investigation will lead in the end to the discovery of something within you which is behind the mind. Solve that great problem and you will solve all other problems.*'

What Sri Ramana means is that you have to solve the problem of the 'I', the false self, and in fact the problem is the identification with the false self. If you can solve that problem, all your other problems will be solved. Not really solved, but they will melt away.

Picture an arched bridge; it is the keystone that holds all the stones of an arch in place. By removing this one stone the whole arch will collapse. In the same way, if we can see our identification with this false self, the 'I', the 'ego', in the moment we see this, the bridge falls down. All the structures that are depending on this 'I', on our identification with the 'I', they all fall down. Sri Ramana calls this investigation Self-enquiry.

The structures might continue to show up for some time but the 'I', the one who we identify with, has been seen to be false and therefore the mini structures that might be showing up cannot bite anymore. We can call this moment Self-realisation. It is the moment we realise the true Self. We are not *identified* with the true Self – we *are* the true Self. It is our very Being and from it the thoughts arise. So the true Self is before the thoughts.

To practise Self-enquiry you look at the thoughts as they arise and you ask yourself, 'To whom are these thoughts arising?' The answer of course is 'to me' because my whole identity revolves around 'me' – 'I'. *I* am driving a car, *I* am talking, *I* am sitting in this chair, *I* am looking now at the question. So we can focus by looking at the thoughts as they arise and this self-awareness, which we've been building up over many years, becomes a tool to see the I. We see that I is an identification with the false self and so we then can ask ourselves: 'Who is this me? Who is this I?'

There are two questions. Question 1: To whom are these

thoughts arising? Answer: To me. Question 2: Who is this me? Instead of just automatically grabbing for the thoughts because we are so identified with them, Self-enquiry reminds us to go before the thoughts, to the source of the thoughts. What is before the thoughts? From where do thoughts arise? Sri Ramana calls Self-enquiry keeping our mind in the true Self, the source. Although it is only two simple questions, it is not so easy to do. First of all it is not easy to remember to do the enquiry because we get so caught up in life. In order to do it a quieter mind is a prerequisite. If you have already achieved this through spiritual practices, then you are ready to make this enquiry. We can also say that this enquiry comes automatically out of spiritual practice.

In the beginning it is easiest to simply sit with eyes closed and look at the thoughts as they arise, asking yourself these two questions. As you begin to get familiar with this you will start to feel the benefit. Then it is time to take this enquiry into your daily life. Our modern European lives are often quite complicated and therefore our minds are always being activated. We think a lot.

All this thinking makes it much more difficult to conduct Self-enquiry. When you become more experienced there will be a moment, where, without really doing anything, you will suddenly see the falseness of the identification. As soon as you see that clearly, Poof! It falls away. This moment is Self-realisation or Awakening.

All is One

We come back to the mind-bending, mystical presence of Neem Karoli Baba, and this quote comes from Ram Dass's loving tribute to his master, *Miracle of Love*.

The best service you can do is to keep your thoughts on God. Keep God in mind every minute.

Neem Karoli Baba

> *Dear John David,*
> *I can feel that I am caught up in following desires for material things. It doesn't leave a good taste in my heart. This quote from Neem Karoli Baba touched me, although I don't really know what it means. Practically, is it about service and devotion, or Self-enquiry? What does it mean to you to 'keep God in mind every minute'?*

Many years ago I was visiting Rishikesh in the north of India and for reasons I can't really remember I walked into a refrigerator and electric cooker shop. There was a man sitting behind a rather tall counter and the rest of the shop was empty. He seemed to be busy with something so I looked over the top of the counter and saw he was writing in a notebook. He was writing the same thing over and over – he was writing *Ram*, which is God. He was writing God, God, God. There you are, there is one technique you can try.

I remember in the story of Papaji's life this part where he came from Pakistan down to what is now called Chennai, and at that time his spiritual practice was to say *Krishna* fifty thousand times a day.

What are they doing? A practice like this doesn't really keep your mind on God; it keeps your mind from everything else. Whether you are saying *Krishna, Krishna* or writing *Ram, Ram* your mind is occupied enough that it can't wander off. Maybe your mind is not completely quiet but equally it's not full of masses of thoughts and if you continue the practice for a longer time, which people do, then your mind will actually become quieter and quieter. When it becomes very quiet you remember God, and because God is also you, you come to your true Being.

In order to remember God, you simply have to remember yourself. You can remember yourself through Self-enquiry; you can do it by finding out what is before the 'I' thought. That's one clear method that Sri Ramana Maharshi offered.

Another way is through devotion, which is a huge yes to life. You approach every moment with a resounding yes and in the process of that yes you are surrendering to what life is bringing you.

There are different ways to arrive at this deep inner space, which we can also call God. It is a wrong idea to think that God is somehow separate from us.

God is not a very useful word because it has become so caught up in religion. Probably we can find other words — in India they use the word Self. I prefer to use True Nature, Being and such things. So actually it's not that difficult to remember God. Of course you could bend down in the evening by your bed and say a little prayer to the God that your mother taught you about when you were a little kid, but now we are big people and we can do something a bit better than that.

To somebody like Neem Karoli Baba, everything was God. He didn't really have a teaching. He would sit with his blanket over him, in front of him would be a crowd of western people, maybe a few Indians also, and he would just play. In this play people's minds would stop and they would have profound moments. Ram Dass and Krishna Das are two well-known Americans who spent time with Neem Karoli Baba.

I was lucky enough to become a friend of the man who translated for these Americans and I would go to him when I was with Papaji in Lucknow. He happened to also live in Lucknow. He was a remarkable man himself. So much heart, I remember. This is one of the beauties that we gain when we go to India: that we can meet these extraordinary people who live quite unlike anybody we know here in the West.

Anyway, the real reason why we can't remember God is that we easily get caught up in certain mind structures, so we need a reminder, like Self-enquiry. Once you become established in this Essence, then thoughts aren't really a problem anymore because although we could say that mind is the problem, mind is also essential for our life.

We could divide the mind into two parts. One part is the functioning, practical mind. We need it for moving the body, for drinking tea. Of course, in order to come to this house you needed to use your practical mind. You decided, 'Well, I'm not going to walk. I'm not going on my horse. I'm not going on my bicycle. I'll go in the car.' Then you don't have to think about it anymore and this part of the mind can again come back to rest.

Then we have the thinking, or conditioned part of the mind. As you sit here maybe you're remembering that you left the stove on in the house and you're wondering if, by now, the whole house is burning. How can you sit here quietly if you're thinking the house is burning even if it's not because you turned the stove off before you left?

There are many things to worry about: 'Well, how am I going to pay my telephone bill?' Now there is the constant distraction of modern technology and social media. There's always something that keeps us from not really being here. This constantly thinking, busy mind, which may not really contribute so much to our lives, has become a habit. Maybe it's become a habit because we have some fear of silence. Sitting here, your mind could be completely silent; we almost don't need anything of the mind, but unfortunately, it's usually not empty, not quiet.

The mind is a wonderful assistant but a terrible boss. If you can live in your Essence, the Essence becomes the boss. This boss is constantly directing your life. It's going to tell you to turn left or to turn right – like a navigation system. Navigation systems are connected to a satellite. This kind of navigation system is connected to everything. It's like a universal wisdom. If you can surrender to this universal wisdom then you can follow it through your life. You can relax; you give yourself to God.

Saying Yes to Life

In Eckhart Tolle's book *A New Earth*, he sets out that for the planet to evolve it will first be necessary for individuals to transform and become more conscious. In this extract below Eckhart beautifully and gently points to the simple truth of human suffering.

Always say 'yes' to the present moment. What could be more futile, more insane, than to create inner resistance to what already is? What could be more insane than to oppose life itself, which is now and always now? Surrender to what is. Say 'yes' to life – and see how life suddenly starts working for you rather than against you.

Eckhart Tolle

> *Dear John David,*
> *I really ask myself what it means practically if you say 'yes' to life. Does it necessarily mean that you say 'yes' to everything that happens, to everything people ask of you? Then I remember what Byron Katie said:* 'Sometimes I say no and this no is a yes to myself.'

That's right. Yes and no are always about our inner Truth. Generally, until we come to some level of understanding, some level of openness, we are often operating from our inner structures. When I want to say no it is probably just a 'no program' in the mind and it may not really come from a deep place. It often just comes in reaction, not from a deeply held sense that you can't do that.

Actually, in our daily lives we are often in reaction. By reaction I mean we are really functioning on old history. Maybe we fell out with Daddy because he did something that wasn't so nice. We decided we didn't like him so we were always saying no to him. So now, any situation that triggers this old 'no to Daddy' will receive a 'no' because we are reacting rather than considering the situation deeply and saying 'No, thank you.' Usually the reaction comes very quickly and for the considered deeper response we need a little pause.

Yes, I understand. It could also mean that saying yes to a lot of things can be a sort of a no.

When you are living in yes you are also living in openness and in a relaxation you can feel in your body. No is a closing, a contraction. You can feel this in your body too. If we become sensitive and aware enough we can recognise the kind of contractions and openings as they happen. In the West there is a lot of talk about stress, which is exactly this contraction. It comes out of a situation where there is a lot of resistance to what is happening.

Why is there now so much cancer in the West? What is so different from the old, more natural, simple way of life? It is about stress! Maybe our grandfathers lived in a small town and walked to their office, if there was an office. Now they are rushing on a metro. A couple of hundred years ago there was no advertising but now wherever you go, you are bombarded by some sort of information. Our senses are completely overloaded and we can't manage to stay relaxed.

We get stressed, and if we are always living contracted it is not surprising that the body responds by giving us cancer or a heart attack or stroke. It seems these things are all modern types of health problems.

Surrender is about accepting the moment, about constantly surrendering everything I know to be 'me' to existence. It is a melting away of the one that knows, the one that judges, the one that does something.

Normally, from moment to moment, we're very much in our ego with all kinds of ideas, desires and judgements. We approach life from the conditioned mind, which we call the ego, with its attachment to all kinds of things. The way of the heart is a different approach. It's the giving up of all this personal story.

If you consider it from your personal 'me' it's hard to see even how it works because we have all been conditioned to live our lives from a fortress-like ego – Me! Me! – and surrender is about saying yes in each moment and deeply accepting what is.

As you gradually move into deeper surrender you experience your heart opening. As the heart opens there's more trust and as there's more trust there can be a deeper surrender. It is a very beautiful way to come to Truth. It's the reason we're so attracted to places like India, Sri Lanka and other Asian countries. Surrender and acceptance are very much a part of those societies. It's all changing now but generally people accept what is. Of course, this can be very frustrating for the western mind because if they don't get your car fixed today they'll tell you 'Oh well, we'll do it tomorrow.' And maybe also tomorrow they don't manage it and they'll tell you it will be a few more days.

There's perhaps another aspect for the western mind because we misunderstand this word 'surrender'. We have the idea that you have to surrender to somebody. With Stalin, with Mao, Mr H – not such good experiences – so we're a little bit concerned when the idea of surrender comes up.

This is a misunderstanding of surrender because the surrender I'm talking about is to something inside you. It's not surrendering to someone on the outside. It's seeing the possibility of accepting what life brings you – without any idea or judgement from your ego.

The western mind thinks surrender is to something or someone on the outside. It is about accepting what life brings – without judgements from the ego. No judgement from 'me'. It's so easy to think that 'I know best!' and it's a little tricky in the beginning, so you have to give it a go. As it gets deeper and deeper it's very beautiful because it's so much easier to accept what's happening. The result of this acceptance is that the heart opens and when this happens you feel tremendous lightness.

Be As You Are

We have another quote from Paul Lowe tonight, in his typical style of cutting right to the heart of the matter.

All our training has to do with change. You pray for change. You go to groups for change. You become a disciple and follow a guru for change. It's all about change. It's all about being better. It's all about you not being who you are. Listen, you cannot change yourself. It's impossible. Your whole difficulty, why you are not at your maximum potential, why you are not bathing yourself in beauty and glory and light, is because you won't be who you are. You want to be different.

Paul Lowe

> Dear John David,
> I have some confusion about this topic of change. I see that the real change comes when the identification with the thoughts, and all the things that normally tie me down, breaks down. I've had glimpses of this. But in daily life it is really not easy to come back to this transcendence and I feel very strongly that I am wrong and should change. Can you please share your understanding of this message to 'Be as you are'?

This is an interesting quotation. It is pointing to a deep acceptance of your True Nature, which is the Self or the silence that occurs when the thoughts become still and when we do not identify with them. This is the goal of our spiritual life – to absolutely be as we are. You mention that in everyday life you have a self-judgement that you are not okay and that you should change. As Paul Lowe says, this is a very common idea among spiritual seekers and it is a subtle mistake because implicit in this idea of changing is that I am going to change because I don't think I am okay as I am.

This is an amazingly egoistical idea because God, divine wisdom, has put you into a particular situation and you are saying no, you want to change it. But it is also a little bit subtle because there is this deep priority or desire to reach Self-realisation and then to live in this realisation. Therefore, as you judge yourself not realised now, you think you need to change something so that you can be realised in the future. There is a paradox! Change has to happen but you can't do the change because the 'you' that wants realisation doesn't exist. This 'you', in fact, is an illusion. You are a creation of your conditioned mind. You are identified with your conditioned mind, and this 'you' simply doesn't exist. You believe that it does exist and therefore you also believe you can change so that one day you can be as you are. Then of course life becomes very complicated.

Sometimes I meet spiritual seekers who I met forty years ago who are still busy trying to change. Yes, something is different but fundamentally there is no change. This idea of change is a completely wrong idea because there is nobody who can do this change.

There is another approach to life. You have an inner desire or longing to become Self-realised, to become unattached to the thoughts. You realise that right now you are absolutely identified with the false self, with the illusory self, and that you are playing out in your life your own particular soap opera. You simply accept yourself, the false self, as you are. A deep self-acceptance that right now you are exactly as you're meant to be, exactly in the place you are meant to be and you are exactly doing what you are supposed to do. See that these things are changing but they are not changing because you are changing them. Change simply happens and if you have the longing to become Self-realised there will be a movement of change to bring you to this Self-realisation.

Life has a tendency to give you exactly what you want. If you want to be rich, you can become rich. If you want to be Self-realised, you can become Self-realised. 'Be as you are' is an invitation to accept yourself exactly as you are in this moment without any self-judgement. 'I am not okay the way I am, I have to change.' This is a completely wrong way of thinking and nothing happens, except that you are constantly making yourself unhappy. You can't change like that and you realise that your judgements about yourself have been going on for a long time and haven't brought you very much.

My recommendation is to completely accept yourself as you are in this moment and at the same time have the goal or longing to come to Self-realisation. When we can accept ourselves in this moment we suddenly discover that life becomes much more easy because we are not putting onto the realities of daily life some kind of philosophy or idea about how we would like to be.

Surrender Just Happens

I lived in India for many years and teach the core spiritual teachings that have been handed down through the centuries. Mahatma Gandhi, a very unusual and unique individual, impressed me deeply as he personified the ancient teachings in the political arena. In the face of British violence he remained steadfast in his philosophy of non-violence.

Surrender means living every moment as if God has given it to you. Whatever happens, with everything that's given to you in your life, live as if everything is given to you by God.

Mahatma Gandhi

Dear John David,

I wanted to surrender so many times, but I have to say I attempted it and nothing happened. I met a friend one day and she said it had been the same for her so she went to bed and talked to God. She said she wanted to surrender, and the next day all the emotional pain disappeared. It was like a miracle.

So I'm wondering if there is a secret to this, this thing called surrender, when all the pain disappears.

We're nearly all absolutely identified with being a separate somebody. This separate somebody has been created slowly over many years, so we didn't particularly consciously choose this somebody; it was kind of given or imposed from our family and society.

Gradually, without noticing, we acquired a certain idea of ourselves and this idea we call 'I' or 'me'. So when you say 'I' tried to surrender, you're talking about this one that's been created over a longer time – this one would now like to surrender. This one is only a packet of ideas and conditioning – a fabrication that we have wrongly identified with. In order to surrender there would have to be somebody there to surrender. The actual Truth is there isn't anybody there – therefore there isn't anybody to surrender. It's a bit like the chicken and the egg. What came first?

The first thing really is to examine this illusory 'me'. When you really become clear about that, when you realise for yourself there is no separate somebody – we're all actually one consciousness – when this becomes your Truth, then surrender just happens. It happens in that moment of Self-realisation.

Thereafter, from moment to moment, you'll find that the surrender is just there. There's no reason not to surrender – it's not an issue anymore, but while we are still identified as a separate somebody, then 'I' would try to surrender: 'I will surrender, I must surrender, I am preparing to surrender.' It's all based on the idea that I'm somebody who could then surrender. It's never going to work.

You say you have a lot of emotional pain. I don't know you well enough to know what your emotional pain was about, but everybody thinks emotional pain is very personal, that it only happens to them. Actually emotional pain happens to everybody and it's often a relationship issue, usually a situation where somebody does something you don't want them to do, or you thought they loved you and then they go and talk to somebody else and start loving that other person. In other words, when the other person doesn't act in the way that we want them to act we feel emotional pain. We completely forget that in the beginning we created a sense of possessiveness of this other person. I'm somebody and then the other person is somebody, so there are two somebodies and blah blah blah.

This gets created all the time – the emotional pain and the lack of surrender and so on. We've actually created all this. We have to look with a new eye, so to say. We just have to look again at what is really going on. You come here with a very good question. So you're a ripe fruit.

I've actually been quite ripe in this context for many years

Right, so you're beginning to get clear about this separation – that we actually create our own separation and after creating the separation we then suffer from it.

It's like knowing something in theory and then wanting it to happen and then it happening.

Yes. It's two things. One is to start understanding what's going on and the next is to be able to live that. It's nice to understand intellectually how something works; then you can become a philosopher. Becoming an unhappy philosopher is not so helpful. Probably you're better off just being an ordinary person, but happy.

I understand you're planning to spend some weeks in the community?

I would like to, yes.

We dash around doing all kinds of stuff, but actually what we're really doing is trying to live this understanding. We're trying to live it from moment to moment, day by day, not just going to a meeting and understanding it as a philosophy. We're trying to see how it works in daily life. So you've probably come to the right place.

Yes, I know I have. So regarding my question, is it all about attachment? I'm attached to my ego, I'm attached to my suffering, would you say?

Yes, basically you're attached to the idea that you're a separate somebody. If you've been doing spiritual work for sometime you must have had moments when the veil drew apart and you were just there, present, and suddenly you felt completely different because it was so wonderful. It can even be slightly scary. Have you had this kind of moment?

Well, I've had five moments in my life where I felt unconditional love, pure unconditional love. There was another moment when I was in America and everything was disappearing, everything before me was disappearing – even my hands. This was suddenly very scary so I started making excuses to myself, telling myself, 'Oh I can't do this now. I'll wait until the lady next door comes back and she can help me do this again.' I wanted somebody with me. I pulled myself back because of fear, and I haven't gone back there since. I know I could do it again, but I haven't.

Basically everybody has the possibility of coming to this space you're talking about because this is our Truth. We're all capable of coming to this Truth. We're all essentially the same. Your fear that came up in that moment, in one way, is totally natural because something was happening that you were completely unprepared for. Even if you'd been doing spiritual work you probably didn't expect your hands to disappear, so that was naturally a scary moment.

One thing you can get out of all that is that some kind of preparation is needed. Something like what you're describing happened two years ago to a woman in the community. Somebody who was with her had an iPhone and was able film her immediate responses. Then we followed her over the next nine months. She was able to dialogue and describe the different things that happened to her over this time and we put it all together into a film that we called *Satori*.

She'd been living for four years in this community and she'd had energetic openings like you describe happen to her before she even met me. I don't think she was so scared about it, but maybe she wanted to understand it. This interest brought her here.

What I'm saying is that she'd had some years of preparation. She had studied yoga and had meditated regularly. Her hands started to shake and she started laughing and crying. She wasn't doing it, it was just happening to her. She was completely taken over by some very strong energy and she was able to trust what was happening to her. These kind of moments are the reason we have this community, not to do philosophy. Philosophy is very safe because you just think about it and talk about it but you never really allow it to touch your life.

CHAPTER 7

The Self

The Self is everything and the Self is nothing. The Self is complete. There is just divine playfulness, a whole life transformed, because you are no longer looking for something. You know you have everything and all desire simply falls away. There is a tremendous contentment, peace and a great relaxation.

The Self

A moment of Self-realisation happens, and in a split second it becomes crystal clear – there never was any separation. We have always been the Truth that we were so deeply yearning and longing for, and devoting our lives to finding. It's all already inside us, in fact it is us. We are not separate from anything.

With this understanding we live our lives knowing that this moment is all we have, and the great divine play of existence just unfolds by itself from moment to moment.

The burdens of the mind and the chains of our conditioning have been seen to be false, and we are released, living in our True Nature.

Life is Miraculous

We have a very beautiful quote from Deepak Chopra, someone we have already met, but who I want to come back to as he always writes in a way that can express the most subtle levels of experience on the spiritual journey.

According to **Vedanta** *there are only two symptoms of enlightenment, just two indications that a transformation is taking place within you towards a higher consciousness.*

The first symptom is that you stop worrying. Things don't bother you anymore. You become light-hearted and full of joy. The second symptom is that you encounter more and more meaningful coincidences in your life, more and more synchronicities. And this accelerates to the point where you experience the miraculous.

Deepak Chopra

> *Dear John David,*
> *I find this quote very beautiful because it's exactly what I see happening more and more in my life. The miraculous things are actually very simple things but somehow they have a profound implication – that there is only one true power and it is guiding the whole of existence. It is beautiful just to experience this, but also it is interesting to ask why life is so miraculous.*

This is an especially lovely quotation. It's also something I can support from my own knowing. You're interested in why life is so miraculous and I have to wonder what you're comparing it with. We only have life as we find it. We open our eyes in the morning and wow! There's a whole world appearing and I can see that as the years pass I more and more find the miraculous in every small thing.

Without bringing judgement, identification and expectations to every situation we find that nothing is a problem, no one is a threat. Who is there to feel threatened or anxious? Each moment is a clean slate.

I've lived in several different countries – about five years in Australia and seven in India. Now I've been about fourteen years based in Germany and when I was younger I lived in Japan for four years. I was even born in Wales to a Welsh father and spent thirty years living in England. A brief two years in the United States, mostly in California. This is actually very interesting because each country opened a new chapter.

When I arrived in Germany I was minus five thousand euros. I had a big suitcase and not many prospects. I remember going for a walk in the little town where I was initially living and discovering that a cup of coffee cost the same as a whole meal in India. That was rather a shock and I couldn't really understand how it was going to work. In fact it did work, but not because I personally did something.

Then things happened and this is, as far as I can see, the miracle of life. Now I don't have minus five thousand euro. I have a nice car, a few computers and I'm busy with three communities. This gives me the chance to fly between Ukraine, Spain and Germany and actually I have a wonderful life.

All kinds of miracles happen. For example, as you see I'm pretty old but I have two babies, two little girls. Last night I was sleeping next to one of them and before I fell asleep and when I woke up I looked at this tiny little creature and it was like I'm sleeping next to God, because she's so innocent, so lovely. This is an amazing miracle for an old guy like me.

I find what Deepak Chopra is saying here quite lovely because it seems to me it's really true. I've had the opportunity to spend quality time with many awakened Indian teachers, initially through interviews for the book and film, *Blueprints for Awakening*. A lot of them were seeing and dealing with many people and had the various pressures that go with that, but one of the qualities I could feel with almost all these people was a lightness in their expression of life. Despite the pressures, they were very relaxed and happy, open to and resting in the moment, dealing with the situations as they arose.

Of course they all have different characters but, as Deepak is saying here, they have some characteristics in common – they are light-hearted and full of joy. They don't worry too much about paying the electric bill and they trust and go with the flow of life from moment to moment.

When you really know the Self, then you live knowing 'I am the Self', and a tremendous playfulness comes. You are happy to be alone and just as happy to run a busy ashram. You can pay the electric bill or sit in meditation. The Self is everything and the Self is nothing. The Self is complete.

Presence and Awareness

Eckhart Tolle is perhaps best known for his simple pointing to Presence, to being fully here in the here and now, and knowing that that is the only Truth. His best-known books are *The Power of Now* and *A New Earth*. I would like to read another quote from him.

As soon as you honour the present moment, all unhappiness and struggles dissolve, and life begins to flow with joy and ease. When you act out of the present-moment awareness, whatever you do becomes embedded with a sense of quality, care and love – even the most simple action.

Eckhart Tolle

Dear John David,
I can imagine that after awakening life becomes very simple because the sense of the personal is not strongly there anymore. The mind is not in the past or the future and so the present moment becomes a focus and a totality – whatever simple or amazing thing is happening.

You say, '*I can imagine that after awakening life becomes very simple.*' It's not possible to imagine. You can imagine away but it won't be as you imagine it, I can promise you. When you're Self-realised, awakened, you don't identify with the false 'I', with the movie, with the ego. So that makes everything much, much easier.

But I don't think Eckhart Tolle is talking about Self-realisation; he's talking about the possibility of developing your awareness to such a degree that you're able to see clearly what is happening. Everybody here is very easily able to see what is happening over there. We can all see that a fire's burning over there. No problem at all. It's very easy. That's a bit of simple awareness. But when we start to turn that awareness around onto ourselves then it becomes much more difficult.

248

Eckhart is telling us that as soon we're not thinking of what happened in the past and not in some kind of hope or fear of what might happen in the future, then we're just simply present and that as long as we honour the present moment all unhappiness and struggles dissolve. He's not talking about awakening or Self-realisation but just about a very simple thing that happens if you become aware enough. With this awareness you catch yourself going to the past and you catch yourself going to the future, and therefore you stay simply present.

Finally, when we're really present, the whole movie that's usually going on, the many thoughts that are churning around inside our minds, they stop. Or at least they become very calm. If we can come into the present moment all our *unhappiness and struggles dissolve* because they are completely dependent on our attachment to the false 'me'.

He then goes on to say that if you're really there in the present moment, through the power of your awareness and your ability to look at what's really happening, whatever you do becomes embedded with a sense of quality, care and love – even the most simple action.

Even the most simple, everyday tasks can be performed out of present-moment awareness, presenting a possibility to break the suffering. Riding a bicycle requires just enough focus to keep you present. Allow yourself to become quiet, and in this quietness things drop away. In presence, notice the movement of the pedals and the wind on your cheeks.

Simple everyday tasks, all the normal, things like chopping vegetables, cleaning the floor or making the bed require a little bit of attention but are not very demanding. This attention is just enough to keep you present and has the enormous benefit of improving your self-awareness.

I remember years ago listening to Osho talking about such things. He was saying that when he was a student he used to wear wooden shoes. Wearing them on a stone floor means that as you walk along there's a 'clack, clack, clack'. He deliberately chose these shoes because he wanted this sound to keep him present. He was aware of the sound, he focussed on it and this taught him awareness. You can use the power of your mind together with the power of your Being to become very self-aware.

I was very grateful to him for this. I came to him without any awareness. I didn't know anything, and over the years I spent with him I could say that gradually my sense of awareness became quite well developed. For example, right now you can think: 'Where did I leave my shoes tonight?' They're probably downstairs with the other shoes. So are they on the top rack or at the bottom of the rack, on the left of it or the right? This is a nice test of your awareness.

If you have no clue about where you left your shoes then you're not very aware. Things like this are happening all day long and you can use them as a teaching device. Like those wooden shoes of Osho's you can find your own particular way to develop your sense of awareness.

Once you start being present it multiplies, leading you to the next and the next and the next. I had a funny example of this just the other day as I was leaving the community in Trypillya, in the Ukraine. Everybody there came to say goodbye to me and we thought: 'Hey! We'll take a picture.' There was a beautiful tree, all covered in yellow leaves. We wanted to get the picture standing in front of this tree. We all wanted to be in the picture so as we stood there we thought: 'Who's going to take the picture?'

Then I remembered there was a guy working there as a carpenter who I had met a few months earlier. He was working nearby so we called him over and asked him to take the photo. And then I remembered what a great guy he was. I had been very impressed by the way he worked and the sense of him being very present with what he was doing. And suddenly – maybe this was creativity or maybe it was about being present, I'm not quite sure – the idea suddenly popped into my head to invite him to the community in Denia, in Spain. He could help us build the rooms we needed down there.

Then of course that led to the next thing … 'Ah! But then we need a plumber. Ah! Satva wants to go to India but he doesn't have the money. So maybe he could exchange doing the plumbing for the trip to India.' Suddenly I've got a team of guys who are ready to fly to Denia and do the work on these two new rooms. See how these things happen. They come out of presence; it is simply presence, awareness. This guy shows up, and then oh! I've remembered what a good carpenter he is and it goes from there. Learning how to be aware, how to simply be here, is one of the greatest benefits you can get in life.

Death

We've already met Robert Adams in earlier talks. While I was staying with Papaji in Lucknow he read the whole of Robert's *Silence of the Heart* in his *Satsangs* over more than a month – an enormous compliment to Robert.

The further existence of his body and the world appears to the jnani as an illusion, which he cannot remove, but which no longer deceives him. After the death of this body, as in life, he remains where and what he eternally is, the first principle of all beings and things: formless, nameless, unsoiled, timeless, dimensionless and utterly free. Death cannot touch him, cravings cannot torture him, sins do not stain him; he is free from all desire and suffering. He sees the infinite Self in all, and all in the infinite Self, which is his Being.

Robert Adams

Dear John David,
Recently someone in my family became very sick and was close to death. I became very afraid and incredibly sad as it seemed so terrible that this family member could die. It seems in the West we have built up a very horrible picture of death, although the reality may be very different. Why are we afraid of it?

Satsang points to our Being, which never changes. And furthermore, my Being is the same as your Being. There is only one Being, only one consciousness, one awareness. It is the eternal Self and the whole universe. Everything arises from the same consciousness, the same Self.

The personal aspect of my life – my particular thoughts, ideas, judgements – is superimposed on this eternal Self. We've become so identified with this personal aspect that we have mostly lost touch with the eternal Self, our Being. Death is happening in every moment. The old moment is dying and the new moment is being born in a continuous process of death and rebirth throughout our whole physical existence.

My first spiritual master, Osho, had this engraved on his shrine: *Never Born, Never Died. Only Visited this Planet Earth between Dec 11 1931 – Jan 19 1990.* Whenever I looked at that I was always perturbed by it. It brought up questions about the meaning of life and death.

We can compare the physical body to our car. We buy a nice new shiny car, the latest model, and we jump inside and drive it around for some years. As it gets older we have to fix it and repair it and one day: kaput! It finally dies.

Then what do we do? We go and buy a new one. We repeat this process continuously. We buy the latest fashions and then when we get a hole in the sleeve we repair it, but finally we look at our clothes and say, 'Well, that's it!' And we go and buy new ones. Our breathing in and out of life-giving oxygen is like birth and death in every moment. When the physical death finally occurs there is no more inbreath.

What about the question of our energetic death? Robert Adams uses the Sanskrit word *jnani* to describe someone who has become Self-realised and is living in freedom. That means living without any desire. Also there is no 'him' or 'her' to suffer anymore, no one to identify with this sweet little movie, which we call 'my life'. This identification has fallen away, melted away.

What is left when this happens? From the outside it looks exactly the same, but inside there's a profound change because the identification shifts from 'my life' to 'my Being', or just 'Being'. There's a profound recognition that we are, in essence, the infinite Self and not 'my life'. This energetic death is not really a death because this movie that we were so identified with never existed. It only appeared to exist, so we were very identified with an illusion.

Sometimes, when people are approaching the understanding of their Being, a lot of fear can arise. Little glimpses that show us that the movie 'my life' could simply melt away can feel like death to our movie … 'I'm not going to exist anymore.' Actually you never existed. This is the illusion. My second spiritual master, Papaji, has a very nice biography in three volumes called *Nothing Ever Happened*.

So what does that mean: *Nothing Ever Happened* in three volumes? You open up the book expecting blank pages, but of course on these pages is outlined the movie of Papaji's life. But Papaji himself understood that nothing ever happened. He also understood that the ultimate Truth is that nothing ever happened.

This can be a bit shocking because most of us are identified with lots of things happening. When Sri Ramana Maharshi got a cancer on his right arm his disciples were very concerned. They introduced different kinds of doctors and healing techniques and he patiently allowed them to do whatever they suggested, but nothing seemed to be helping him and finally the doctors said the only way to save his life would be to cut off his arm. At that point he said, 'No thank you.' He preferred to let nature take its course. He had no fear of death.

I had my own experience of what I imagine death might feel like. One night I was sitting with a group of people in meditation. At the end of the meditation everybody left and in that moment I realised something strange was going on and I couldn't really move, but nobody noticed I was struggling and everybody disappeared up the path.

I managed to get to my feet and I started walking after the group. Finally I reached my partner and I said, 'Umm … I think I may be dying. Could you take me to the doctor?' It happened that we were in a very large community and there was a doctor living there, so she was quite cool about it.

We got in her car and I had this experience where I felt all the energy withdrawing from my body. Naturally, I don't know what's going to happen in the moment of death but previously I'd had the idea that it would feel very much like this energetic withdrawal.

It was about a ten-minute drive to the doctor's and I was sitting there in the car feeling completely relaxed. But then I thought about my partner and I found myself saying something along the lines of,

'I'm sorry for all this trouble. It's going to cause you some difficulties. I'm sorry for that.'

But inside there was no fear; there was no anxiety, nothing, just very peaceful. Anyway, finally I got to the doctor. I took all my clothes off and lay on the doctor's couch. He got a flashlight and searched my whole body for a paralysis tick and even though he couldn't find one, that's all he could suggest. After a while I began to feel a little bit foolish, so I went home and went to bed. Next morning everything was back to normal.

That was my experience with death. It was fairly intense, but actually when I look back it's clear that the moment of realisation was much more powerful. I'd been wanting it for many years. I didn't have any fear about it and when it happened it was a strong energetic explosion, as if a typhoon had picked me up.

There was a month of strong inner energy processes and when the feet got back on the ground there came a realisation that 'I' had disappeared and, luckily, have never come back. So this is also death. This is the death of the ego, the death of the idea that I am a separate somebody.

There's a very famous passage in the Indian spiritual text, *The Bhagavad Gita*. It's the beginning of a great battle between two families. The king of one family is *Arjuna*, a great warrior. As he's waiting for the battle to begin he suddenly gets cold feet and he says to his chariot driver, *Krishna*, 'I can't start this battle. I have many friends on the other side, even family. I can't start this war because some of these people who are very dear to me will be killed.' And then there's the famous speech by *Krishna*. He talked about destiny and he urged *Arjuna* to start the battle.

About seventeen years ago I was busy with my project, *Blueprints for Awakening*. Through that I met about twenty Indian masters. I had a meeting with one of them, Thuli Baba, and I explained my situation. I was about to leave India and go to Europe and I had this strong inner message from Papaji, my direct master, that I had some work to do, that I should begin teaching. I was asking Thuli Baba whether he would support this idea. He told me something rather shocking, something along the lines of: you should only teach if you understand that nobody ever dies.

I think it's a very strong topic because it's not so easy to let go and accept this. It seems natural that there would be a fear of death because it is connected to loss.

The fear is clearly not natural because the death of the body is a part of the cycle of life.

And we have a natural instinct to keep this body alive. So when there's a fire, we run away. But at the same time we know the body is ageing and dying.

This is not always easy to see because when you look inside you don't feel any age.

In our culture there is something sad and heavy and dramatic about death. Is there a culture that celebrates death?

During the first couple of years that I lived in India in Osho's ashram, there were two western disciples who died. I was completely shocked because we had a great celebration with dancing and singing and lots of flowers. Together we made up a procession to take the body down to the riverbank to be burnt. We all sat around in the night, singing and dancing and celebrating, and I could feel inside what you're suggesting. I could feel that this was different from my idea of death. So yes, there are cultures where death can be celebrated.

I recently lost a parent, and to meet death is something very powerful and also can be beautiful. When you spend time with or support a person who is dying it raises the question: What is life about? Because in very strong moments unnecessary suffering and worry, or whatever, can absolutely drop.

256

When someone close to us is dying many people experience the possibility of a deep meeting, which wasn't always possible in the active life.

I have one question. When you want to become free, do you have to face and overcome the fear of death, because finally there will be a kind of death happening?

No, I don't think so. It doesn't really work like that. As you become more conscious, more aware, more self-aware, there comes a moment when you realise very clearly that actually, nothing exists. This is revealed in the natural flow of life.

We don't need to do anything about that. So all these spiritual practices and spiritual books and meetings like this one, they all seem to be giving us some tools to do something. But in Truth, there's nothing to do because we're already free. There's nothing to get. It's about the realisation of that. We're always the Self, the eternal Self, but we forget. We're looking in the other direction, believing that 'I'm doing my life'.

Truly Free

I'd like to read a quote from Sri Ramana Maharshi's *Nan Yar –
Who Am I?* Every year in January in India we visit his ashram, even
though he has passed away. It's always a beautiful time. We go every
year because we are very focussed on Sri Ramana's teachings and we
enjoy the ambiance of Indian culture.

Sri Ramana Maharshi was asked: *The residual impressions
(thoughts) of objects appear unending like the waves of an ocean.
When will all of them get destroyed?"*

Question 13 Nan Yar

*As the meditation on the Self rises higher and higher, the thoughts
will get destroyed.*

Sri Ramana Maharshi

> Dear John David,
> I still have a misunderstanding about this destruction of
> thoughts. When thoughts come there is also a voice saying
> they have to be destroyed. It becomes something you have
> to do. Is it more seeing them at a distance and asking the
> question, 'To whom are they arising', and with this question
> they fade rather than being destroyed by my doing?

If we think we can destroy our thoughts then we are still coming
from the position of 'me', from the sense of there being somebody
who can make the mind calm, who can free themselves from all
thoughts. This in itself is a false position, and unfortunately here in
the West we usually pick up this idea and then we want to do a lot
with it.

There is no you. Don't forget there is no you, nobody to do
any destroying. Thoughts simply fade, many less thoughts appear
and your identification changes from the thoughts to the source

of the thoughts, the Self. When you engage in Self-enquiry, your whole identification shifts. That's what really happens. There is no question of destroying thoughts by your own doing.

In India they are always talking about destroying the mind. What they mean is destroying the *thinking* mind, not the *functioning* mind. The thinking mind is the aspect that identifies strongly with the 'I' thought, with the 'me'. Until the identification with this false self, or the sense of 'me', has been cut, it will continue to hold onto experiences from the past and endlessly re-run the old movies. The functioning mind is needed in order to live and function as a human being. It doesn't give you a problem.

If you try to understand *Advaita* with your mind you'll have many questions, but gradually you start to see there are no real answers to your questions because it is not about your mind understanding some kind of answer. It is about your mind disappearing! So in the end the person will stop asking questions and they will find themselves sinking deeper into stillness, and that is the answer to all their questions. Questions disappear.

If you remember, there was a moment in the *Arunachala Shiva* film where I was interviewing David Godman. He said that when he was at university he was spending all his money on spiritual books until he bought a book about Sri Ramana's teachings. He said, '*This book answered all my questions*', and then he said, '*No no, it didn't answer my questions, it simply took them away. It took away my questions.*' There is a difference.

This is the beauty of Self-enquiry and *Advaita*. It is an instantaneous non-teaching, directing your identification from outside to inside, to your Being.

There is no need to learn something new from the outside. It is saying, 'Don't turn right; turn left.' We are completely identified with always turning right. Turning left after forty years of turning right is not so easy. And when you turn left 'WOW!' That's it. There is nothing really to learn.

When you turn your attention from the dramas of life to the Self the mind calms down, judgements and attachments to philosophies and ideas drop away. Then you are available and it is very easy to turn left. You don't have to be a great spiritual seeker to wake up. In fact sometimes people who've been doing spiritual practices for many years become conditioned to certain 'spiritual ideas' and can't make a left turn.

Sri Ramana Maharshi was asked: *Is it possible for the residual impressions of objects that come from beginingless time, as it were, to be resolved, and for one to remain as the pure Self?*

Question 14 Nan Yar

Without yielding to the doubt 'Is it possible, or not?' one should persistently hold on to the meditation on the Self. Even if one be a great sinner, one should not worry and weep 'Oh! I am a sinner, how can I be saved?' One should completely renounce the thought 'I am a sinner' and concentrate keenly on meditation on the Self alone; then, one would surely succeed.

There are not two minds – one good and the other evil; the mind is only one. It is the residual impressions [thoughts] that are of two kinds – auspicious and inauspicious. When the mind is under the influence of auspicious impressions it is called good; and when it is under the influence of inauspicious impressions it is regarded as evil.

The mind should not be allowed to wander towards worldly objects and what concerns other people. However bad other people may be, one should bear no hatred for them. Both desire and hatred should be eschewed [avoided].

All that one gives to others, one gives to one's self. If this truth is understood who will not give to others? When one's self arises all arises; when one's self becomes quiescent [still] all becomes quiescent. To the extent we behave with humility, to that extent there will result good. If the mind is rendered quiescent, one may live anywhere.

Sri Ramana Maharshi

Sri Ramana tells us not to even bother doubting if it is possible or not. It's all mindy stuff. Just get on with the job. Even if you are a sinner, even you can come to your own Self, because everyone's core nature is the Self.

Mind is like a garbage place where there are many kinds of garbage. There is not good garbage and bad garbage. It is all just garbage. We like to believe that our mind is a wonderful thing, with wonderful thoughts. Just remember it is not a question of good thoughts and bad thoughts. All the thoughts are garbage.

His advice for keeping the mind quiet is not to allow it to wander towards worldly objects and what concerns other people. That of course has a lot to do with desire. In the last years, even in India, there is an enormous desire for material things, for objects. Everybody is busy trying to get the latest car or iPhone.

You can ask yourself what effect that has. I've been coming here now for a long time, forty years, and India has transformed amazingly. If you are Indian you would probably find the proliferation of new scooters, cars and motorbikes very positive but it has an effect on the culture. As far as I can see, there is not as much interest in spiritual matters as there was forty years ago.

One of the things I found a bit confronting this year in Sri Ramana's ashram was the age of the resident *poojaris* (Hindu temple priests). The guys who do the *puja* on Ramana's shrine are getting very old. They have probably been serving for almost their whole lives, since they were young men, or even boys. There is one very big man who I've seen there since twenty-five years. I was watching him the other night, taking his food home. He lives in an ashram room and I feel a bit sorry for him because it is not easy for him to even walk. The whole ashram is getting old and I wonder if there is really new blood coming. Most young, middle-class, well-educated Indians simply don't have the interest. They are busy trying to buy a computer or a car.

Sri Ramana also says something quite interesting in the second-last sentence. He says, *'To the extent we behave with humility, to that extent there will result good.'* Jesus said, *'The meek will inherit the kingdom of God.'* Meek is an old-fashioned word for humility. Both Sri Ramana and Jesus remind us to behave with humility. There must be some reason why they would both say that. In the last twenty years of teaching I've met many people who see themselves as spiritually advanced, who think they know. Thinking you know can be a barrier to really knowing.

If you are humble, innocent, there is more likelihood of availability. This is one of the reasons why most ashrams in India have something called *karma yoga*, which basically means spiritual work and it provides opportunities for devotees to work for the ashram. That's also the reason we do most of the kitchen cleaning and tidying while we are in this retreat. We are very advanced, educated people from the West with lots of money, so why should we be doing the cleaning? It reminds you to be humble, it reminds you to be ordinary, it reminds you that you are not special. Nobody is higher and nobody is lower. If you want to come to spiritual Truth you have to be very vigilant about arrogance.

Sri Ramana's last sentence: *'If the mind is rendered still, one might live anywhere'* teaches us that freedom is not dependent on your circumstances. When I left Papaji I was flying to Australia where I had some friends. I had told them when I would arrive and they had arranged a dinner to welcome me. The flight went from Delhi to Bangkok and I arrived in Bangkok very early in the morning. I was very tired and I was celebrating with a few alcoholic drinks, which I wasn't used to drinking any more, and had about six or seven hours in transit before my flight to Australia.

The airline offered me a hotel for the day, and in my unclear, rather unconscious cloud of alcohol and not enough sleep I thought 'Wow! That's great, I'll do that.' So I went to passport control and I was immediately arrested and ended up in a Thai jail for a month. That was a pretty tough experience. I remember being marched through the airport in handcuffs with my laptop hanging off between my hands.

One minute I was dreaming of a nice Thai hotel room and the next moment I was in a pickup truck being driven downtown into a cage. So life doesn't always go as you plan it, but what became very interesting later was that even though I was in jail I discovered I was still free. This was a very important thing to discover, and maybe it's the reason I was sent to jail the day after I left my nearly five years with Papaji.

Actually I discovered two things in jail. Firstly, I was free even in jail, and secondly, I was absolutely taken care of. It wasn't a very nice situation because it was full of very nasty Thai criminals – rapists, murderers and such people. One of the first shocks was that they wanted to cut my very nice trousers into short pants. I probably hadn't worn them for many years but I had put them on especially to travel to Australia, and they wanted to cut them! Before that they offered me lunch. I'll never forget it. It was a bowl of fish soup. Hungry as I was, its smell was so terrible I couldn't eat it.

It was a big crisis, how could I live there if I couldn't even eat the food? The next day, out of the crowd came this middle-class Thai man who wanted to be friends. Then after sometime he said, 'You know, my wife brings me food everyday. If you like you can share it.' Wow! Then she brought this delicious, home cooked, really good Thai food.

I was in prison but eating very nicely. After some time they moved me to another building in the same prison and again I had the fear of not getting food I could eat. There was an American who'd been there quite a few years and he'd started teaching the prison officers how to speak English. For this he could cook his own food. He invited me to share it, so I discovered that even in prison I was free and I was essentially taken care of.

Once you are free, it doesn't matter where you go or what happens. You are always free. Your freedom doesn't depend on anything.

The Pointless Joy of Freedom

So we have a very nice quote here from Adyashanti. During a period of a few months, including some retreats, I often read extracts from his book *The End of Your World*, as there are many parts which beautifully express the phenomenon of awakening, and which are very close to my own expression.

Freedom is not necessarily exciting; it is just free. Very peaceful and quiet, so very quiet. Of course it is also filled with joy and wonder but it is not what you imagine. It is much much less. In order to be truly free you must desire to know the Truth more than you want to feel good.

Adyashanti

> *Dear John David,*
> *This is a very beautiful quote, but I have a question about the end. Is it just about being in the present moment and not running away from whatever the moment holds and seeing, after enough experience, that there is no separation at all so we should just accept everything in life as it is, even if we feel inside that something should change or something should happen?*

Lovely! This question illustrates the problem of being attached to your mind and looking at the world from this position. It is the same old stuff – you want to do something and you feel you should do something. Who's going to do something?

Adyashanti is saying here that freedom '...*is just free. Very peaceful and quiet, so very quiet.*' Perhaps we should ask ourselves what we actually mean by freedom. What I mean by freedom is that I am free from my conditioned mind. I am not attached anymore; I am not in the movie of 'I' anymore. So very quiet, very very peaceful, very very empty. How this manifests in daily life is of course unique for each person. We will all have a different expression, but when you become free of this non-stop attachment to a personal somebody, when this attachment is cut, then suddenly it is like you become a child – spontaneous, innocent, with an easy joy in each moment. This joy doesn't depend on anything.

It is difficult to talk about but this joy is just welling up inside and expressing itself. One of the metaphors I like to use is some kids playing on the beach. They are building a sand castle and having a lot of fun building it higher and higher and then at some point Mummy comes and says, 'Sorry darlings, we have to go home now.' Then all the kids jump on the sand castle and break it down and they have as much fun breaking it down as they did building it up. So this is the pointless joy of freedom!

Once the attachment to the movie is cut there is still a deepening that happens. I don't know if there is any end to this process of maturing. It's something like a child growing into an adult, the adult growing into an old man and the old man growing into an even older man. It seems to be without end. If you perceive this from your 'me' then you might well imagine there is no point even to wake up, because all you get when you wake up is what you started with, but it is not quite like that.

There is a shift that we can call awakening, or Self-realisation. It is the deep realisation about duality, about this illusory 'me'. This is a sudden change in the way that we perceive everything. It is the end of the spiritual seeker. You could also say it is the beginning of the spiritual life, but this is not the spiritual life that many people are busy with. They want some techniques, but these belong to a beginner's stage.

In the beginning of the journey we think we need all kinds of techniques. We need to be busy with being a spiritual seeker and maybe we like to see that our spiritual life is different from our ordinary life; we make it special. Awakening happens when there is clear understanding about duality, clear understanding that the 'me' we have this fixation on is actually not true. It is a very strong change.

It can be a gradual change over some time or it can be a sudden experience. In my case it was both ... a sudden movement followed by a gradual unfolding. After this strong thing happened – which I would call Self-realisation – I stayed in Papaji's *Sangha* for four-and-a-half years. I continued to live there and I continued to get lots of benefits.

At the time I was running a guesthouse, at Papaji's suggestion, and into this guesthouse walked a variety of guests who provided me with all kinds of situations that allowed me to see all my structures. I saw how I dealt with each guest – how I got pissed off with some, how I loved others. Many things were happening at the guesthouse. Looking back, I see it was one of the most important times of my life. The staff and the machinery were always breaking down. With all this, and the dramas of living in India, it created a mirror that showed me my structures. In those days I was very intensely involved in that process of seeing and understanding. It was amazing because there was no longer anyone left inside me to do anything with the structures and they would just drop away by themselves.

During this intense four years I had the support of the energy of the *Satsang*, the community, and particularly from Papaji. When I went off to Australia the re-entry into a normal society brought up a whole new set of situations that had to be assimilated.

I was in Australia about five years and most of that time I felt quite vulnerable and I lived quite alone, but still a lot was going on, a lot was being seen and things were dropping away. I would say it took nine or ten pretty intense years of deepening. Everything is perceived in a new way. It is almost like you are being reborn and you have to learn all about life again and it happens in a new way.

It is different from the way our parents brought us up and suddenly it's 'Oh! How does this work, how do I do things, how do I manage in the world?' I used to feel very vulnerable a lot of the time, childish and innocent.

So actually this deepening, or if you like you could see it as a disappearing, went on for a long time and I don't think it ever stops. There is no sense of separation anymore, and this whole idea of spiritual life has completely dissolved. For a long time now I don't see any division between spiritual life and life. There is just life unfolding.

Be the Sky, Not the Weather

Tonight's quote is from Meister Eckhart, the Christian mystic. He was not just a Christian religious figure but he was actually deeply spiritual and was one of the earlier Christian writers. He was clearly somebody who had become Self-realised and lived in this beautiful way most of his life. Amazingly, his writings are very similar to *Advaita*, which had its roots in India.

For the person who has learned to let go and let be, nothing can ever get in the way again. There exists only the present instant. There is no yesterday nor any tomorrow, but only now.

Meister Eckhart

Dear John David,
I find it hard to balance letting go and letting be with the need to function in the world, to plan and make decisions. I feel these things are all part of my movie, and happening in my mind, and yet they also seem important and necessary. Maybe I don't see how attached I really am. Can you share about how you understand these words 'to let go and let be'?

Here he is telling us that if we can really see how much attachment we have to this false movie, we can fully enter this present moment. If the attachment would really break, if it would really collapse, as it would do depending on your priority and your clarity, then of course there is no past and no future because these things are both from time.

So suddenly, when you are completely free of this movie, you exist out of time. Have you noticed that time often plays tricks? Sometimes it seems to go very very slowly and sometimes very very fast. He says, '*For the person who has learnt to let go and let be*', but of course we can't really learn that. There is a moment where we no longer live from the mind but from the Being, and this we call Self-realisation.

Self-realisation is a particular moment when the attachment to the thoughts is cut and this is of course very beautiful because it puts you completely in the hands of the divine. From that moment your life will continue to flow and you will find that it is not the mind deciding, it is not you deciding, but rather the divine revealing your destiny from moment to moment.

You live in the moment with no past and no future, as Meister Eckhart says. This is the way we've always lived but on top of that there is a kind of overlay in which we say, 'I am doing my life.' This 'I' is what we call the ego.

The Truth doesn't change and it is quite simple. Now-a-days we are constantly bombarded with massive amounts of input. This keeps our minds very busy and it gives us a lot of material to create really interesting stories. We love it, and we become very attached to our stories.

We are not easily going to give all that up. Everybody here understands what has happened, that they are free and there is nothing to get. There are no special pieces of a jigsaw that you have to get from somewhere. You don't have to meet a special truth or special teaching because we are all complete. We are all already free and in fact our nature is love, not romantic love of course but authentic love, unconditional love. So there is nothing to change, there is nothing wrong. Everybody is exactly good enough, everybody is doing exactly what they are supposed to be doing and everybody is exactly where they should be.

The beautiful alternative way to live is very simple because if you keep being aware of what is going on in your mind and you understand it in a clear way, if you understand it with some kind of distance, then you will find yourself living more and more in the present. You don't care too much about the future because if you feel content in this moment now, why wouldn't you feel the same in some more moments? You don't have worries about how it will work out in the future because you feel completely peaceful, you feel love and silence inside and so you are not much interested in the future. You are not much interested in the past, and you find yourself just naturally getting more and more into presence.

———————

I have another beautiful quotation that follows on quite nicely here. It is from a Tibetan Buddhist called Pema Chödrön. It is lovely to have people from different traditions who are actually pointing to the same Truth. Pema Chödrön was a student of Chögyam Trungpa, and I have been touched in the last years by the warmth and compassion in her teachings and also by her clarity and insight.

You are the sky. Everything else is just the weather.

Pema Chödrön

Living as the sky, becoming identified with the sky, you realise that as your life is unfolding you are always okay, you are always good. It doesn't matter what kind of weather it is. Some days the sun shines, some days there is a rainstorm. The weather may change but the sky is constant, untouched.

One of my strongest structures was the belief that I wasn't good enough. For fifty years I believed this, but the beautiful thing is that when it changed in the moment of awakening it didn't change to 'I am good enough.' It changed to 'There is nobody home anymore.' There isn't anybody to be good enough and there isn't anybody to be not good enough. This person simply disappeared.

There is no need to worry that you won't be able to do your job or to relate to people because suddenly you are in the moment. You accept whatever it is that happens, and things are constantly happening. Life is full of happenings; they never stop, but you know that this is not who you are and you discover that who you are is something that never changes.

It is hard to describe what this is but we can use words like peace, love or emptiness, and you recognise this. Often when people become realised – particularly if it happens suddenly – they laugh a lot because they realise that what they had been struggling for years to understand, they always knew. There is nothing new. You don't get something new, you just suddenly realise what you've always had. It is like 'Oh! I've got two legs! Wow! That's good.'

The weather is always changing and in daily life we have constant challenges – we have to meet people, we have difficulties with some people, the electricity stops, things break down, we don't have enough money to pay our telephone bill. This never stops throughout the whole of life, but it doesn't matter because we are not identifying with paying the phone bill. We know that the phone bill will get paid, so we can relax knowing that the whole show is taken care of. An amazingly beautiful way to live.

This is easy to say, but we can't quite get there. We can't get around the edge. It is almost like the bad fairy waved the magic wand and hypnotised us all but we didn't know that we'd been hypnotised. It is only afterwards that we realise we were living for many years in a kind of hypnosis, which we can call the regular attached way of living.

So this waking up is an enormous moment and actually it is not something that has to be really understood. We are always awake, we've never been asleep, we've always been free, we've always been love, we've always been peace. This is our Being; this is our True Nature. It has always been there but unfortunately we identified with something else and we lost touch with it. We don't need to get something.

There is nothing new to get. We only need to see our wrong identification. We are always complete, we are always perfect, we are always doing exactly what we are supposed to be doing and we are always where we are supposed to be. Life is very very simple, everything is just happening. What we can call the divine is an enormous wisdom, intelligence, and this is who I am. We are not separate from that.

So be the sky and don't care about the weather. It doesn't matter. Just put your umbrella up when it rains and put on your sunglasses when the sun shines. You don't have to care about the weather. There is nothing to care about. The invitation is to fully accept each moment.

Awakening

We have another beautiful quote from Adyashanti that expresses the first moment of spiritual awakening, a glimpse:

The experience of awakening differs from person to person. For some, the awakening is sustained over time while for others the glimpse is momentary. It may last just a split second but in that instant the whole sense of self (by self, I would say false self) disappears. The way they perceive the world suddenly changes and they find themselves without any sense of separation between themselves and the rest of the world. It can be likened to the experience of waking up from a dream, a dream you didn't even know you were in until you are jolted out of it.

Adyashanti

> Dear John David,
> I desperately want to wake up from the dream, but it is not happening. I am on the spiritual path but I don't know how to step out of my mind.

The only true way to step out of all the stories and all the nonsense is to really see with great clarity that this 'me' that we are so fond of referring everything to, simply doesn't exist. Once you see it doesn't exist then the whole thing falls away. Everything just falls away and you're left with what is. You are not going to die; nothing is going to happen really.

Often there is a tremendous release of energy. You can see this in our film, *Satori*, where a resident in the community, Indira, had a spontaneous and powerful awakening experience while sitting in her office, and some residents were actually on hand and filmed it.

In the 'normal' situation of life where we are identified with 'me', then the conditioned mind acts like a lid on a pressure cooker, always pushing our energy down, holding our natural energy in a reasonable, controlled flow. When an awakening happens the lid of the pressure cooker is removed and very often this happens in an explosive way, because the realisation is usually happening very suddenly. This is perhaps the more normal way. Just suddenly, 'Bang!' The lid blows off and there's a tremendous amount of energy released. It can also happen over time, in an imperceptible way.

Then it is quite common, and I also experienced this, that the physical body doesn't function for some time, perhaps for a few hours or a few days. So with this suddenly greater flow of energy the body doesn't function, but very quickly the energy – or you could say the vibration or the frequency – is absorbed and rises up.

Then the amazing thing is that you can function extremely well afterwards, even better than before because there isn't the constant filter and static of the mind. In Indira's case she is running our community every day, a tough job. She manages me everyday – that's a pretty tough job too, and she still does her own external work in the world. You almost never see her tired. So this is not something to understand with the mind. If you try to understand it from 'me' you can project some sort of understanding, but unless you have had a glimpse then it really has no meaning.

When you are limited by a strong attachment to a separate me it is almost impossible to imagine how that would be. It is very difficult therefore to talk about because the person is listening from a certain reference point. You are listening from 'me', which you perceive as separate, and this is why some students have heard me talk about it for years and still don't get it.

It is not a criticism of anyone. I was listening to this for many years and I didn't get it. It takes some time to understand this and when you do, it just happens. So in the end there is nothing you can do and that is why I started this talk by pointing out that there is no one to do anything. You can say, 'Well, I am on the spiritual path, I am doing my meditation everyday', and so you have a feeling that if you keep doing it for some years you will get some absolutely concrete benefit. But what I am talking about is that there is no formula, there is no practice.

I know a lot of people who have had such an opening, even if it was only for a short moment. It is tremendously life-changing because once this small moment has happened then you know something that you didn't know before. If you like, you know yourself in a new way, but then the self we're talking about is no longer this rather small illusionary self. It is suddenly another self, the Self, the authentic Self, vast, a feeling of oneness, tremendous love, tremendous connectedness.

Once this is experienced you can never really be the same again. After a few seconds the normal self, normal 'me', usually comes back very quickly because the glimpse in that moment is frightening, shocking, completely unexpected, magnificent.

I can still remember sitting on my balcony in my house in India. I was looking out on the trees, the birds were singing and suddenly a glimpse happened and I was so afraid! The fear closed it down almost immediately. It was only a few seconds but it was like experiencing an amazing passion and incredible fire. Similar things happened a few more times, always a bit different, but they all just happened.

When you look back on your old false self, which you've been believing for many years, you can only really laugh. Five minutes before you completely believed in this false self and five minutes later it is just ridiculous. It is extremely difficult to talk about, to give a sense of that change. You can read about it, but reading about it doesn't really help to prepare you for when it happens. When it does happen it is completely fresh, something that you just didn't know.

During the day the basic colour of the sky is blue but very often, especially in northern Europe, it's covered in clouds. So you can't see the blueness of the sky but occasionally the clouds part, even in Germany, and you get a glimpse of the blue sky. Then of course the clouds come back.

So this is the glimpse, but you can't forget it. There is this enormous motivation inside you now and you look at the weather forecast hoping that the blue sky will come back this summer. This glimpse is indescribably beautiful. It is the best moment of your life.

Even so, there is often fear and the fear closes down the glimpse.

In the beginning it will just be a glimpse, a flash where the clouds (the structures of the mind) in the blue sky part, and you get a glimpse of the blueness. You feel this very deeply. It is very beautiful but it is not something you can do, it just happens. In that instance the whole sense of self disappears.

This is what is really important. The sense of self – this 'me' that we are so attached to – disappears. It is a completely shocking moment. Adyashanti's words explain it: '*The way they perceive the world suddenly changes and they find themselves without any sense of separation between themselves and the rest of the world. It can be likened to the experience of waking up from a dream. A dream you didn't even know you were in until you are jolted out of it.*'

We've all experienced super-realistic dreams, often with familiar people and scenes. Suddenly we wake up and are amazed that what seemed so real before was only a dream. As a spiritual seeker you probably expect an awakening to be amazingly special, but when you awaken it is completely ordinary.

Ending the Search

Anandamayi Ma was one of the great Indian female spiritual masters. She left her body in the early 80s, as an old lady. When she was younger she was an extremely beautiful woman, everyone's idea of what a goddess would look like. She has a very beautiful and powerful *Samadhi* in her ashram in Haridwar.

When by the flood of your tears the inner and the outer have fused into one, you will find Her whom you sought with such anguish, nearer than the nearest, the very breath of life, the very core of every heart.

Anandamayi Ma

Dear John David,
This seems to me a funny paradox. I have been searching intensely, desiring to live from my True Nature, and while I know that ultimately the search is for what I already am, still it continues, and there is a constant angst inside that drives me on. It seems that all I can do is to persevere, to keep focusing on the priority of waking up until 'the inner and outer have fused into one'.

A spiritual seeker is a funny paradox, because he or she is searching for something, looking here and looking there, spending time with this person or that person and normally having the idea they have to find something on the outside. While they're searching for this something they are already themselves, whole and complete, so what they are searching for is what they already are. This is the paradox.

We are all awakened, there is nothing to get, to be different, but in our daily experience we can't always feel this freedom. So what does she mean by *the flood of your tears*? She means that in order to come to this understanding you have to go through some kind of process. There are rare cases when someone becomes spontaneously realised, for example Sri Ramana Maharshi, but in order for most of us to come to something very close to us, we often have to walk around the whole mountain, or maybe even the whole planet. We have to search here and there, and all this searching seems to be a necessary process for us to give up and discover that we are already what we were searching for.

We go through challenging moments on the path as well as the moments when we feel the beauty of life, the beauty of our inner world. Then of course we can laugh, and we can also laugh at the joke of searching for something that in fact is already our inner Truth.

Papaji used to say, 'If you say you are free, you are free.' This was always hard to grasp with my mind. What does he mean? I say I am free and I am free? How does that work? The beauty of what Anandamayi Ma is suggesting, and actually what every master is suggesting, is that this is very very close. There is not really any teaching; you just have to look. Where do you look? Not in your mind. You don't need to do anything.

Western people find doing nothing almost impossible. We believe we have to do a lot to get this Truth. After spending years searching, going to this ashram and that ashram, going to this teacher and that teacher, watching now YouTube videos, so much effort, piles of spiritual books and suddenly being told do nothing! What kind of a teaching is that?

'I like being a spiritual seeker. I don't want to stop. It's lots of fun. Now do nothing!' What does that suggest? It suggests that you are already free. 'No I am not free. I didn't feel very good after lunch today. I am not free.' Then another five years of searching. This is an enormous paradox, and it's so easy to misunderstand.

You hear the message that you don't have to do anything. Then of course you can get the idea that you'll just sit here and have a few beers and not do anything and tomorrow you'll be Self-realised. That's one kind of response, but that doesn't work, unfortunately. What is being suggested is very subtle and most of the people I have met who became Self-realised have done years of spiritual seeking, spiritual practice and intense inner work. They are experts.

So it seems that most of us need to do all this spiritual seeking in order to come to a kind of exhaustion, when everything doesn't seem to work. Just like Buddha. He did years of spiritual practice, years of living in a tough situation, not enough food, alone in a cave. Finally he gave up. 'It is enough; I can't anymore. No more ideas how it should be. I give up, I stop.' In the moment he stopped, 'Poof', something happened.

We have all kind of ideas: how it should be, how we think it should be, and it's very hard if not impossible to stop this habit by yourself. But, like Buddha, if you do stop, if you are truly living 'do nothing', the result is this moment of awakening. Our ideas will never get us there.

Somebody like a master is not interested in these ideas at all. They are a monster, a complete monster, because they are trying to kill your mind, to kill all the ideas standing in the way, to kill this sense of you being somebody separate from life. Not many people want to be killed, so that kind of master is not going to be hugely popular. It's a tough job! We love all our ideas, we love our philosophy, we like being a nice guy or nice woman. We have all kind of spiritual ideas and we also have all kinds of spiritual ideas about the teacher.

It is very beautiful work because whatever is going on around me there is always an opportunity to show something. So this is why we have to have our ego confronted because that is the only thing that prevents us from seeing what Anandamayi Ma is saying here, '*... nearer than the nearest, the very breath of life, the very core of every heart*'. Nothing to search for; you just have to drop all the nonsense, and as the nonsense drops, there you are. You have always been there but there was so much nonsense in between that you couldn't see it. You simply couldn't see it.

Our True Nature

I first came across the Third Zen Patriarch, Seng-ts'an, during my time with Osho. Later someone gave this quote to Papaji. In one *Satsang* meeting Papaji read this beautiful quote below, which clearly lays out how we can live in the Self, in peace, with just a simple understanding.

On reading more about Seng-ts'an I liked very much how he apparently led a very ordinary and humble life, and how his spiritual message can be so touching and fundamental after fifteen hundred years.

> *The Great Way is not difficult*
> *for those who are unattached, no preferences.*
> *When love and hate are both absent,*
> *everything becomes clear and undisguised.*
> *Make the smallest distinction, however,*
> *and heaven and earth are set infinitely apart.*
> *If you wish to see the Truth,*
> *then hold no opinion for or against anything.*
> *Seng-ts'an, Third Zen Patriarch of China*

Dear John David,
When I meditate, or when I am sitting quietly or doing something that I find beautiful, then often this lovely quiet, peaceful space comes over me. Is there something to do to keep this in the daily life, when it feels so difficult to stay in touch with it, or is any doing just taking me further from this space?

This is the most beautiful meditation – coming to what doesn't change, and what doesn't change is you, your True Nature, your Essence. The unchangeable Self.

If you are really there in the Self it is very likely you will experience a vast blackness, without any borders or boundaries. Infinite space. Black, shining, luminous, infinite space. It is not the blackness of death or of dark forces. It is a brilliant, shiny, luminous blackness, full of light, and it is very attractive. You don't have any movement away from this. You can stay there forever and ever. Once you become a little experienced you can stay there and have your eyes open and move your body and walk around and do some tasks, but in the beginning you have to sit. You have to close your eyes and find this place that never changes.

If you have a busy mind you need to do a spiritual practice that we've talked about before to quieten it – different kinds of meditation, mantras, breathing. If you are a very emotional person, then again some effort needs to happen to calm these emotions, which are also part of the mind. When you don't have much disturbing you inside, if you are calm and relaxed, then in any moment you will be directly and easily aware, in the Self, of what doesn't change.

The Self has no boundaries – a tremendous feeling of infinite space, completely empty. Sometimes there may be some thoughts passing but they look a lot like rocket traces through the blackness, completely not disturbing anything. The beautiful thing about this infinite, shiny, luminous blackness is that we feel amazingly good. We feel so good that we don't want to change anything. We don't even want to open our eyes. We just want to stay there in the Self. This is a wonderful mirror in which to see that in our every-day lives we are always discontent.

We are not content with here and now so we want to move, we want to go somewhere, we want to do something, we want to get something new. If we really do a deep enquiry about the nature of this 'I' that always wants something else, then in the fullness of this investigation we will discover that we are not who we always thought we were. We discover that in Truth we are that which doesn't change. In that moment there is Self-realisation.

When you come to the place that doesn't change you don't want to do anything. When you fall very deeply into the Self it can become very intense as it is possible that the energy passing through your system is so strong that your body doesn't function. You can't lift your arms or legs but inside you are connected to this amazingly beautiful space of the Self. It is not about happiness; it is beyond happiness. Tremendous ecstasy, a tremendous feeling of oneness. You feel like the master of the universe.

Most people never experience the True Nature of life. But once you have had at least a glimpse of this place, you know the Self, and therefore it is easier to make it a priority. Still you can push it away, because there are all kinds of demands that appear to be more important, but this beautiful space where you had a glimpse is always waiting inside you. It is your Essence.

Before you've had a glimpse you're just projecting some idea you have of what it might be like. So the glimpse is very important because it gives you clear knowing. Why do you lose contact again? Because for many, many years you've been identified with the movie of your life. It's very hard to give this up. It's such a strong habit. I have experienced many good people who have had a glimpse, then forget under the weight of old structures.

When Sri Ramana Maharshi was asked about these structures of the mind he said if they are very strong you won't be able to remain in contact to the Self. They can be powerful enough to prevent a settling into the Being.

There is just love, tremendous love. We can live our whole life in this love. It has nothing to do with anybody, it is just love that is moving; it is moving, it is here, it is presence. In the here and now a presence of love – this is our Essence as human beings. Our True Nature.

Life After Awakening

I met Ma Souris about fifteen years ago at her small ashram a couple of hours north of Chennai. I spent three days with her and made an interview for the Indian *Blueprints for Awakening* film. She was an interesting, very salty eighty-five-year-old lady. She was a little bit of an acquired taste, but she was amazingly honest and we had quite a sweet time together.

Each morning her assistants would bring flowers from the garden and she would put them into small pots for the altar. It was something very ordinary, but the way she did it was so beautiful.

This is the beauty of someone who is living in the moment, because when you're in their presence you experience this amazing feeling of NOW.

She was very connected to Sri Ramana Maharshi and was introduced to him by her father, an unusual man who was a well-known poet and writer. Later he became her disciple.

The waves fall upon the shore and they leave behind a pool: that is the mind. When the waves dash back upon the shore, where is the pool? The pool is submerged into the ocean. That is what happens. There is nothing separate. Self is everything: the world, and you and me; it is everything

Ma Souris

Dear John David,
Could you try to share how your inner life is today compared to the years before Self-realisation? What is it inside that changes when this moment happens?

This happened about twenty-five years ago. Today we were looking at some photos and it seems that twenty-five years ago I looked very energetic, very shiny, but now after having Open Sky House Community for fifteen years I realised I look like an old carpet!

Well, I'm joking a bit – that is not completely true!

I would say one very clear difference is that I have a lot more energy since the moment of awakening. For example these days I am looking after things in the three communities on a daily basis and I am also completing a new book. The last two nights I worked till about 4 o'clock in the morning and three or four days ago I flew from Spain. Tomorrow I fly to Ukraine and I come to see that it is not completely easy to go from one country's energy into another's. But basically I am very energetic and can manage very well, even at seventy-two.

It is very difficult to really talk about all this because if I look inside and try to explain about my life it is basically ordinary and pretty quiet and there is nothing really that exciting going on.

If I go back twenty-five years to when this shift happened, I can remember some pretty dramatic changes. On the physical level, almost from one day to the next, my penis stopped working and it didn't work again for about one-and-a-half years. This was quite a strong phenomenon because I had always had an active sex life. I discovered that actually women are quite okay without sex. Me too!

I think what really started then was a lot of fun and it wasn't like special fun – everything ordinary was simply fun. For example, I had a scooter that sometimes broke down or got a puncture. Before, I would have got slightly pissed off about that but now it was just fun. I had lots of lovely moments when the scooter broke down and a whole bunch of Indians came to help me and then they discussed together what's the best thing to do and we ended up having a kind of party, repairing my scooter.

Particularly in the first three months – but continuing in some way for about a year or so – a lot of my mind structures turned up again. This was slightly disappointing because one of my ideas was that I would be sitting in silence forever. But gradually I saw that because the attachment to those thoughts and structures had been cut, they didn't really have anywhere to land. They didn't have anywhere to attach and therefore most of the smaller ones disappeared fairly quickly.

I would say in the first months a big pile of them simply evaporated, and you'll be pleased to know that my most difficult structure, which probably continued for a year or so, was 'I'm not good enough'. I had this pretty strongly throughout my life and by watching what was happening inside I could see how I was still getting caught by it – but not really getting caught. There was a different quality you could say.

Then after I moved from India to Australia, to Sydney, I woke up one morning and I realised that this pattern of thoughts hadn't come to me for quite a long time. It has never come back. What replaces that? It is not that I suddenly became good enough. I simply became myself and any idea of good enough and not good enough simply disappeared.

You could say I was being who I was, and this continues. I am maybe not so good at seeing it, but sometimes I can see my energy is simply much too strong for another person. Things like politeness disappeared and were replaced by something like directness. Sometimes that is very good, but if the other person needs a bit of politeness or a little bit of social care it can create problems. Unfortunately I can see that after twenty-odd years I don't have any real strong control mechanism. There isn't much sense of John David. It is more like a sense of an energy phenomenon. So in any particular moment, in any particular situation, there will be a very spontaneous response to that moment.

I live in any particular moment, allowing and dealing with whatever it is that arises in that moment. I very rarely say 'Oh, we'll talk about it tomorrow.' I tend to deal with stuff now, even if it is difficult. In these last twenty years I've spent a lot of the time alone. This may sound strange when I have been living in the Open Sky House Community for fourteen years, but in the end the reference is here and it comes from here. So whatever is going on here I am ready to express that.

I am very conscious of my destiny. I have lived in a few different countries and every time I moved to a different country it was like starting a new book or a new chapter. When I left Australia and came to Europe, ending up in Germany, I arrived with minus five thousand euros and one big suitcase.

When I was younger I was forever doing these calculations to work out if I would have enough money to cover all my expenses, but now it is not like that. In fact, at some point along the way I discovered the more I spent, the more would come to me. That was a rather nice discovery!

I always liked shopping, but I hardly need anything anymore. I've discovered that I can have just as much fun buying stuff for other people as I used to have buying for myself. All the feelings I might have had in the past about having something new, a special whatever it was, I can still have all those nice feelings but it is not personal anymore.

The other thing I've noticed happening more and more as my life in the community has been happening is that if I am quiet enough, if I am present enough, I can pretty much get any answer I need from my divine navigation system. Actually it works better than the Internet. I can get help with things from how to screw in a particular screw, to making very big complex decisions.

Last year in Spain I wanted to buy some beautiful Japanese carp for our pond. I was told that their sale had been banned by the Spanish government and it was not possible to buy them, but within a couple of weeks I had bought thirty of them!

I trust the divine mystery, and it's amazing to see how the divine mystery wants to serve you, how in any moment it wants to give you what you apparently want, or maybe it is what existence thinks you should have.

Over the last many years I see how my functioning has moved from mind orientated to increasingly open hearted. This began when meditation started forty years ago. Since realisation it has accelerated and now there is a huge energy available that manifests in a capacity to care and support those many people who seek me out. There is a deep caring about the human condition and a compassion that supports my work as a teacher.

I can see that I am pretty unconventional. About four years

ago I decided to have some children and when I told my sister she told me don't be ridiculous, you are so old, just think of the children having such an old father, it would be terrible for them. But actually there was a very nice young woman who was ready to join me in this project.

Now we have two little girls. It is an enormous gift. The girls seem to like me as my sense of freedom makes up for my old bones. Things like this happen pretty regularly in my life.

In the last fourteen years I have to admit there have been some moments where I would have liked to pack all my bags and drive away from the communities, but that was absolutely impossible. First of all I couldn't think of anywhere to go, and secondly there was just this very clear sense that my life is unfolding as it should be unfolding and I don't really even have any means to interfere. Over the years there is more and more trust that everything is working as it is supposed to be working, and of course this gets tested sometimes.

Sometimes I get caught up in pretty tough personal situations, but not for very long. Very quickly an overdrive kicks in that sees that everything is fine.

In the past I used to not like 'boring'. You could even say it was a bit of a torture. But that also disappeared and there is no real issue about boring anymore. It is pretty hard to be bored with a lifestyle that is always pretty exciting, full of pointless joy. Constantly moving between communities in three countries, relating with an intimate group of disciples from many cultures and a yearly visit to India, my spiritual home.

I have been sharing now for about twenty-five years and I would guess that there was never one week where existence didn't send somebody for me to share with. I can see that a few of these people received the same gift that I got from my masters. It's not hundreds of people but of course when it happens it is very touching and it gives the energy to continue. Just when I would like to stop sharing, existence has this way of creating a beautiful meeting.

So anyway, to answer your question, I had a head full of ideas about what it would be like when this shift happened, but when it happened I discovered that it was very simple and very ordinary. In one way it is ordinary, and yet in other way it is extraordinary. A lot like those Zen stories about before and after enlightenment – carrying water and chopping wood. However in my case it's about carrying my iPhone and tapping a computer.

Open Sky House Communities
A Radical Path to Awakening

Recently, a close disciple of mine who has been with me for six years in the community, Kabir, was inspired to write an article about the community, about how he experiences the life there, and how it has transformed him. It is a lovely first-hand account, and an insight into the process of awakening.

I wanted to again include the quote from Thich Nhat Hanh we have already explored in the book, as it is so fitting in this personal account of transformation in the support of a community.

It is possible that the next Buddha will not take the form of an individual. The next Buddha may take the form of a community, a community practising understanding and loving kindness, a community practising mindful living.
Thich Nhat Hanh

Open Sky House *comprises three spiritual and creative communities in Germany, Ukraine and Spain under the guidance of the English non duality teacher John David. The focus of the communities is to allow people the space to investigate the Truth of human life, to become free of identifying with a false, conditioned persona, and to be nourished by living consciously from their own Being.*

I became aware of the Open Sky House Community while I was living in China and working as an English teacher. I felt deep down that I didn't want the life that was apparently laid out for me by the world I grew up in. I wanted to find out who I really was, and find a way out of the suffering I was experiencing in my life. I started watching spiritual meetings on the Internet and discovered John David and the Open Sky House Community.

I stayed some time as a volunteer and decided to move in. A few months after my initial excitement of joining the community, knowing that this was a great chance to look deeply inside, I was strongly confronted with my ideas about life, and my patterns of behavior that covered something I didn't want to see about myself.

I was working in the community's publishing company, Open Sky Press, helping with the distribution of spiritual books and films. John David and the people who worked close to me could see that I often avoided finishing things and didn't really take care about what I was doing. I couldn't connect to anything. I knew this side of myself and had experienced a lot of suffering from it, but I had never wanted to look at it or step out of it.

At this point I am reminded of Chögyam Trungpa's words.

*The **Sangha** is a community of people who have the perfect right to cut through your trips and feed you with their wisdom, as well as the perfect right to demonstrate their own neurosis and be seen through by you. The companionship within the **Sangha** is a kind of clean friendship – without expectation, without demand, but at the same time, fulfilling. True **Sangha** is only possible within a container of love, intimacy and trust. It takes commitment, willingness, time and patience to create this much-needed environment.*

Chögyam Trungpa

In such a vibrant community where twenty people live closely with a teacher, everybody gets the exact mirror they need for whatever structure they have inside them that is standing in the way of them being free, being whole and fully alive. In my life before the community I always took it incredibly personally, like a criticism, if someone pointed out my inner structures.

In the community I also took it very personally in the beginning, but over time, and with such a loving, supportive and nourishing field of acceptance, my mind and energy became very open to the process of looking inside and dealing with the patterns that keep me in suffering.

Unlike friends who understand us in our suffering and usually confirm and support our ego, John David sees his role as a strong mirror, showing people what is really going on inside them, even if that may be difficult or uncomfortable to hear. Working and living closely with residents he continuously creates situations in everyday life that expose the workings of the ego and shine light onto areas of unconsciousness.

Before I moved in, I got tremendous support from John David's regular public *Satsangs* that take place in all the Open Sky Houses and which are streamed live twice a week through the community's website and iTunes app: SatTV (www.sattv.tv). They are still profound reminders for me that we are the silence that is always present. In absolute Truth there is nothing to teach, there is no teacher, and no student, but in the reality of our daily lives we hardly ever live that Truth because we are so identified with our minds and who we think we are.

One of my stronger issues concerned relationships. I often would get very painfully lost in a romantic falling in love which I could see for myself was actually not an authentic way of relating. I was living in a story made up by my mind.

Through bringing awareness, giving advice and creating challenging situations, John David guided me away from falling down again and pointed me towards finding my own love, my own ground to stand on, instead of always looking for it in 'another.'

A year ago, I started feeling the incredible benefit of his advice and the constant inner work. Now there is love, peace and a spring of confidence and ease, which doesn't depend on the outside world. This is such a beautiful and radical transformation that sometimes I hardly recognise myself.

The most profound mirror in this journey has been John David. A true master, with a deep, unconditional love and caring for the processes of each person, he manifests an enormous energy and power that is utterly devoted to provoking the people around him to wake up.

At the beginning, working with a teacher sometimes went against my nice ideas of what 'spiritual' life is about. It was incredibly strong and uncomfortable to have someone relentlessly and honestly showing me what was really going on inside of me; someone who constantly pointed to what is false, what I am attached to, what I don't want to let go, where I cause separation.

As in many traditional ashrams, the communities encourage two paths: The Way of Knowledge, which is the intense work of self-awareness that leads eventually to a quiet mind, and the Way of the Heart, which is about service and devotion. Self-enquiry and service are strong foundations of all three communities. In this way the Open Sky Houses are a cross between a traditional ashram from the East and a modern western lifestyle.

To support the Way of Knowledge we have three silent meditations each day, but the silence we are really interested in is not the silence of 'doing' meditation. It is the deep silence that is the core of who we really are and from which everything that is 'done' arises.

Various successful businesses have been set up over the years in the Open Sky Houses, including a hotel and seminar house, an art gallery and a publishing company. As well as providing the financial means for the communities these businesses also create a platform for service, which is simply about giving, with no expectation of a direct return.

After some time I discovered that giving without intention opens the heart and allows trust to come. This results in a natural way of life where you work, share, and live free from egoistic identity and intention. Through this 'love in action' the sense of a personal 'me' gradually dissolves.

Another effect of working with these two paths is the creativity that arises. I had always played the piano or written poems, but some time after joining the community I began playing and writing with an incredible spontaneity and inspiration, often amazing myself with what was coming out of me. Creativity gives birth to beauty, the very important third path to awakening that John David constantly encourages and invites into the communities.

Over the years the Way of Beauty is clear to see with the annual arts festival, the art gallery exhibiting art made from stillness, the publication of many beautifully designed spiritual books and films, the transformation of the communities' buildings and gardens and the zoo in the main community house which is full of exotic birds and animals that wander freely in the inner courtyard.

In my own case I've had many moments when there was a profound opening, a dropping away of what I normally considered 'me' into something incredibly beautiful, simple and peaceful, my Being, my True Nature. Such a glimpse is a reminder of what is possible in one's life, a true potential, and is a great support and encouragement to continue the inner looking. Maybe one day the glimpse doesn't go away and we remain in our Being, not re-identifying with the mind and ego. This is what you could say the spiritual work is about, returning to our Being and working to remove the patterns that pull us out of the present moment.

The combination in community life of intensive self-awareness and an opening heart immersed in beauty lets the false identity fall away and invites Truth to make itself known.

In my past six years there has been a profound and life-changing transformation. I know the trust in life that comes from just being there for the moment, and I feel it becoming more and more grounded in my daily life.

All are welcome to come and taste this magical, amazing place as a guest or volunteer. A wealth of information about the Open Sky House Communities and John David can be found on www.opensky.international.

There is no doubt that over the last fourteen years the community has served its intention – a very rare and successful embodiment of conscious living. My deepest gratitude and love to John David and the residents of the Open Sky Houses.

Kabir

John David
Biography

After a typical English, middle-class upbringing, John David found himself in his early twenties working as a structural engineer and later training as an architect, developing his career and enjoying the fruits of life like any ambitious young man. He had a nice apartment, a curvy Volkswagon Beetle, sometimes a girlfriend, and a good job in a well-known architectural office in the centre of London. Everything looked pretty set for him to live a comfortable, successful, even rich life. His mum was very happy with him.

However, during his teens and early twenties he had developed a question that seemed to be about not knowing what to do with his life, not finding meaning in the world around him. On a deeper inner level he had the strong feeling that he never really fitted in and that he didn't actually want what he had apparently chosen in his life.

One evening he was waiting at an underground station in London during the rush hour, heading back from the centre of town after another long day's work. There was a strong voice inside him that suddenly said this was not the life he wanted. He decided to move abroad, finding an opportunity with an architectural office in Tokyo, Japan.

On his arrival in Tokyo he experienced a huge culture shock and his internal question became even stronger. He again felt this overwhelming sense of not fitting, something he thought he had moved away from by coming abroad. There was something missing in his life, and it brought a great sadness and confusion. He went into a 'dark night of the soul' that lasted several years. He stayed on in Japan because he was engrossed in an internal dialogue that was provoked by being in that alien culture.

At twenty-eight John David still had no idea about spiritual life, but while in Japan he met a German architecture professor who introduced him to his first master, Osho. At the time he had no interest, nor any idea of the significance of the meeting. Twelve months later, through a series of inexplicable events, he arrived at Osho's ashram in Pune, India. As he walked through the gate, which was called 'The Gateless Gate', he immediately felt at home.

He had found his place. The feeling was energetic, powerful and strong and it was without any reason. It was as if the question he'd had for more than ten years was answered. For the next fifteen years he lived as an Osho *sannyasin* in India, England and America. Taking part in transformational workshops led to self-awareness, and the years of meditation developed a quiet mind.

Two years after Osho's death, John David was living contentedly in Pune, close to Osho's ashram when he heard about another teacher, the great *Advaita* master Sri Harilal Poonja, known to his many devotees as Papaji. He read an interview with this man and also saw a video, but the real interest came when he started noticing people who had come back from visiting him. He saw an amazing transformation in these people. There was a glow and internal smile coming from them that touched him.

Although he had not been looking for another master, he arrived in Lucknow and was surprised by Papaji's enormous availability. John David found Papaji almost shockingly available. Shocking, because his immediacy confronted him with the questions, 'Who am I?' and 'What am I doing here?'

In the first three weeks, John David formally sat with Papaji in *Satsang* each day and three times asked him a question. On the occasion of the third meeting he saw with amazing clarity the thing that, during fifteen years of spiritual searching, he had never understood. The Self revealed itself and it was seen that this was his True Nature, which had always been known. Without any doubt, that moment marked a total change in his life. Instantly the identification with John David and his story were cut. From one moment to the next there was an enormous shift, which can only be described as Self-realisation.

John David stayed on with his teacher for five years, then he moved to Australia. On the night Papaji left his body John David was conducting a residential Reiki weekend. At lunchtime he received a powerful, energetic internal 'fax' message seemingly from Papaji telling him that he had some work to do. He was incredulous about this, even though the messages continued for two days. At the time he didn't know that Papaji had left his body at exactly that time. This was in 1997 and marked the beginning of John David offering *Satsang*.

At that time John David was living in Sydney, Australia. He had already collected a group of students for his meditation and Reiki classes. He offered them an informal 'new' kind of meeting. The group expanded rapidly and a building was offered out of the blue. Then for three years he offered regular *Satsang* meetings, weekends and retreats in and around Sydney as well as on visits to Melbourne and the Byron Bay area.

Since 2003 John David has been back in Europe and travelling widely, wherever he is invited, confronting the conditioned mind – the prison we build for ourselves from our identification with thoughts, emotions, beliefs, and desires. The demolition process begins as John David lovingly and humorously guides participants to see that they are not the many experiences of 'my life', but rather the awareness in which the experience happens. He focuses his meetings on this awareness, the Self, which is our true nature and is revealed when the mind becomes quiet.

Some years before meeting Papaji, John David found a hand-tinted photograph in a room he was renting in his last years with Osho. Although he had no idea who this person was, the beautiful eyes gradually made their way into his heart and Being. Later he discovered this was Sri Ramana Maharshi, whose saintly presence and teaching of Self-enquiry, 'Who am I?' had made him famous.

On meeting Papaji he was deeply affected to see that he had the same photograph on his wall behind his *Satsang* chair. John David sees himself as a messenger for the ancient wisdom of India, the wisdom that forms the basis of most spiritual traditions. He is deeply grateful to his direct masters and to many others in both the East and the West whom he has met and befriended through his project, *Blueprints for Awakening.*

Surrounded by twenty close disciples, John David now travels between the three Open Sky House *Satsang* and Arts Communities, in Hitdorf, near Cologne in Germany, in Denia near Valencia, Spain, and in Trypillia near Kiev in Ukraine.

In all three communities John David holds regular retreats and weekends. He has three *Sangha* groups around him by his invitation, consisting of people who have a strong longing to become free. They meet with him on a regular basis. The communities are open to anybody who has come to the point in their life where they want to know themselves – not their stories and dramas, but rather their true nature. 'Who am I?' is the focus of the community and the motto is 'be as you are'.

From his deep love for India, John David was led to meet and befriend many Indian saints and masters, collecting rare interviews, which can now be found in his book and its companion film *Blueprints for Awakening – Indian Masters.* After the support and feedback he received, he embarked on another book and film project *European Spiritual Masters – Blueprints for Awakening. Arunachala Shiva*, a book and film about the life and teachings of Sri Ramana Maharshi, followed.

John David's experiences with communities and spiritual seekers in Europe encouraged him to make the film *Satori – Metamorphosis of an Awakening*, the book and film *The Great Misunderstanding*, the film *Art from Inner Stillness*, and this current book and film about his life and teachings, *The Pointless Joy of Freedom.*

His other projects include a homage to his master, Papaji, in the form of the book *Papaji Amazing Grace*, and a selection of his *Satsangs* given in India, *Arunachala Talks.*

He enjoys art and beauty and is himself a painter, and the curator of the Flow Fine Art Gallery. As an artist, John David has exhibited his paintings in India, Australia and Germany. They are in private collections in several countries. His joy-filled abstract paintings are an expression of the playfulness at the core of his Being. They can be seen throughout this book. He encourages and facilitates many forms of creativity in the Open Sky House Communities.

He is actively available in these International Communities to meet you as a guest or volunteer and to invite you to live with him if your passion for living in freedom is great enough. He offers online *Satsang* two evenings a week through SatTV, which can be viewed live around the world. You can engage in dialogue with him by entering into the meeting live through Skype. The Skype address is: meetingjohndavid. There is also a comprehensive archive of six hundred *Satsang* meetings given since 2009, in seven different languages.

John David is no longer caught up in his conditioned mind, believing he is a somebody. Out of the emptiness, Self manifests as enormous energy and presence in each moment. Through his example, John David shows us that spiritual life is every moment. There is no 'spiritual life', there is just life. Presence in each moment. He is an unusual character, full of fun and lightness with the possibility of a sudden storm at any moment. Many love him to bits and others find him outrageous. He is never boring but not always able to see when he is too much. He would love to invite you to come and make your own assessment!

See the film *The Pointless Joy of Freedom* for a visual biography of John David.

www.sattv.tv
www.openskypress.com
www.opensky.international
www.johndavidsatsang.international

Glossary

Advaita Vedanta   One of the three systems of *Vedanta*, a philosophical interpretation of the *Vedas* (Four collections of ancient Hindu history and scripture). *Advaita Vedanta* emphasises the non duality of everything. That is, everything – subjective and objective – is nothing but the Self.

Arjuna   Main male figure from the *Bhagavad Gita* who receives instruction from Lord *Krishna* about the nature of being and the meaning of life. *Arjuna* represents the human being caught in ignorance.

Arunachala   Holy mountain at Tiruvannamalai in South India. Considered to be *Shiva*. Sri Ramana Maharshi called Arunachala his guru. He arrived there aged sixteen and never left.

Bhagavad Gita   A portion of the *Mahabharata* (a major Sanskrit epic) in which Lord *Krishna*, an incarnation of Lord *Vishnu*, gives spiritual instructions to *Arjuna*.

Bhagavan   God. Respectful title for a realised being.

bhakti   Devotion, love. Traditionally it is one of the main approaches to Self-realisation.

Bodhisattva   One who has gained complete liberation; an enlightened being who is no longer caught in the cycle of birth and death, yet continues to incarnate out of compassion until all sentient beings are awakened.

Brahma	The creator. With *Shiva* (the destroyer) and *Vishnu* (the preserver), one of the Hindu deities.
dharma	Practice or path to Truth.
guru	A teacher in the religious or spiritual sense, commonly used in Hinduism and Buddhism.
jnani	One who has realised the Self. From *Jnana*, knowledge. Discrimination of what is real from what is not real. A principal, traditional path to Self-realisation.
karma yoga	The yoga of action. Achieving Self-realisation by performing one's duties in an unselfish manner, being fully dedicated yet detached from the reward.
Krishna	Incarnation of *Vishnu*, who is considered the Supreme God. Usually depicted as a young cowherd playing a flute or as a youthful prince giving philosophical instruction. Represents knowledge and bliss.
nirvana	Blowing out, such as a flame. Annihilation of desire, passion and ego; liberation, characterised by freedom and bliss.
puja	Worship. Ritual in which offerings are made and prayers said.
Ram	In Hindu mythology and tradition *Ram* is considered an incarnation of *Vishnu*, revered for qualities of righteousness and bravery. More commonly used as a term for God, used in greetings, prayers and mantras.
sadhu	A pious or righteous man. Traditionally a renunciate, a wanderer with a bare minimum

	of possessions, who relies on alms for daily needs.
Samadhi	A non dualistic state of consciousness. Also the name for the burial place of a saint or guru.
Sangha	The community or gathering of devotees around a teacher.
sannyasin	In the traditional sense, a renunciate who has abandoned ties with society and lives an ascetic life, detaching from worldly desires and what is born of the ego.
Sanskrit	Ancient language of the *Vedas*. In Hinduism and Buddhism it was regarded as 'the language of the gods'. Nowadays used mainly for religious and scientific discourse. Origin of Indo-Germanic languages.
Satguru	The guru who leads one to freedom – Self-realisation.
satori	Awakening to the profound understanding of the True Nature of existence.
Satsang	Abiding in the Truth. The gathering of the guru with his students.
Shiva	The destroyer and creator, associated with fire. With *Brahma* (the creator) and *Vishnu* (the preserver), one of the main Hindu deities.
Upanishads	The concluding portion of the *Vedas* consisting of 108 verses. The *Upanishads* are the texts from which all *Vedanta* philosophy is derived.
yogi	One who practises some form of yoga. A path to awakening.